American
Conquistador

American
Conquistador

Daryl Arden Ferguson

American Conquistador: An action-adventure that is more Robin Hood than Robin Hood. And the story is TRUE!

For information about this title or to order other books and/or electronic media, contact the publisher:

Fragata Publishing
Beaufort, South Carolina
www.Fragatapublishing.com

ISBNs:
978–1-7371575–0-2 (hardcover)
978–1-7371575–1-9 (softcover)
978–1-7371575–2-6 (eBook)

978-1-7371575-3-3 (Spanish Edition softcover)
978-1-7371575-4-0 (Spanish Edition eBook)

Printed in the United States of America

Cover and Interior design: 1106 Design
Chief Graphics Illustrator—Sandy Dimke
Nautical Graphics Illustrator—Richard Schlecht

I dedicate this book to two exceptional historians and explorers . . . the late Dr. Eugene Lyon and Dr. Paul E. Hoffman. They had the stamina and willpower to buck a 400-year-old belief that it was the English who first settled our country. They were more than historians. They were explorers and the most unselfish of mentors. Their work revealed our "lost century."

CONQUISTADOR:

A conquistador was a noble knight who was charged with conquering new lands for Spain.

When a conquistador was ordered to fund the expedition on his own, and then pacify and govern that new territory, he was called an **ADELANTADO**. The personal risks that he would have to take were enormous. But success could deliver enormous honor and wealth. Pedro Menendez de Aviles was one of Spain's most fabled Adelantados.

He was an **American Conquistador**.

Table of Contents

A Personal Note from the Author

I have always been drawn to the story of how America became a nation. It's like researching our family's bloodline. It allows us to understand what it took for us to make this quilt of different colors. Our ancestors risked everything just to come here. But there was a payoff later. We began to understand why our parents and grandparents still have many of those same traits. And that helps us understand the character of our nation. I will never forget the words of a friend of mine from Spain. He said, *"How can you understand your country if you don't know where you came from?"*

This historical adventure starts in the 16th century . . . one century before England landed on Plymouth Rock. Europe was leaving the feudal age. Hundreds of little kingdoms were merging into countries such as France and Spain. Compared to today, life was very, very different. Ships lasted from three to four years before they rotted away. Most of Europe was made up of peasant farmers who didn't own the land that they harvested. They used a hand scythe to harvest their grain.

The crossbow was still being used by the European armies. But then everything changed dramatically when Spain's Cortes discovered gold and silver in Mexico.

The story that you are about to read is an historical thriller. The air is heavy with two of Europe's most powerful monarchs constantly fighting each other. That sparks espionage, piracy, and a Spanish conquistador who has to challenge his own country before he can counterattack the pirates. And that leads to a real-life cross-Atlantic race—a race that will decide whether it is Spain or France that will have the right to first control North America.

I can almost guarantee you that you will remember this story long after you read it. **That's because the entire story is TRUE.**

I spent eight years researching the history behind this story. It was like solving 100 complex puzzles that eventually came together as one. Most of the primary documents that I cited were written more than 450 years ago. My research began in 2012, when I was part of a volunteer economic-development team that was intent on improving tourism in southern South Carolina. While studying a list of assets that the southern part of the state had to offer tourists, the name "Santa Elena" surfaced. I asked the question, "What is Santa Elena?" After checking with the historian in our group, I got this answer: *It was a 16th-century Spanish settlement that we believe is located on Parris Island.* That drew a strong response from me. *"How could a Spanish settlement be located on our coast in the 16th century (the 1500's)? The English pilgrims only landed on Plymouth Rock in 1620!"*

With an overwhelming curiosity, I dug deeper and contacted the nation's top two 16th-century Spanish historians—Dr. Eugene Lyon and Dr. Paul E. Hoffman. Dr. Lyon was more than a 16th-century historian; he was also an explorer. He found the location of the Spanish gold ship *Atocha*, when Mel Fisher asked for his help in the early 1980s. Dr. Hoffman was equally adventurous. If he could not find a key 500-year-old document in Seville's Archives of the Indies, he would scour the smallest Spanish villages for those precious records. What made Drs. Lyon and Hoffman especially important was that they were part of a team that actually determined in the fall of 1978 that Santa Elena was on Parris Island. In short, if there was a basic primer on the history and importance of Santa Elena, it was written by Dr. Eugene Lyon and Dr. Paul Hoffman. And those two historians unselfishly mentored me during my research.

After eight years of research, a historical thriller surfaced. I believe that it is even more exciting than the battle of the Alamo. The story becomes so fascinating that you would think it had to be a make-believe novel. But it is not. It is a TRUE story . . . and one that will change our American history forever.

The story follows the boyhood lives of two European boys who are the same age. These two boys, one from France and one from Spain, grow up on the opposite side of life. Young Gaspard Coligny comes from one of the wealthiest families in France. He lives in a castle and plays with the king's son. Seven hundred miles southwest lives a young Spaniard of the same age. His name is Pedro Menendez de Aviles. For centuries, his family survived by working as seamen on the Bay of Biscay. Pedro Menendez's family had some "honor," which was important to Spanish families. But they were peasant-poor. The lives of these two boys would come together within ten years. And eventually they would find themselves in a cross-Atlantic race that would determine which country, France or Spain, would be the first to place a European colony in North America. Happy reading! I do not believe that you will put this book down.

—Daryl Arden Ferguson

Acknowledgments

he author thanks these historians and students of history for their immense contribution to this book.

Dr. Sally K. Boese

My "Jewel of the Nile," the author's editor who painfully made the initial editing of this book. She was instrumental in making this book a thriller that you will never forget.

Jeannette Thurber Connor (1872–1927)

She did the research and translations that allowed America to see the most important documents that impacted our early history. These documents included Gonzalo Solis de Meras' *Pedro Menendez de Aviles: MEMORIAL*; Jean Ribault's *The Whole and True Discouerye of Terra Florida*, and her two-volume collection of *Colonial Records of Spanish Florida*.

Sandy Dimke

An extraordinary art director who knows the history. She developed the race charts and coordinated all graphics. When we see her work, we understand why she was selected as a member of our country's most talented female artists.

Dr. William Kelso

Bill Kelso put historic Jamestown on the map. As the chief archaeologist of *Jamestown Rediscovery*, he made Jamestown the most exciting presentation of America's early history. His work uncovered the story behind the first English settlement and how the first English settlement was established.

Howard Heckrote and Douglas Nelson

Exceptional ocean navigators who worked for three years to confirm the most-likely configuration of the 1565 French-Spanish race. As one of the nation's few forensic navigator teams, they confirmed the author's belief that Spain and France actually raced to North America to decide which country would first control North America. Douglas passed away in March of 2021. He will be missed by everyone who knew him. Before he left us, the author said to him, *"Through your research, you and Howard have actually changed our American History—and all to the better."*

Dr. Carla Rahn Phillips

More than anyone, she had the background to show us what life was like in 16th-century Spain. She put reality into this book.

Jim DeFelice

A *New York Times* best seller and author of *American Sniper*. A friend of the author who unselfishly mentored him through his research.

Dr. Chester DePratter

The University of South Carolina archaeologist who discovered the location of France's Charlesfort on Parris Island. A tireless protector of Charlesfort and Santa Elena.

Stan South

The University of South Carolina archaeologist who said on July 4, 1979, *"We found the old Spanish fort San Felipe II (1572–1576). Santa Elena is here!"* It proved to be the first European settlement in North America and "where our America actually began."

Dr. John de Bry

A noted historian of French and Spanish history. As a direct descendant of the original engraver of Fort Caroline (Theodore de Bry), he provided the author with the graphic detail that surrounded Fort Caroline . . . its ships, fort, native Americans, and plant and animal life. He was a rare source of 16th-century French and Spanish North American history.

Dr. Lawrence Rowland

Renowned historian of the South Carolina Low Country. He became the first to encourage the author to dig behind the Santa Elena story and assess its value to our country. He was the first to pioneer this book.

Dr. Michael Francis

Considered by many to be one of today's most knowledgeable and influential historians of the 16th- through the 19th-centuries Spanish settlement period. Ferguson relied on Dr. Francis' voluminous research, opinion, and contacts as he wrote this book.

Colonel Christopher Allen (U.S. Army Special Forces Retired)

A brilliant "young" historian who brought life to the Santa Elena story. With an insatiable curiosity, Allen showed us the value of addressing the question: "What did Europe and our emerging country look like in the 16th century?" By matching historical maps to the events of the day, he exposed some of the greatest myths of the time . . . "China was located above the lower 48 states." "France believed that one could reach the Pacific from the Outer Banks of North Carolina."

CHAPTER I

A Tale of Two Boys

he sea was quiet. A calm, cool morning it was, the mists not yet fled from the sun. In the light air, the Spanish coast guard vessels drifted, sails furled and sweeps at rest. Behind them, the harbor was a cleft in green hills that swept upward from the rocky coast. This was Galicia.

The three ships were pataches,* small but fast row-sailers, fine for the coast patrol. Their mission was against corsairs, of course, for in the 1540s, the Spanish coasts were never free of these sea robbers, and fighting them was a fair way to make a living in the King's Service.

Or so it seemed to the youth. His name was Pedro Menendez, and he captained one of the little ships. He watched a trio of freighters making slow passage to the next port. Obviously, there would be a wedding soon. On the hindmost ship was a bridal party happily escorting a young woman to her betrothed. Ribald jests were bandied about as this craft, her rails heavy with people, nosed past the Spanish patrol.

Then out of nowhere loomed the corsairs, sails spread and oars flashing as they came on after the freighters. There were four attackers—a ship and three swift zabras,* the Biscayan frigates of that day. The powerful zabras soon overtook the bride's crowded transport.

With mounting concern, Pedro saw it all. These were French enemies. He knew what would happen to the bride and the other women. "Come!" he shouted to the men in the three patches. "We go to save the maiden and her women . . . or we die!"

"Don't be a fool," the other ship captains told him. "We are badly outnumbered," they muttered. So only his craft pursued the pirates—he alone with his fifty men, relying on them and his own clever strength, and on the nimbleness of his vessel. It was a daring thing and done with a flourish. With the shrill of the fife and the beat of the drum, and the pennants hoisted aloft, the oarsmen plied their blades with a will that fluttered the pennants astern. Then the sails were loosed in the promise of a livening breeze.

Seeing a lone patache approach, the Frenchmen waited, sniffing another easy victory. The three zabras clustered around their prize. Their ship was now a league away, outdistanced during the chase.

The incongruous sight and sound as the patache came on—fife whistling, drum thundering, flags flying, and a little company of armed men on her deck—entertained the corsairs. Out of curiosity, they fell quiet as she neared, and her young captain picked up the trumpet.

"Yield this prize," Pedro shouted, "else I will hang you all!" Of course, they laughed at him, this cocky figure whose beard could not hide his youth. When the roar subsided, one of them mocked him. "Why sure, Captain, sir. Just you come aboard and take it. We'll give it to you, all right!"

Two zabras moved to grapple the patache. There was nothing to do but run, so run he did. And as the old account says, the first zabra was faster than the second, and the patache faster than either. Pedro ran until

---

* See Appendix I for frequently used terms that may be unfamiliar.

he had well separated from the two pursuers. Then he turned fiercely upon the foremost and took her. Next he put half of his fighting men aboard this captive and used both her and his own vessel to capture the second zabra.

The crew of the third, still guarding the bride, saw him coming back. Suddenly they realized he intended to carry out his promise of the hangman. In quick council, they reached a logical decision: the prize should be yielded and without risking another encounter with this madman, they should depart. And they did.[1]

There was something very unusual about this 24-year-old young man. Yes, Pedro Menendez de Aviles was a skilled seaman. That's what many young men did when they lived on the Bay of Biscay. But Pedro Menendez had a fire within him that made him a strangely unique leader.

One of Pedro Menendez's biographers put it this way. "His deeds soon became a matter for conversation in the waterfront wine shops of France and Spain, as well as in royal palaces. Depending upon one's viewpoint, either Menendez was a brash and ruthless foe who was destroying 'freedom of the seas,' or he was a brave and talented leader who was freeing Spanish waters from piracy. Since he threatened the livelihood of so many sea ruffians, they continuously sought a way to kill him. Whether in war or peace, he was in danger."[2]

Maybe young Menendez's inner passion came from the dire economic conditions within Spain. Maybe it came from his strong belief in God. Or maybe it just came because he was a simple hidalgo. And hidalgos never had a path to real success within Spain. The Menendezes may have been poor, but they did have distant relatives who once served an earlier king. In Spain that made Pedro a minor hidalgo . . . a part of a family that had some honor. And honor meant everything to a Spaniard in the early 16th century. In reality, however, it still meant that he was likely to remain poor. One historian put it this way: *"Unlike the grandee (noble), the hidalgo did not have vast territories and vassals to govern; huge taxes and high command were not for him. He did not take part in palace intrigues, or seek royal favors, and was not embarrassed by the need for compromise of those who wished, to 'arrive.' His sole capital was his honor, inherited from ancestors who fought for their faith."* There were actually two elements that made up the soul of every 16th-century Spaniard . . . the Catholic faith and the concern for one's honor.[3]

In the 1530s, all eyes were on Spain. Their treasure ships were returning once a year with tons of silver and gold from Mexico and Peru. Spain's nobles were prospering, but not the typical peasant. And not the lowly hidalgo family.

More than ninety-five percent of Spain's people worked on small farms. For most of Europe, people's lives were organized around the rising and setting of the sun. When the sun set, they returned to their villages and their one- or two-room thatched-roof homes. Then they would go to bed. There was no light in a peasant's house. Few peasants had the means to pay for candles.[4] These tenant farmers were just eking out a living on the 8–12 acres of land that they were working.[5]

The 16th century had a few other disadvantages. One was the lack of medical help. When a member of the family became sick, the doctor would make his diagnosis by either taste or smell. Another problem was the simple lack of job opportunities. When a young man or woman reached an age when they wanted (or had to) leave the farm, they only had a few options. They could enter the Church as a nun or monk. They could join the army. They could be a mariner. They could be an apprentice to an artisan. Or they could be a noble's servant. Many of them preferred to work for a noble. That automatically gave them housing and food. But they could almost never advance from any of these manual-labor jobs to become a noble. And unless they were a noble, real success was never possible in Spain . . . or in France.

Times were difficult for any family that lived along Spain's northern coast . . . the Bay of Biscay. Work centered around the sea. Historian Dr. Eugene Lyon may have best described the situation: *"The very nature of the rugged shore*

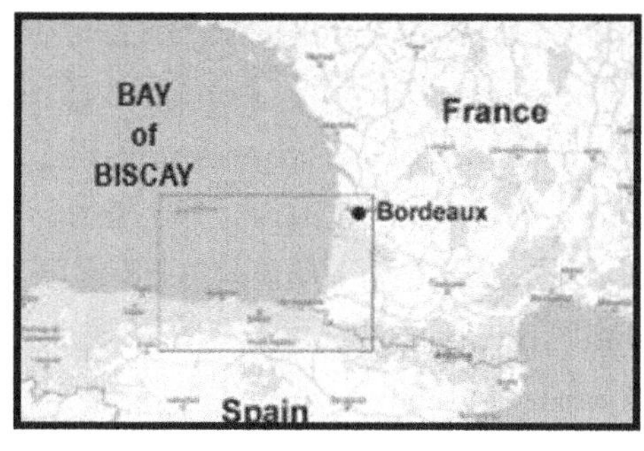

(of the Bay of Biscay), cut by endless inlets alternating with rocky headlands, thrust men onto the oceans for livelihood."[6]

Many families along the coast had a small acreage where they could raise vegetables or a few farm animals. However, the loss of one pig or the unexpected addition of one new baby could push a family into poverty. When Pedro Menendez was just a young boy, his father died. As was the custom for survival, Pedro's mother remarried. Now young thirteen-year-old Pedro Menendez had a newly blended family of twenty brothers and sisters. His family could not feed that many mouths. Young Pedro Menendez was soon farmed out to a relative, but that did not work for him. He quickly left and joined a nearby crew as a seaman for a ship's tender.[7]

Unfortunately, being a mariner was looked down upon by the nobles in Spain, as well as in France. It was manual work. One could certainly not become a noble, or a fleet admiral, if he chose the life of a mariner.[8] However, the men of Asturias did have their strengths . . . and reputations. Pedro Menendez's biographer, Bartolome Barrientos, noted in 1567: *"The men in northern Spain are honest, not tricksters, truthful, not babblers, most faithful to their King, generous, friendly, light-hearted and merry, and warlike."*[9]

SEVEN HUNDRED AND FORTY MILES TO THE NORTHEAST

Seven hundred and forty miles to the north-northeast of Aviles is the tranquil small French villa of Chantillon-Su-Loing. The village is located about 100 miles southeast of Paris. It is a very quiet little village. The twenty-foot-wide little Loing River runs through the village and makes it one of the most picturesque walled villages in France. What makes it stand apart from others is the castle . . . the castle of the Colignys and the home of Louise and Gaspard I, and their sons Gaspard II, Odet, and Andelot. As one of France's most recognized families, the family was served by its own knights, pages, and men-at-arms, plus the maids and servants that are needed to serve the family. Chantillon-Su-Loing was, in fact, the home of one of France's most important "grandee" noble families.[10]

It is February 16, 1534. In this small village, Gaspard II (hereafter only called Gaspard) is only one day younger than Pedro Menendez de Aviles. What young Pedro Menendez does not know, however, is that one day in the future, this young French boy will be his most important enemy. He will, in fact, lead France in a race that will determine which country, France or Spain, will become the first to settle North America.

THOSE WHO PRAYED, THOSE WHO FOUGHT, AND THOSE WHO LABORED

Young Gaspard Coligny lived in a time when France had three distinct classes of citizens: the clergy, or those who prayed; the nobles, or those who fought; and the lower class, (the "third estate"), or those who labored.[11]

Gaspard Coligny

He was one of only a few young men in the country who could trace his family back to the time when a distant ancestor was serving as "the first baron" of an early French king. For that early service, the Coligny family was awarded vast lands, giving them extensive wealth and income. Thus, when another war arrived—and there were many in the 16th century—such "grandee' nobles had both the income and the time to serve their king in a knightly fashion.

In 1534, when young Coligny was only 15, French nobles paid no taxes on the land that they owned. They had other special privileges. They could sit in the front pew at church. They could hunt where others could not. And their legal court cases could be heard before others. Most importantly, "grandee" nobles had direct access to the Crown. They acquired that influence because they were also members of the king's court. There was only one other group that had the influence of France's nobles. They were the high-level Catholic bishops, whose income could match most nobles. That was possible because the Church was charging the common peasants for just about everything, including a price to bury their dead.[12]

THE MOST POWERFUL NOBLE IN FRANCE

Gaspard's mother Louise was considered the backbone of the Coligny family in 1534. Part of the respect that others gave her came from the simple fact that she was a "Montmorency" before she was a Coligny. That made her a "grandee" noble and the sister of France's most powerful noble, Anne (pronounced An-nay) Montmorency. But her family loved her because

Anne (An-nay) de Montmorency

she was a pillar of independent thought and righteous courage. She taught her boys, Gaspard, Odet, and Andelot, to question concepts that they did not understand. She urged them to become knowledgeable about alternative solutions, even if they were not popular ones. Thus, at a time when France was finding the Reformed Protestant Church a threat, Louise Coligny was exposing her boys to both Luther and Calvin. However, this new Church was based on a theology that was directly focused on 'salvation by faith alone,' not on a dictatorial Church, artifacts and Papal edicts. Outside of their mother, their uncle Anne de Montmorency was the most important mentor in the lives of the Coligny boys. He had great influence simply because of his vast wealth. He reportedly owned 600 fiefs or estates.[13] But more importantly, he was the Constable of France. He commanded the entire Army. In the 1500s, if one led the Army, he had more power than anyone in the country, except the king. The Constable was also the Grand Master of both King Francis I and his son, King Henry II.[14] That also made him the most trusted friend of the king. As Grand Master, he managed everything that touched the king's day-to-day life: his servants (which totaled almost 2,500 by 1550); his palace, and the king's Court (which included several thousand nobles).[15]

To the Coligny boys, the Constable was just their loving uncle. To anyone else, he was the second-most-powerful man in France . . . a stern and inflexible man who could apologize but who would never change his position on a decision he had made. He was also a diehard Catholic. He believed that France and the Catholic Church were one and that a true Catholic should never eat meat on Friday.

As one would expect, young Gaspard Coligny grew up in the most privileged of situations. His friends—Henry (later to be King Henry II) and Francois de Lorraine (later to become the powerful Duke of Guise)—were all of the same pedigree. Although they played together like most young boys, their personalities were quite different. Gaspard tended to be a little more serious . . . not quite as fun loving as young Henry. Yet even young Henry could be "down" at times. Francois Guise had the more infectious personality. Everyone loved him.

These young grandee nobles would often play in the halls of the king's palace. They soon had a common view of Henry's father, King

Francis II. They saw him as tall and regally handsome. Yet, by Gaspard Coligny's standards, he had to have asked himself, *"Why does the king walk down the halls of the Palace with his hand around a woman who is not his wife?* Young Gaspard also had to wonder why the king was planning an alliance with the one group that had constantly been attack-

*King Francis I
by Francois Seraphin Delpech*

ing Europe . . . the Muslims.† What young Gaspard was witnessing in the halls of the royal palace was often the exact opposite of what his mother had taught him . . . except for one thing: Young Gaspard agreed with his king. France's most important enemy was Spain and their Habsburg cousins.

A Boy with a Well-Planned Career

Unlike Pedro Menendez, Gaspard Coligny had his career path well-manicured. Once he was tutored in both the arts and military, he would join the Army as a junior officer. From there he was expected to rise quickly in the ranks. However, he faced a future where his country was being squeezed by a large mechanical vise. One pressure came from how King Francis I saw his plans conflict with Spain's and their Habsburg family. The other pressure came from within. Martin Luther's more

---

† Young Gaspard Coligny had to notice one other thing when he played with the king's son in the royal palace. The building was loaded with household servants, guards, and helpers of every kind. In fact, by 1535, Francis I had 622 members just in his household staff. That included a confessor, almoners, chaplains, doctors, surgeons, bread-carriers, cup-bearers, carvers, squires, grooms, pages, quartermasters, porters, musicians, sumpters, coopers, spit-turners, sauce-makers, tapestry-makers, valets, and hundreds of bodyguards, archers, and royal troops. See R. J. Knecht's *Renaissance Warrior and Patron: The Reign of Francis I.*

democratic reform religion was gradually being spread throughout the realm by John Calvin. And that reform challenged the very basis of France's government of absolutism, in which the king and the Catholic Church were "one."

Increasingly the nobles began to talk about the need for religious reform in the 1530s. The sins of many within the Catholic Church were apparent everywhere . . . public drunkenness and every other vice known to man. Luther and Calvin exposed the real problem. The Church had built itself on a shaky foundation . . . centralized laws, edicts, and top-down guidelines rather than the Bible. Throughout Europe, the more educated citizens began to ask questions. Why do we have to pay for the atonement of our sins? Why are statues and artifacts so important? Why do the clergy get paid for jobs that they never do? Why are France's Catholic Bishops so wealthy? Why is the Pope more important than the individual's simple belief in the Bible? These were only questions in the 1530s. France had not yet felt the pressure from the masses, but this minor problem was about to explode.[‡]

ENVY CAN TEAR A FAMILY APART

France was more than Europe's strongest country by 1500. With Francis I at the helm, the country also wanted to ambitiously expand into the territory of other continental countries . . . like the Netherlands and the Italian Peninsula. Unfortunately, most of the Netherlands was under the firm control of the Archduke of Austria, the Habsburg family's Maximilian I. And that made Maximilian I France's enemy. Outside of Austria, the Habsburgs controlled a number of cities in

---

[‡] As French families died and willed their land to the Church, the Catholic Church became landowners of about one-third of the property in France. They paid no taxes on this land. By the mid-16th century, the Catholic Church in France generated approximately forty percent of all of the country's income. The Church became a huge economic powerhouse in France. See Frederic Baumgartner, *France in the Sixteenth Century*, 34.

southern Germany. They also controlled the Netherlands and Hungary, and they remained in charge of the Burgundy lands bordering western France.

But it was France's plan to conquer the Duchy of Milan and the Kingdom of Naples that created their second major enemy . . . the allied countries of Castile and Aragon. By 1515, Castile and Aragon had a combined population of about 6 million people. Aragon, however, only had a population of 1 million. However, they also controlled the Kingdom of Naples, Sicily, and Sardinia on the Italian peninsula.

Since 1499, France was intent on capturing both the independent city-states of Milan and the Kingdom of Naples. To the French noble, Italy represented everything that they wanted in a heaven on earth. Instead of dull gothic French architecture, Italy had countless estates with open courtyards. Women's wardrobes had brighter colors. Their ladies were more expressive and seemed more attractive. It became a

great deal easier to modify one's morals when visiting a land across the Alps. And the "grandee" nobles could not forget that the Duchy of Milan was also a strong economic center. Its products reached both northern Germany and the Netherlands.

France's plan to acquire the Duchy of Milan and Kingdom of Naples was a copy of what other strong countries did in the late Middle Ages.

They would make a claim that a distant relative (sometimes 200 years distant) had been on, or near, the throne of the country that they desired to control. Then, they would use the intimidation of their military to get the targeted government to submit to their ownership. The French king's claim on Milan was both distant and thin. Very thin. It did not stick when France's Charles VIII attacked the Kingdom of Naples in 1494. And it did not stick when France's Louis XII tried to strong-arm Milan and Naples in 1499. That, however, did not deter Francis I. He continued to use the same argument.

It did not take long for the Habsburgs and Isabella and Ferdinand II to see the French threat. Although Isabella and Ferdinand were married, they also ruled Castile and Aragon as separate allied countries.

And as allies, they married their daughter, Joanna, to Maximilian's son, Philip I. This was a typical strategy that monarchs used in the 15th and 16th centuries. It was called "matrimonial imperialism."* This simply meant, "If two countries were threatened by a third, unite the two through marriage and better defend yourself."[16]

Their first offspring, Charles, was, therefore, first in line to rule both Castile and Aragon when his parents died. And in 1516, Charles V became king of both countries, which he called Spain. [17] Now France faced a young king who was both emperor of the Habsburg-Austrian dynasty and king of Spain. France no longer had two enemies. It had one large one that literally had France surrounded.[18]

Charles V, King of Spain, now found himself in an awkward position. Unlike France, his empire was not in one cohesive area. It was spread over a thousand miles. To go from Spain to Austria, Charles's

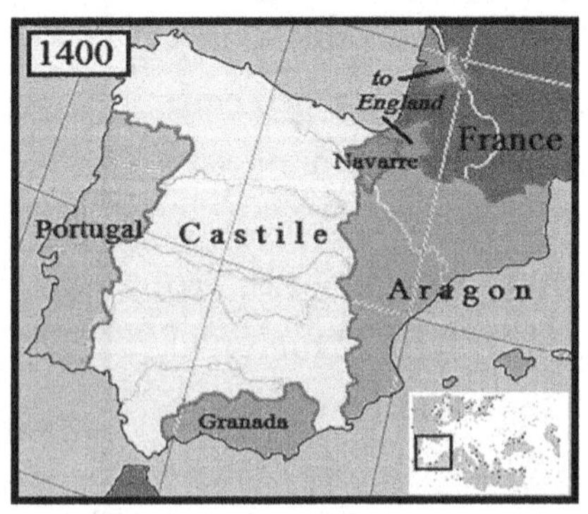

Prior to 1516: Castile and Aragon were two separate countries

safest bet was to take a ship from Barcelona to Genoa and then go a few miles inland to Milan and cross the northern border into Austria. That reality forced Charles V to realize that the control of Milan was also important to him. Milan became, in fact, his lynchpin in traveling between the two major parts of his empire.[19]

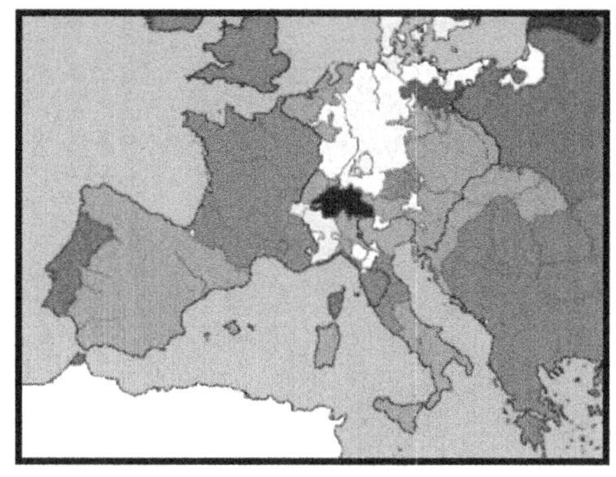

Charles V has France surrounded.

By 1516, King Francis I made his major objective the control of both Milan and the Kingdom of Naples. He informed the French Court that he intended to have one of his sons be the king of Milan and another the king of Naples. But that goal ran right into the face of Spain's Charles V, who controlled the Kingdom of Naples and Sicily.

Chapter II

Is It "Discovery" or "Effective Control"?

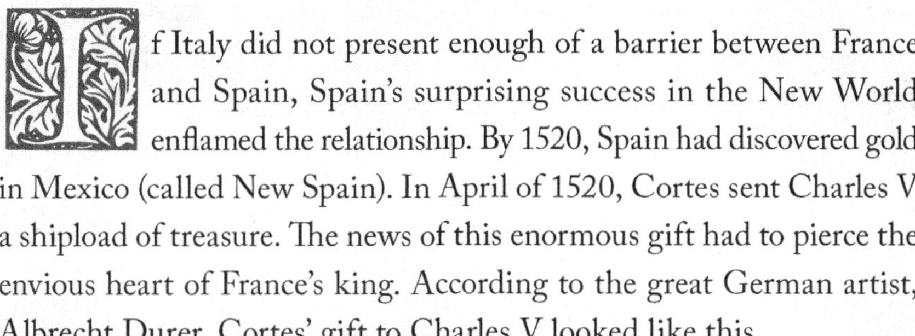

If Italy did not present enough of a barrier between France and Spain, Spain's surprising success in the New World enflamed the relationship. By 1520, Spain had discovered gold in Mexico (called New Spain). In April of 1520, Cortes sent Charles V a shipload of treasure. The news of this enormous gift had to pierce the envious heart of France's king. According to the great German artist, Albrecht Durer, Cortes' gift to Charles V looked like this.

"A sun all of gold six feet wide, and a moon all of silver of the same size, also two rooms full of armor from there, and all manner of wondrously designed weapons, equipment and missiles, strange clothing, beds and all kinds of wonderful things in everyday use, much more seeing than prodigies. These things are so precious that they are valued at 100,000 florins. In all of my life, I have seen nothing that rejoiced my heart so much as these things for I saw amongst them wonderful works of art, and I wondered at the subtle ingenuity of people in foreign lands. Indeed, I do not know how to express what I thought about it."[20]

Cortes' Gift To Charles V.

If this 1520 event was not enough to stir the envy of France's king, a second show of Spanish New World wealth was showcased in January of 1534. Francisco Pizarro had just conquered the Incas in Peru. He discovered an unbelievable treasure. On January 9, Francisco's brother, Hernando, presented Charles V with 100,000 castellanos of gold and five million of silver. Then he presented the king with thirty-eight vessels of gold and forty-eight vessels of silver. Together the Pizarro brothers had melted in their forge 13,420 pounds of gold and 26,000 pounds of silver. One Spanish minister quickly commented, "If this influx of gold lasts for just ten years, this city will become the richest in the world."[21]

FRANCE ATTEMPTS TO CHANGE THE RULES

All of Europe was watching as Spain was collecting an increasing amount of silver and gold from the Indies during the 1520s and 1530s. Up until this time, Europe accepted the fact that the Catholic Pope would resolve issues that involved "newly discovered lands." Once both sides made their case, the Pope would issue an edict or Papal Bull. That approach worked in the 1520s, because all of Europe was Catholic.

In May of 1493, Pope Alexander VI issued the Bull *Inter Caetera*. This Papal edict recognized Columbus' discovery of the Indies and the northern corner of South America. The Pope's ruling gave Spain the exclusive right to all lands west of a north-south line that ran one hundred leagues west of the Azores and Cape Verde.[22]

The premise of the Pope's edict was that "the country who first discovered the land (meaning landed on the undiscovered territory and planted its flag), owned the land." Furthermore, this Papal decree said that no other country shall trade with the claimed territory unless they have the permission of Spain. This edict was widely accepted by all of Europe when it was issued in 1494. That included Charles VIII, who was king of France at the time. Yet, thirty years and two French kings later, Francis I objected to that Papal edict after he saw the silver and gold flow from the Americas into Spain's pockets.

North America after the Treaty of Tordesillas

In Francis I's mind, the new guideline should be "effective occupation." And it carried one meaning. Instead of awarding a country on the basis of discovery, it should be awarded ownership only when they created a settlement.[23] Francis I clearly introduced this new standard for one reason—to say that Spain had no right to the rich territories that they had already discovered. Spain, however, had what it believed was an even stronger argument. It not only had a Papal-supported claim for North America, it invested in at least five expeditions to make that first settlement. In other words, Spain actively "worked their claim."

SPAIN BEGINS TO CONNECT THE DOTS

By early 1500, Spain's Caribbean ship captains began to venture north of Cuba. Once the CASA* had received enough of these ship reports, they connected the dots. By 1511, they began to see a rough sketch of a North American coast line. But there were holes in that sketch between Panama and Florida. Ponce de Leon had discovered the eastern point of this possible coast when he discovered Florida in 1513. But Spain had no firm idea of what was between Panama on the West and Florida. Then in 1519, magic came together. The Spanish ship captain, Pineda, had made enough observations to say "There is an entire coastline above Cuba." Now Spain's interest in the land mass above Cuba noticeably jumped. Could this newly discovered North American land mass be a source of even greater wealth?[24]

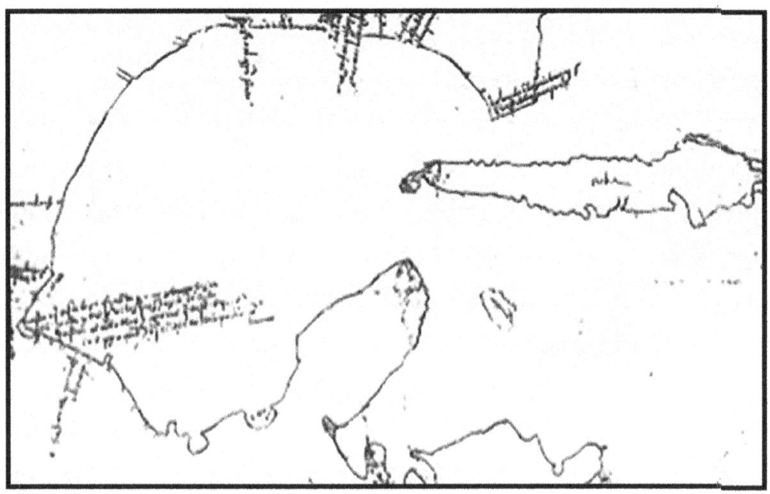

The Dots Come Together in 1519.

---

* The CASA, or Casa de Contratacion, was the Spanish department that organized all trade and movement of treasure between Spain and the Indies. They trained the navigators, secured the charts and changed them when necessary, collected the needed ships, and tried to prevent the smuggling of bullion. Aside from that, they appointed all Captain-Generals of the treasure armadas. They were large enough to have their own police and courts.

However, no European had yet penetrated this southern coast of North America. Then in 1521, Lucas Vazquez de Ayllon, a judge in Spain's royal court in Santo Domingo, became involved in the slave-trading business. He soon dispatched a slave trader called Francisco Gordillo to the Bahamas to search for Indian slaves. But before he departed, the judge suggested a fallback strategy if Gordillo did not find any Indians in the Bahamas. Ayllon informed Gordillo that he had heard a story of a man called Pedro de Salazar, who'd sailed northwest from the Bahamas between 1514 and 1516 and found a large land mass. The judge recommended to Gordillo that if he was unsuccessful in the Bahamas, he should consider sailing northwest and check out the Salazar story. If there is a land mass, it might have Indians.

Gordillo was unsuccessful in finding any slaves in the Bahamas. The islands had been thoroughly scoured by other slavers. But he did find another slave trader who was also unsuccessful . . . Pedro Quejo. Together, they decided to check out the Salazar story. On June 24, 1521, the two slave traders landed south of today's Myrtle Beach, South Carolina. The Salazar story was real. They found the land mass, and it had Indians. Salazar, in fact, may have been the first "European" to have penetrated the southern shores of North America. By September, the two slave traders returned to Hispaniola with 30 unusually tall Indian slaves.

Judge Ayllon sensed a big opportunity. He knew that he would need a contract from King Charles V to further explore this new land mass and determine if it could sustain a Spanish settlement. Charles V gave him that contract, but it came with two restrictions. He had to complete the exploration trip by 1526, and he could not capture Indian slaves. Spain was in the process of eliminating slavery . . . unless, of course, there was a special situation where it was needed.

The judge ordered Quejo to return to the shores of southeast North America in 1525 to make that assessment. Quejo returned to Hispaniola with good news. There was an area in the northern part of today's South Carolina that appeared to support a settlement. King Charles V was intrigued. He authorized Judge Ayllon to make a settlement attempt as an Adelantado. Furthermore, the king would pay for his expenses.

On August 9, 1526, Ayllon entered the northern waters of what we today call South Carolina. With him were five ships and 500–600 men, women, and children. Under royal contract, he would attempt to make a settlement. Soon after he landed, he examined the area in more detail. To his dismay, it did not have either the soil or Indian activity to support a settlement. He knew from the 1525 expedition that he may have better choices further south. Within a few days, he dispatched three ships to find that "better" location. One ship headed south to an area near today's St. Augustine. Then it looped back and landed on an island that we now call Tybee Island. The second scouting ship entered Port Royal Sound on August 18, 1526, after passing the island that we today call Hilton Head Island. The ship's pilot named the harbor behind the island the River of Santa Elena, after he checked his Calendar of Saints. Saint Helena was to be honored on August 18, and it was August 18. She was the mother of Emperor Constantine and recognized for rediscovering the true crucifixion crosses. Today we call this deep harbor Port Royal Sound. The third scouting ship made landfall on Hilton Head Island on the same day, August 18, 1526.[25] The ship's captain named the island Cabo (or Punta) Santa Elena. Any ship that entered Port Royal Sound (or the River of Santa Elena) from the south, had to pass today's Hilton Head Island on it's port, or left, side.

After the three ship captains circled back to the Santee River in today's northern South Carolina, they made their report to Judge Ayllon. He made the decision to settle his 500-plus settlers south of Savannah at a site he called San Miguel de Guadape. It lasted only four months. Cold weather, starvation, and other diseases decimated the new village. Only 150 lived to return to Hispaniola.

When Spain read the report from the failed 1526 expedition, **one point got their attention** . . . news of a deep-water harbor behind what is now Hilton Head Island. From at least 1530 to 1566, Spain would give today's Hilton Head Island and Port Royal Sound the name *"Punta Santa Elena."* It would soon become the most important strategic target in North America. Spain placed it on its master chart, the Padro Real, for good reason. It was the prime location where its Treasure Armada was vulnerable to a French ambush attack as it turned east to return home.

Spain's 1529 Master Chart

France had little interest in investing into a North American exploration plan in the 1520s. France was focusing on trade within Europe, managing its many Italian wars, and gaining the release of the king's two hostage sons from Spain. Francis I did authorize Verrazzano to make a 1524 expedition to North America in hopes of finding a northwest passage to the Orient. Verrazzano, however, went to the king. Francis I did **not** go to Verrazzano for help in implementing a New World plan. He had no "New World Plan."

However, during Verrazzano's 1524 expedition to North America, he did report that he discovered a passage that would lead to the Pacific. He based that claim on the fact that he discovered an "isthmus" behind the North Carolina Outer Bank islands that had deep water. He believed that "the other side" was the Pacific Ocean.

France's Understanding of North America in the 1530s
(Based on Juan Verrazzano's observations in 1524)

Verrazano's voyage did have one lasting effect on France's future relationship with Spain. In 1529, the French map makers printed a map of North America that had one name on the Atlantic coastline stretching from North Carolina's Outer Banks to the cod-fishing grounds of Newfoundland. That name was *Francisca*.

Then in 1543, they replaced *Francisca* with *Terra des Bretons*, a name that would honor the French province of Brittany. But on that map, they also acknowledged Spain's ownership of the southeast and mid-Atlantic regions when they placed the name *La Florida* on it. Later in 1562 and 1565, France's Queen regent, Catherine de Medici, would use those names as proof that France was **not** landing on Spanish soil. *"France was only landing on the soil that Verrazano had discovered in 1524."*[26]

ONE FRUSTRATED MONARCH

By 1525, Francis I was one frustrated monarch. Spain had just pushed France out of the Duchy of Milan at the Battle of Pavia. And Spain was in firm control of the Kingdom of Naples and Sicily. Furthermore, Francis I was witnessing Cortes' unparalleled success in giving Spain's treasury an influx of millions of dollars in gold. That, of course, only increased the envy of

Francis I. It also prompted him to find another way to damage Spain and the Habsburgs during the Italian war. No country in Europe at the time had their own Navy or government-owned fighting ships. However, Francis I took the treacherous step of licensing owners of merchant or fishing ships to attack and seize Spanish vessels. France outfitted

Drawing by Richard Schlecht

these privateer ships with the necessary weapons and paid the merchant for the use of his ship. If the privateer captured a Spanish ship, the owner, captain, and crew would receive most of the value of the ship and its cargo.[†]

That was a very cost-effective way for France to have a Navy. And in 1520 and 1521, French privateers descended on Spain's northern coast of the Bay of Biscay. But someone was waiting for them . . . Admiral Alvaro Bazan of Spain.[27]

A NAVY OF PRIVATEERS

By the time Pedro Menendez de Aviles was in his early twenties, he joined Spain's Bazan "coast guard" fleet. The role of this newly formed

---

† Between 1536 and 1568, French and English privateers captured 189 Spanish ships either in the Indies or entering or leaving the area. Shady Island Pirate Society, "History—French Corsairs" (March 31, 2017), http://bbprivatgeer.ca/?q=French_Corsairs

coast guard was to defend Spain's northern coast from these invading French privateers. By 1545, young Menendez was gaining a reputation within the Bazan armada as one whom the French pirates wanted to avoid.

Meanwhile, young Gaspard Coligny was rising up the ranks in the French infantry. In 1545, he led a successful attack on English-controlled Boulogne, France. Both twenty-six-year-old fighters were getting experience in battle.[28] Yet, at this age they both displayed tenacity, courage, and a personal commitment that was somewhat rare in both countries. Before they faced each other, however, they would have to deal with other leaders who did not necessarily value independent thought and honesty. Young Gaspard Coligny would soon see that when Francis I died in 1547.

WAR, WOMEN, ENVY, AND TREATIES

Francis I, King of France, died on Thursday, March 31, 1547. He was fifty-two years old. At his funeral, even his son, the new King Henry II, could not conceal his joy at his father's death.[29] He left a legacy that was largely a failure. One could sum it up in four words: war, women, envy, and treaties. Or, put another way, he chose war over peace. He had a mistress and loved women. His envy of Charles V and hatred of Spain was well known. And he rarely kept his promises in the treaties that he signed.‡ Unfortunately, his son Henry would rule with only a slightly better reputation. Nonetheless, the next ten years would set the stage for France to join Spain in a race . . . a race that would determine which European country would be the first to settle what would one day would become the United States of America.

---

‡ When the King died, the focus of the funeral ceremony shifted from the king's body to his effigy. His attendants made the look-alike effigy as real as possible. They dressed it in state robes. It wore the imperial crown. The strangest part of the ceremony was that, for 11 days, the effigy of the dead king was seated at a table to eat as if he were alive. Then the servants would bring in different courses and serve the effigy samples. An attendant would then wipe the king's hands and serve him wine twice during each meal. At the end of the meal, grace was said by a cardinal. Knecht, *Renaissance Warrior and Patron: The Reign of Francis I* (New York, Cambridge University Press, 1994), 545.

Henry II did not waste any time in getting started. He immediately reached out to his old friend Anne (An-nay) de Montmorency, the Constable of France. Anne had been sidelined by Henry's father in 1541 over a difference in foreign policy. The young king, however, remembered the Constable in very fond terms. He had negotiated his release from a Spanish prison when his father offered his two sons, Henry and Francis, as hostages when he was captured in a battle near Milan in 1525.

Now at the age of 54, Anne Montmorency returned to power as both Constable and Grand Master of France. Very quickly, Henry II replaced his government's leadership with two powerful families . . . The Montmorency-Coligny family and the Guise family.

By 1552, Henry II had appointed the Constable's nephew, Gaspard Coligny, as both the Admiral of France and Governor of the province of Picardy. As Admiral of France, Gaspard held one of the most prized positions. He was responsible for collecting and outfitting the private ships that would be needed when the country went to war. Maybe even more importantly, he was responsible for organizing the country's privateers . . . those private merchants and fishermen who would agree to arm their ships and go after the Spanish ships in Northern Spain and the Indies.

Henry II also looked after his second family of friends . . . the Guises, Francois and Charles. Francois was not just a boyhood friend of Henry and Gaspard Coligny. He had a reputation of being an exceptional Army commander. Within a few months, Henry II promoted Francois to "Duke of Guise," and his brother, Charles, was elevated to "Cardinal of Lorraine." Now both families were members of the King's Council.

Like his father, Francis I, Henry II had both a wife, Catherine de Medici, and a mistress, Diane de Poitiers. But Diane was much more than a mistress.

She used her influence to move the king toward the actions she favored. Knowing this, Francois and Charles Guise patronized Diane for any support that would favor them over that of the Constable or his Coligny nephews. This continuous use of political manipulation became increasingly resented by the Montmorency-Coligny family.

Gaspard Coligny, in particular, began to see his boyhood friend, Francois Guise, in a new light. Francois was now willing to do anything to pursue his family's interest. That included manipulating, lying, and working against anyone who could stop his enormous ambitions. It also included forcing the new Protestant faction out of France. This was exactly opposite of how Gaspard was raised.

Diane de Poitiers

Meanwhile the threat from the Reformed Church continued to grow. Henry II lost no time in showing where he stood in the growing Protestant vs. Catholic conflict. In October of 1547, he set up a special Tribunal to hear cases of heresy. Between May of 1548 and March of 1550, the new court handed down 37 death sentences. The Huguenot issue was becoming more prominent, and Henry II continued to fuel the flames.[30]

Between the start of Henry II's reign in 1547 and up until 1552, the balance of power between the Montmorency-Coligny family and the Guise brothers remained about the same. But that changed in September of 1552. By January of 1553, Henry II had declared war on Charles V. With German mercenaries leading the charge, he ordered his troops to attack the emperor's western border cities of Toul, Metz, and Verdun.

Toul and Metz opened their gates to Henry's generals. However, Charles V was eager to lead a counter-attack. In late September, Charles V advanced on Metz with 55,000 troops. The Duke of Guise was defending the city, however, and he was a brilliant tactician. With only 6,000 men and substantial assistance from a cold winter, Guise turned back Charles V. It was a humiliating defeat for Charles V and a huge win for the ambitious Duke of Guise. Now the balance of power between the two French "Grandee" families shifted farther to the Guise side. But it would shift even further in August of 1557.

BACK IN SPAIN

By mid-1552, King Charles' frustrations with his treasure fleet had risen to a point where he was about to explode. Paying for an almost continuous war with France was very costly. The king could repay his war loans only if he had quick access to the gold and silver bullion in the returning treasure fleet.

But it was taking an unusually long time for Philip's treasure fleet to return from the Indies. The king was constantly receiving news of delayed departures, delayed arrivals, and lost ships. Spain's Council of the Indies and the CASA responded. They developed an interesting protective strategy. They would try to prevent the French from getting any of their nautical charts. And they would allow only true Spaniards to crew their ships.[31]

Those steps were important, but they did not attack the heart of the problem. The CASA's approach to protecting the treasure fleet had fundamental flaws. First, they looked upon their treasure fleet as an extension of the Army. In their mind Spain was not a seafaring country. It was a land-based nation. Thus, they preferred to appoint "captain-generals," or fleet admirals, who had a background as an Army general. Or they would just appoint a noble. Nobles had the natural elements of leadership and courage. Only a noble had the bloodline that proved that he could rule others. The CASA would certainly not hire a lower-level hidalgo for the position of Captain-General of the treasure armada. They had some honor, but not enough to lead an armada. And they would never appoint one who had a background in manual labor . . . like a farmer or seaman . . . or even a ship captain. There was only one problem with the CASA's selection process. These former Army generals and nobles had no experience in navigating a cross-Atlantic route, fighting attacking pirates, or establishing discipline at sea. Furthermore, the hiring of these "nobles" gave them the best opportunity to smuggle bullion for themselves.[32]

As the CASA pulled an armada together, they exercised an unusual right . . . the right to sell key officer positions. That included the captain-general of the armada and his admiral. That move made cash more important than competence. The CASA was also too far "in bed" with the merchants who financed the ships and the cargo they carried. Some called it "selective enforcement."[33] When a merchant could benefit by the delay of an extra day, or two, or three, the CASA would often look the other way.

Pedro Menendez witnessed this problem firsthand. When he was outfitting his ships at the Bay of Biscay port of San Juan de Luz and preparing to depart for the Indies, certain merchants offered him a thousand ducats a day to postpone his departure for three days and double that amount for every additional day of delay. Menendez showed his moral compass. He responded by saying, *"That is "good money."* Then he ordered his chaplain of the fleet to say mass. He boarded his flagship and got the armada underway, but not before he said in a very public way: *"No one knows what the loss of an hour could bring in the service of God and the King."*[34]

The real situation was more serious than what the king believed. The historian Woodbury Lowery summed it up well:

> *"Discipline had grown lax; the masters and captains of the ships were insubordinate and disobedient, and sometimes deserting the fleet in the attempt to arrive ahead of it, their vessels fell a frequent prey to the French pirates."*

The king's son, Prince Philip, however, saw it in more simple terms. *"The CASA was appointing weak Captain-Generals."*[35]

THE FRENCH CAPTURE PEDRO MENENDEZ

Pedro Menendez de Aviles' timing could not have been better. In 1552, he not only witnessed the problem, he addressed the Council of the Indies with some answers. The notes from that meeting went straight to the

Pedro Menendez de Aviles

king. It happened this way. When Charles V saw the unique talents of Pedro Menendez de Aviles in capturing French Corsairs off of the Bay of Biscay, he quickly gave the thirty-one-year-old sea captain a commission to privateer in the Indies.

That is where the king needed the most help. In 1552, Menendez's ship was captured by a large French Corsair. For fifteen days he was held in captivity on the ship until he could raise his ransom. But that was enough time for him to overhear the conversations of the French officers on the ship. They talked of one thing . . . France's plans to raid the Indies on a large scale.[36]

As soon as Pedro Menendez de Aviles was released from the French galleass, he went straight to the Viceroy of New Spain (Mexico) Luis de Velasco. Then he went to Seville to the Council of Indies, where he informed them of France's plans.[37] This time he went a step further. He suggested solutions to the problem. Just envision the setting. When Menendez entered the Council of Indies' conference room in Seville, he would have seen a handful of nobles, all staring intensely at him.

Menendez had a muscular, compact frame. When he moved, he walked very erect . . . like the nobles in the room. His nose was a little long, similar to that of the king. His chiseled face was deeply lined from living on the sea. His eyes were bright and alert. He was not a handsome man, but he looked like his reputation . . . a very successful privateer. Most of them were acquainted with his background but they also knew that he wasn't a true noble. Some had to be thinking, *"What is he doing here? Hidalgos do not make presentations to the Council of the Indies."* But once Pedro Menendez started talking, all eyes were on him and what he said.

He spoke from experience and with a subdued passion. We can almost hear him deliver this message.

"A few weeks ago, my ship was captured by a large French corsair. I was held on the ship for fifteen days before I was able to raise the ransom that they demanded. During that time the French allowed me to go to the main deck at least once a day for fresh air. After a few days, the French officers forgot that I was not one of them. Soon I heard their conversation and the message that France would soon mount a massive privateer attack on the Indies. They intend to attack both our ships and our ports. Clearly, we are not prepared for that. We need to quickly upgrade our defenses. But we must also change the entire way we are protecting our treasure armadas.

Let me share my experience with you. Today we are losing ships and cargo because we have captain-generals who do not have the maritime experience to know how to lead a convoy of ships. Most of them are former Army generals. They do not have the experience to know how to sail an armada in the most efficient way. They take months to sail a leg of the trip that should take weeks. They have no idea how to fight an attacking group of privateers. Too often they allow ships to leave formation because a ship captain wants to be the first to return. That may help him economically, but it weakens the armada. We need an armada that will do more than escort ships. We need one that has the sole responsibility of attacking any foreign privateer that enters our waters. We need to repeat what Admiral Bazan successfully accomplished at the Bay of Biscay."

Pedro Menendez was preaching to the choir. The Council of the Indies, as well as the king and his son, Prince Philip, were as frustrated as Pedro Menendez. It was crystal clear to Charles V that he needed some immediate changes. He needed captain-generals that would lead and tighten the discipline within the treasure fleets. The king had to be thinking, *Who could best fill that position?* Menendez's name had to quickly come to mind. But he also had to be thinking, *How do I get the CASA to move in that direction?*

CHAPTER III

The Claws of the CASA

Spain's King Charles V and his son Philip quickly realized that Pedro Menendez de Aviles' report on the ineffectiveness of the CASA was right on target. They also knew that the CASA was a highly bureaucratic organization. It was almost like a country all by itself within the Spanish government. Its mission was to ensure that Spain achieved the trade monopoly that the Pope had given it. It was Spain's infrastructure for getting the maximum income from the gold and silver that it was mining in the New World. Thus, the CASA had unusually broad powers. They protected the Indies' navigational charts as if they were the crown jewels. They were responsible for collecting all silver and gold from the Indies and preventing any smuggling. They collected the taxes.* They scheduled all ship voyages, armed the protecting ships, trained all ship navigators, and appointed all ship captains and fleet admirals (Spain called them captain-generals). They

---

* Spain first received 20% of the bullion once it was mined. Then they were paid a lease fee by the private company that mined the bullion, and another tax, the averia, for the treasure-ship protection that they gave the merchants who shipped the bullion. The Spanish government ended up with 25–33% of the mined bullion. Robert Marx, *The Treasure Fleets of the Spanish Main*, 22.

even had their own police force and courts. They had jurisdiction over all treasure fleets and their personnel, with one exception. They had no jurisdiction over anyone who reported directly to the king. And that was soon to become a problem.

Charles V realized, however, that he had a near-urgent need for cash to pay those bankers who had been financing his wars with France. Moreover, his blood pressure was rising as he reviewed the dire situation in the Indies. France was increasing its attacks. Instead of one or two ships making planned attacks, France was now making attacks on both Spanish ships and their ports. One official wrote home to Spain that *"a bird cannot fly without being seen by a Frenchman."*[38]

When Spain's regent, Prince Philip, got the news of each pirate attack, he had to remind himself that it was the CASA's captain-generals who were responsible for the late arrival of his treasure ships. The problem, however, was much deeper than what Philip understood. The CASA was managed by four "royal officials."[39] These leaders strongly believed that only nobles had the proven bloodline to rule others.[†]

Finally, Charles V threw a virtual hand grenade into the CASA. He was fed up with its inability to appoint captain-generals who could deliver bullion on time and without losing valuable ships.[‡] Charles V bypassed the CASA for the first time in history.[40] He appointed Pedro Menendez de Aviles to be his next captain-general of the Treasure Fleet. One can only imagine the firestorm that he ignited when those

---

† Sixteenth-century people generally believed that social distinctions reflected God's will. They saw inequality among humans as an exact reflection of the inequalities visible in the animal kingdom. A nobleman was held to have inherited the virtue without which his status counted for nothing. R. J. Knecht, *Renaissance Warrior and Patron* (Cambridge. Cambridge University Press. 1994). 40.

‡ Philip's frustrations from these French attacks grew to the point where he sent a message in 1556 that ordered that all French officers and seamen captured in or on the way to the Indies, or even merely while lying in wait in the Azores for ships returning from the Americas, were to be thrown into the sea or hanged without mercy. See Paul E. Hoffman, *A New Andalucia and a Way to the Orient*, 140.

officials received word that the king had taken away one of their most important prerogatives . . . the selection of the captain-general of the Treasure Armada. Even more inflammatory, Menendez's profile did not match the job description. He was not, in their minds, a true noble. He was not a former Army general. He was a lower-class hidalgo. He did not have the bloodline to lead. He came from manual labor. He was a mariner. His hands were rough, and his brow was wrinkled. He didn't dress like a noble, and he did not have a noble-size estate. In their eyes, Menendez was not a noble.

The royal officials of the CASA immediately made it known that the king's appointment of Menendez was absolutely unacceptable. Yet, they also knew that they had no ability to overturn the king's decision. They knew, however, that they could do one thing. They could make Pedro Menendez's life miserable. And that might encourage Menendez to decline the appointment. Before the CASA could pounce on Pedro Menendez, they had to wait until he escorted Prince Philip to England to marry Queen Mary Stuart. While Prince Philip's wedding in England delayed Pedro Menendez's first official trip to the Indies as the next captain-general, the French continued their piracy. Three ships were lost off of Texas' Padre Island. The French pirate Jacques Sores thoroughly sacked Havana and put many of its residents to the sword. Two ships from the returning Treasure Fleet had sunk in the infamous Bahama Channel. The tensions around those losses had everyone in Spain on edge and worried.[41]

The CASA's orders for Menendez were simple. Depart from Seville in September 1555, with a combined armada (New Spain and Tierra Firme) of six men-of-war and seventy merchant ships. The CASA's orders were specific. Pick up the treasure bullion at Panama's east coast port of Nombre de Dios and from Mexico's (New Spain) Gulf Coast port of Veracruz. Meet in Havana, and return in the early summer of 1557.

Menendez had a good idea of what was ahead of him. Spain had excellent intelligence reports on the French corsairs that were leaving from its two major Huguenot ports . . . Dieppe and La Rochelle. Menendez was well informed that it was Gaspard Coligny, the Admiral of France, that dispatched every French privateer. Menendez had not yet personally met him, but he knew him as well as General Patton knew the German General, Field Marshal Gerd von Rundstedt, who fought him at the Battle of the Bulge.

Again, Pedro Menendez de Aviles used his seasoned judgment. He knew that King Philip II had a critical need for the bullion. There was no reason in his mind why he could not return earlier. On September 12 of 1556, Pedro Menendez de Aviles arrived at Seville . . . nine months earlier than ordered. He returned with a huge amount of bullion worth seven million ducats. However, by amending the CASA's orders, he also gave them a reason to arrest him. The CASA seized the opportunity. They arrested Pedro Menendez and his brother on multiple charges . . . returning with a half million ducats' worth of cochineal and sugar outside of legal registry and allowing passengers to travel disguised as soldiers. Philip II responded. He applauded Menendez's initiative and rescinded the charges.[42]

ESCAPING THE CASA

Before Pedro Menendez de Aviles could take his next Treasure Armada to the Indies, Philip had a more critical assignment waiting for him. On May 23, 1555, the Vatican had appointed an 80 year-old cardinal, Giovanni Pietro Carafa, as the next Pope, Pope Paul IV. He was no friend of the recently crowned King Philip II. The ascension of Giovanni Carafa was a surprise to almost everyone. The Vatican had 45 cardinals. Twenty of them were from Spanish or Habsburg countries. Nevertheless, they voted for the older cardinal, who hated anything Spanish. Pope Paul IV quickly made it known that he had two primary goals . . . extend Catholicism and diminish the power and prestige of the Habsburg-Spanish family in the Italian peninsula.[43]

The new Pope had two things in his favor. First, he knew that Charles V had just retired in January of 1556 and turned over everything except the Austrian empire to his son, Prince Philip. He was also aware that the new king was very unsure of himself. He also knew that France had a long-time interest in gaining control of both the Duchy of Milan and the Kingdom of Naples . . . both Spanish-controlled possessions in 1556. In the mind of Pope

Pope Paul IV

Paul IV, the time was right to remind Henry II that France had long promised to come to the aid of the Papacy whenever they were in need. What was clear was that Pope Paul IV would not listen to anyone about the risks of declaring an open war on Spain. For example, in August of 1556, Cardinal Giannangelo de Medici listened to the Pope extol the power of his Italian troops. After hearing the diatribe, the cardinal responded: *"Since the first arrival of the French King Charles VIII in 1474, never has an army composed exclusively of Italians won one single battle."*[44]

By October of 1555, it was clear that Pope Paul IV was prepared to go to war against the new king of Spain. When the Portuguese ambassador expressed his hope that his Holiness would be reconciled with Spain, Pope Paul IV cried out, *"Lord ambassador, let there be no more talk of peace, but of war!"*[45] Thus, it was not long before the Pope contacted Henry II and suggested that they develop a mutual French-Papal alliance to push Spain out of the Italian Peninsula.[46] That was like offering honey to a bear. Henry II, like his three predecessors—his father, Francis I, Louis XII, and Charles VIII—had long desired to control both Naples and

Milan. By the very detail inside the formal alliance, the ambitious Duke of Guise would be the commanding general of the joint attack forces. The Duke's brother, Charles, Cardinal of Lorraine, would be asked to negotiate the final "attack" alliance. With a decisive win, the "alliance" would promise that the Duchy of Milan would be ruled by one of Henry II's sons. Another son would rule the Kingdom of Naples. And France, for the first time, would own its long-desired prizes.

The young, nervous, and untested Philip II knew the details of the proposed alliance by late 1555. With 20 of the 45 cardinals originating from either Spain or Spanish-controlled countries, Philip had a direct pipeline to the Vatican. By the early winter of 1556, the young king, Philip II, knew that he had a huge "first" decision to make. Surprisingly, Philip stepped up to the challenge and in an ingenious way.

Philip knew by the fall of 1556 that Henry II would send the Duke of Guise, and the heart of France's army, into Italy to attack the Duchy of Milan. Philip also knew that he had his best fighting general, the Duke of Alba, already stationed in the peninsula. And he had 20,000 well-trained fighting men under his command.[47] But that might not be enough. Philip designed an intriguing plan. Spain would attack the northern French city of St. Quentin at the same time that France was about to attack the Italian provinces. If timed correctly, Philip should be able to pull France's Guise out of Italy just when his troops were most needed. Philip II was well aware of the difficulties inherent in the plan. He could get some of his troops from the Spanish Netherlands and his English allies. But most of the 45,000 men would have to come from Spain. He would also need a constant infusion of supplies, money, and ships to make the Spain-to-Flanders "run." The problem? The armada would have to be commanded by a captain-general who could pass 800 miles of French coast . . . a coastline where French privateers would be waiting outside of every French port. In other words, Philip II needed the best captain-general that he had. He needed Pedro Menendez de Aviles.

From April to August of 1557, Menendez literally did the impossible. He turned back or sank every French ship that attacked his supply armada. His impact was so effective that the word was passed from port to port, *"Don't attack Menendez's convoy if it passes your port. It is not worth the risk."*[48]

By August 2, 1557, Spain's Emanuel Philibert reached St. Quentin with 45,000 troops. Gaspar Coligny, who was also governor of the province that included St. Quentin, was immediately notified. He immediately raced from Abbeville, the prov-

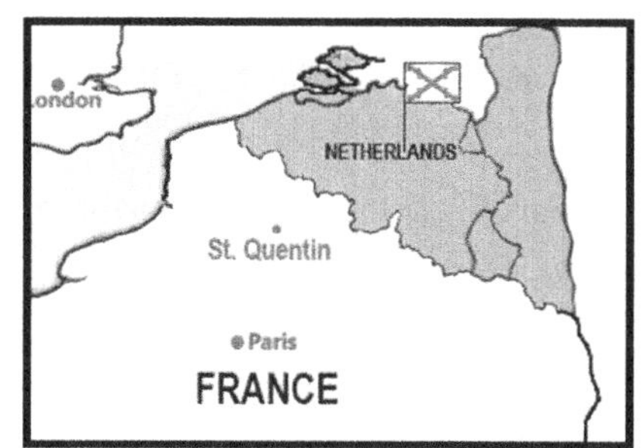

St. Quentin Is about to be attacked

ince's capital, to St. Quentin. But before he left, he sent a courier to his uncle, Montmorency, with a message that asked for immediate assistance. As Constable of France, Montmorency was head of the French Army. He arrived with an army of thousands on August 10, 1557. As France's supreme Constable, he was certainly loyal and courageous. But he was not an effective front-line general.

THE DUKE OF GUISE GETS THE MESSAGE

As the Duke of Guise was moving toward Spain's Kingdom of Naples in late August, he received this message from Henry II: *"The whole French Army was routed at St. Quentin, and 12,000 of the Constable's men were killed."*[49] The king ordered Guise to immediately return home. Paris was only 80 miles away from St. Quentin. It could be Philip's next target. Philip II's plan could not have been more effective. As soon as Henry II received the news that Spain had destroyed France's army at St. Quentin, he immediately ordered the Duke of Guise to pull out of Italy. In the mid-afternoon of August 23, Pope Paul IV received the same news. *"Spain had wiped out the French Army at St. Quentin."*

Three days later, Spain's Duke of Alba was at the gates of Rome, ready with scaling ladders and artillery. Pope Paul agreed to an unconditional peace on September 11, 1557. France would lose almost everything on the Italian peninsula.

WHERE IS GASPARD COLIGNY?

Philip II's strategy worked. But there was still one unknown. Where was Gaspard Coligny when Montmorency was defeated? The answer: He was still inside the walls of St. Quentin, defending the city against a Spanish force of 45,000—with no more than 800 soldiers and volunteers. At his side was his brother and best friend, Andelot. Although the French Army had been defeated on August 10, Gaspard Coligny, his brother Andelot, and 800 soldiers and volunteers held out for another two weeks. It was an unbelievably courageous stand by Gaspard Coligny. It allowed the French Army to regroup and block Spain from attacking Paris. It also defined the true character of Gaspard Coligny.[50]

ONE ISSUE WAS ON THE MIND OF PHILIP II.

The thirty-year-old new King of Spain, Philip II, had brilliantly passed his first test of battle with France. However, he never forgot what his father, Charles V, told him, *"The Nature of the French is never to keep any part of the promises that they make, unless they are forced to do so."*[51] That advice certainly had to remind Philip that the financial situation within Spain was still dire.

By 1557, the Indies were sending Spain approximately 974 thousand ounces of silver and 137 thousand ounces of gold each year. Spain needed all of that to pay the interest on its war debts. Philip could not afford to have one treasure ship captured as it returned to Spain. Thus, even while his men were attacking St. Quentin in 1557, Philip was thinking about how to strengthen his defenses in the Indies. He knew that France, and their Huguenots, would continue to launch pirate attacks. He also knew that his most vulnerable position was the Punta Santa Elena . . . located at the mouth of today's Port Royal Sound.

A LETTER THAT WILL NOT BE FORGOTTEN.

Soon after Philip won the battle at St. Quentin and the Papal war, he received administrative updates at his Flanders office. One had to be an update on Spain's income compared to its ongoing war debts. The picture was not good. His war debt was now more than 25 million ducats. More important, the annual interest on that debt was approaching one half of the country's annual budget. Philip was not well versed on how to read financial statements. But he did know one thing. If he could not protect his returning Treasure Armada at the Punta Santa Elena, he could not depend on the income from the Indies.[52] Knowing that, he fired off this letter to the Viceroy of New Spain (Mexico).[53]

December 29, 1557

Don Luis de Velasco, Viceroy of New Spain

Know ye, our officials of New Spain who reside in the city of Mexico, that we are sending orders to Don Luis de Velasco, our viceroy of that country, that he is to provide for making a settlement on the point of Santa Elena, which is in (the colony of) Florida. He is to send the people who it seems to him should be sent and with them some religious who understand how to bring peace and to bring to the knowledge of our holy Catholic faith the natives of that country. In order that the people may be taken in ships to the said point of Santa Elena, as the provisions which it is advisable that they carry for use until they may sow and reap enough to sustain themselves.

Signed under orders from the king,

Francisco de Ledesma,
Personal secretary to King Philip II

PUBLIC OPINION

To recover from his embarrassing losses at St. Quentin and in Italy, Henry II ordered the Duke of Guise to attack English-held Calais in January of 1558. England had held this important city on the coast of France for 250 years. In a masterful attack, Guise received the surrender from the English commander on January 8, 1558. Ironically, the French public soon forgot about the Duke's major loss of Italy. The focus of the French populace was that Montmorency lost St. Quentin and the Duke of Guise won Calais. Virtually nothing was mentioned of Coligny's heroic "last stand"—a "stand" that may have saved nearby Paris.[§] Henry II, however, was beginning to see the Duke of Guise in a new light. He was tiring of his self-promotion and willingness to achieve any goal at any cost. The king was beginning to lose all respect for the new national hero.

A peace treaty with Spain was signed on the second of April, 1559.[54] There were few benefits for France. England would hold Calais for only eight more years. Then Calais would transfer to France. France would also retain Toul, Metz, and Verdun. France, however, would lose almost everything in Italy. Henry had just lost the one goal that had driven him, his father, and two prior kings . . . the conquest of Milan and the Kingdom of Naples.

THE BENEFITS OF PRISON

Gaspard Coligny's eighteen-month stay in Ghent's Spanish prison was a period of both reflection and decision. During that time, he had to accept the public's outcry, and his king's, that he had failed at his mission. Those who knew him, however, had a much different opinion. The painful part was that Henry II did not acknowledge what Coligny had

---

§ What is remarkable is that the plan to capture Calais originated from Gaspard Coligny. Two years earlier, Coligny had shared his ideas in great detail with Henry II. The King remembered that conversation. Before he ordered Guise to attack Calais, he sent a courier to Coligny's home at Chatillon to get those plans. Guise followed them and captured the city. Eugene Bursier, *COLIGNY* (London, 1884), 117.

done to basically "save Paris." By holding out and extending the fight an additional two weeks, France had the time to reinforce Paris, which was only eighty miles from St. Quentin.

Prison confinement was also a time when he had to sit quietly on the sidelines and hear that the Duke of Guise was advancing in reputation and power. Coligny was not the type of man who wallowed in self-pity. He simply knew that the man who was being given such public acclaim was morally corrupt. He would do anything to achieve his goals. And one of those goals was to prevent any Protestant from worshiping in France. The positive

Gaspard Coligny

part of his imprisonment was simply that Gaspard was in a very quiet place . . . a place where he could contemplate whether he wanted to remain a Catholic or become a Protestant. He certainly knew that if he became a Huguenot, he would immediately fall into disfavor with Henry II and most of the King's Court. He also knew that he would lose most of his political influence. By the time he left prison, Gaspard Coligny was a confirmed Protestant . . . a French Huguenot. He left prison dejected and very solemn, but he was certainly not defeated.

One of Coligny's biographers, Sir Walter Besant, described his situation this way. *"There were no smiles lurking in his depth, but a great capacity for sorrow. His face was one of a grave man, stern at all times, just, even to harshness, and trusted because of that justness. He was willing to push the priest aside and stand solemnly, face to face with God."*[55]

France's eighty-five-year attempt to conquer the sweet spots of Italy died. Henry II agreed that France would pull out of Italy, except for a few fortified towns in the Piedmont. Overall, France lost almost all of its Italian possessions when it signed the 1559 peace agreement.[56]

The fallout from the loss of St. Quentin hit the Montmorency-Coligny family hard. The Constable, although still loved by the King, was out of power. The power of the crown now shifted to the Guise family. Under strong public pressure, Henry gave the Duke of Guise the title of Lieutenant-General of the Kingdom. His brother, Charles, took over many of the Constable's duties. He became, in effect, the new Prime Minister, but it was the Guise brothers who were now running the French government. And Gaspard Coligny had little respect for either of them.

CHAPTER IV

A Very Bold Strategy

oligny knew that with the growing power of the Guises, the French Catholic Party would do almost anything to push the Huguenots out of France . . . including the creation of an inquisition blessed by the Pope. Coligny had to find a strategy that would weaken France's hard-line Catholic faction. Otherwise, the Protestant movement would die. It was not long before that strategy emerged. In Coligny's mind, Spain was France's natural enemy. Along with Spain's Habsburg family, they had France surrounded. They pushed France out of Italy. They had a king, Philip II, who saw himself as the policeman of Christianity. They claimed all of the Americas simply because the Pope signed an edict.

In the past, most historians believed that Gaspard Coligny's plan was to develop a settlement in Spain's La Florida for one reason . . . to provide the Huguenots a home away from home . . . a place where they could peacefully practice their religion. But in 1879, Sir Walter Besant penned a book that suggested that Coligny's strategy was much broader than that. He believed that Coligny's real intent was to start a major conflict, or a war, with Spain in North America. His objective? To strengthen the French Protestants by indirectly weakening Guise's Catholic hold on France. Besant put it this way:

> *"It was thus with mixed motives that he (Gaspard Coligny) designed his Florida colony. The Protestants were to have a place where freedom of thought would be conceded to them without dispute. The Spaniards were to be braved on their own soil (La Florida). The King of Spain was to be provoked to become an enemy to the whole, instead of an ally to half of France."*[57]

THE STAGE IS SET FOR A COUP D'ETAT

Was this the Admiral of France's real strategy? That answer emerges when we review what happened next. Forty-year-old Gaspard Coligny may have been lost in the dust of St. Quentin, but he demonstrated to anyone who knew him that he had the moral courage and the leadership ability to nearly do the impossible. He may have left prison as a defeated and unpopular Huguenot, but he left stronger and more willing than ever to address what was ahead of him. In the process, he also got to know the one Spaniard whom he would one day race to America . . . Pedro Menendez de Aviles. And Pedro Menendez de Aviles got to know him. Coligny was responsible for recruiting the French privateers who attacked Spain's ships in the Indies. Menendez was in the Indies attacking those French corsairs. He led the Spanish armada that moved thousands of soldiers and supplies along the French coast to St. Quentin. He was also the one about whom the French warned, *"It makes no sense to leave port and attack Menendez as he follows our coast. You will simply lose."*[58]

Moreover, by the nature of the office of the Admiral of France, Gaspard Coligny would have received dozens of reports that mentioned how his privateers were turned around, damaged, or sunk by Pedro Menendez de Aviles. When Menendez was part of the 1543 Spanish

Coast Guard, he became a hero of Spain and a threat to France. As the captain-general of the Spain-to-St.-Quentin Armada in 1557–1559, he showed the same tactical skills that he used in the 1540s. He could outmaneuver any ship, or armada, and win the day. To the Admiral of France, following Pedro Menendez was like watching an exceptional young football star moving from high school ball to college and then to the pros. What made him exciting to watch was that he did not always follow the rules. And he was completely willing to do the one thing that Spaniards would never think of doing . . . change the king's order when he thought it would help Spain.

A Celebration Like No Other

Henry II was ready to make the best of his losses at St. Quentin and Italy. He ordered a lavish one-week celebration in honor of the new peace accord. As was customary in the 16th century, all major treaties were usually sealed by the marriage of a family member from each side. As part of the treaty itself, that rule was followed. Spain's Duke of Savoy, who led the attack on St. Quentin, would marry Henry's sister, Marguerite. And Philip II would marry Henry's thirteen-year-old daughter, Elisabeth de Valois.[59] Philip, however, would throw some cold water on the planned celebration when he was reported to have said that *"kings of Spain do not go after their brides."* That triggered Philip's decision to remain in Spain and send the Duke of Alba as his proxy groom.[60]

Henry planned a five-day jousting tournament to cap off the festivities. Against all advice, he entered the friendly tournament. On the third day of the tournament, the lance of Henry's captain of the Scottish guard, Gabriel de Montgomery, splintered and struck the King's visor. Several needle-sharp splinters entered the King's forehead above his right eye. In ten days, Henry II was dead.[61]

With Henry's death, the unexpected happened. While Henry II was lying in state, both his queen, Catherine de Medici, and the Admiral of

France were at his bedside. But the Guises were not. They were planning a coup d'etat . . . an illegal surprise takeover of the government.[62] The young new king, Francis II, was not the problem. He was physically weak and more than willing to let the Guises do his job. Catherine played it smart. She played along with the Guises, giving them tacit assistance, however, the Guises gave her little respect.

But this takeover did not play well throughout France. The King's Court was well aware that, according to custom, the Princes of Bloods, the Bourbon family, should have been part of any discussion that dealt with the handoff of power. They were the junior family that could also trace their lineage from the first king. Now for the first time, Antoine Bourbon, King of Navarre, and Louis, the Prince of Conde, were more than upset. Furthermore, many saw the Guises as making an unlawful seizure of the government. Yes, the Guises had some royal ties, but their family was a relatively young royal family. It had not been that long since they'd migrated from Lorraine to France.

BACK IN SPAIN

Philip II was pleased that the Guises had taken the behind-the-scenes power from Francis II. That would only enhance France's willingness to deal with the heretical Huguenots. On the other hand, Philip was still wary of France's constant privateer attacks against his Indies and the Treasure Armada. In fact, there were an increasing level of pirate attacks coming from Huguenots leaving from the port of La Rochelle, France. That again triggered the king's concern about controlling his most vulnerable position in the Indies . . . the Punta Santa Elena. "Where was his Viceroy, Luis de Velasco, in following his order of December, 1557, to establish a settlement at the Punta Santa Elena?" On December 18, 1559, Philip went around the Viceroy and sent this letter directly to the governor who had the responsibility of establishing a settlement at the Punta Santa Elena.[63]

December 18, 1559
Don Tristan de Luna

As you know (from the King's letter of December, 1557), it was fitting and very necessary to make a strong settlement at the Punta de Santa Elena, which is in the land of La Florida, in order to make an effort from there by means of preaching and good treatment to bring the people of that land to our holy Catholic faith, and in order that the ships which come from New Spain and other parts of the Indies to these kingdoms and make port there may find shelter instead of being lost on account of there being no settlement at all at the Punta; and also in order to prevent people from France or any other foreign kingdom from entering there to settle or take possession in our lands . . .

. . . 'But though it may be by order which the viceroy gave you that you have made first another town than that which is to be placed at that Punta de Santa Elena, this appears here not to be suitable. The first of all settlements we have ordered must be made at the Punta before any other town whatsoever. For notwithstanding that we are at peace with France, we have learned that Frenchmen, under pretext of going to Los Bacallaos (the cod fishing grounds near Newfoundland), may possibly be desirous of going to that land of La Florida to settle in it and take possession of our lands. This it is necessary to prevent them from doing, and I therefore command you, notwithstanding whatever other order you may have to the contrary from our viceroy, to make first a town at the Punta de Santa Elena rather than at any other place.

Francisco de Eraso
Signed for King Philip II

The Guises Are in Control

No one was surprised at the changes that the Guises made when they seized power in July of 1559. The Constable, Anne de Montmorency, was out. The Duke of Guise placed the Army under his command as well as the title of Grand Master. That gave him control of the personal life of Francis II and the Court. In reality, it gave him the same power as the king. The Duke of Guise's brother, Charles, assumed the responsibility for all financial and state affairs. They allowed, however, Gaspard Coligny to remain as Admiral of France. That helped them show some appearance of political fairness. An aide to the leader of Geneva's Reformed Church, John Calvin, wrote a letter in September of 1559 that captured the working situation:

> *"The Guises have so parceled out the power between them, that they have left the king nothing more than (his) name."*[64]

With a sick, frail, and disinterested 16-year-old king under their hand, the Guises had to work quickly to plot their course of action. That trajectory soon became clear. They would move France from being anti-Spanish to anti-Protestant. Spain's King, Philip II, would move from being the enemy of France to their advisor. By taking that position, Charles Guise could see himself as the future head of the French Catholic party. Given peace with Spain, it might even be possible for the Duke of Guise to be a future king. In fact, Charles Guise wrote to Philip II in August of 1560, that *"he was prepared to serve him with no less affection than the King of France."*[65] The only thing that might stop this ship would be if Gaspard Coligny was able to execute his strategy . . . or if the frail Francis II would die before they had a chance to develop their new Guise strategy for France.

With this new anti-Protestant strategy, Charles Guise moved rapidly to tighten the screws on all heretics. The Guises also intended to demonstrate that they had now aligned themselves to Spain. The Cardinal of Lorraine, Charles Guise, organized a vast espionage system to uncover the location of where the Huguenots worshiped. He employed endless devices to determine who was and was not a heretic (or Protestant). Statues of the Virgin and other saints were placed at the corners of the streets. Crowds congregated. If anyone refused to pay or to uncover his head, or tried to slip away, he or she was denounced as a heretic and arrested. Death was the almost certain doom of the heretic. Spies were locked up with prisoners to listen to their conversations and to try to discover where they held their meetings. The Guises began exactly what Spain had so successfully executed since the day of Charles V. They started a practice of giving no space for any anti-Catholic sentiment.[66] Their only problem was that the vast number of France's nobles would not tolerate this change in their national culture.

THE UNIMAGINABLE HAPPENED!

The one thing that the Guises needed to make this strategic change was time. But the unimaginable happened. On December 5, 1560, after a reign of only sixteen months, the fragile young king, Francis II, died. Catherine immediately contacted the Constable (Anne de Montmorency), who had been the titular head of the Army. Francis I had given Montmorency the title of Constable for life. However, he removed his authority to that title when they had a policy difference in 1544. Now Catherine restored that authority. She needed both his reputation and power to prevent another unauthorized seizure of the government.

The Guises did not attend the funeral of their young king. *"Gentlemen,"* said Coligny, to the courtiers standing around. *"The king is dead; let us learn a lesson how to live."*[67] Almost immediately Catherine took command of the government as the regent of the underaged ten-year-old Charles IX. She was driven by one goal . . . to keep her sons in power. At this point she had not defined her leadership style. All of a sudden, however, the Court took notice of her for the first time. She certainly had a memorable persona. "She was a large, tall, and powerful woman, with a full, round, red face. Her hair was curly, and lay well forward on her head before her cap. It made some think it was false. Her eyebrows were yellow. She had light eyes, a somewhat large and colorless mouth, and large, long teeth. Her speech was unfeminine, almost that of a rough country-woman."[68]

The King's Court was just stunned, waiting for the next shoe to drop. Catherine did not bother to seek the support of the Princes of Blood (The Bourbon family that had a direct bloodline claim on the Throne). She correctly assessed that Antoine of Navarre, the senior Bourbon, was not strong enough to make a play for the regency. Nevertheless, the situation she was in was a literal powder keg. Catherine de Medici had virtually no credentials other than being the mother of a ten-year-old king, Charles IX. Her late husband, Henry II, virtually ignored her. When he died, the Guise brothers pushed her aside and with a coup d'etat ran the government. Now she was literally claiming to be the interim "king" of the nation.* And she was doing it at a time when one wrong move could ignite a national religious war.[69] Unfortunately, she did not pull the minority royal Bourbon family into the discussion of succession. And with Gaspard Coligny's announcement that he had become a

Catherine de Medici
(By Edouard Debat-Ponsan)

* France's Saltic Law specified that the oldest son of the king would become the next king. Women were excluded. If the dead monarch had no sons, the next closest living male, in the male line of the family, would be crowned king.

Huguenot, the Bourbons became closer to the Colignys. That, in turn, triggered the junior Bourbon, Louis, the Prince of Conde, to look for a religious alliance with Gaspard Coligny. For the first time, France had a leadership team for the Huguenot movement: Gaspard Coligny and Louis, the Bourbon Prince of Conde.

At this point, Catherine de Medici had little use for the Guises. If they had not already left the Court, she would have probably asked them to leave. After her daughter assumed the role of Queen of Spain, she wrote her a letter that included this statement: *"I want to tell you, for it is the truth, that all this trouble has grown out of the hatred which this whole kingdom bears to the Cardinal of Lorraine and the Duke of Guise."*[70]

By January of 1561, Catherine had made a clear break with the Guises. Once Antoine Bourbon agreed to give up all claims to be regent to the young king, Catherine installed him as the new Lieutenant-General of the Kingdom. That neutralized Antoine from being an untimely dissident. Then she began to work more closely with The Admiral of France. It was a show of moderation toward the growing Huguenot population. None of this sat well with either the Duke of Guise or Gaspard's uncle, the Constable, Anne de Montmorency. Although they were poles apart on moral principles, they agreed on one point. To survive as a kingdom, France could only have one monarch with one faith . . . the Catholic faith.

Catherine's new policy of moderation began to tear the empire apart. On April 5, 1561, the Constable agreed to join the Duke of Guise and the wealthy noble St. Andre in an attempt to block all further Protestant inroads. The three soon acquired the name the "triumvirate." In Montmorency's mind, it was a call to return to the "old religion." The country should never tolerate meat being eaten on fast-days.[71] When the Constable's nephews, Odet, Gaspard, and Andelot, heard of their uncle's new political affiliation, they were shocked. Guise may have had a magnetic personality, but he was impetuous and violent by nature.

It took just one move by Catherine, however, to implement her first step toward religious moderation. She introduced the "Edict of January." It passed on January 15, 1561. It was a huge appeasement to the Catholic Guises. It would, in effect, kill the Huguenot movement in its tracks. The Edict recognized the Protestants' right of citizenship. They could practice their religion, but only outside town walls. It also required the Protestants to restore all Catholic churches and ecclesiastical revenue of which they had taken possession.[72] The order irritated everyone, but it lit the fuse for the Guise brothers and Coligny's uncle, the Constable, Anne de Montmorency.

The Duke of Guise

By the summer of 1561, the Triumvirate had thrown their first hand grenade. They countered with the Edict of July, 1561. Under severe penalties, this edict would prevent any Frenchman from assembling to worship in a manner that was different from that of the Catholic church.[73] When the Constable's nephews, Odet, Gaspard, and Andelot, heard of their uncle's new political affiliation, they were more than surprised. Guise may have had a magnetic personality, but he was impetuous, self-serving, and violent by nature.

WHERE SHOULD FRANCE MAKE ITS FIRST FOOTPRINT?

France was feeling the strain. The Admiral of France, Gaspard Coligny, was working well with the Bourbon Prince of Conde as the new leadership of the Huguenot effort. Overall, the Protestants were pleased that the Queen-mother was moving toward reconciliation. The country, however, was still a tinderbox waiting for a spark. During the autumn of 1561, monks were being killed and churches pillaged in the southwest of France.[74] Despite this carnage, it was also a time when the Admiral of France could begin to contemplate the initial step of his strategy. Where in Spanish North America should France place its first footprint? Historian Paul E. Hoffman notes that the rumor within France was that Coligny wanted a site where the Huguenots could settle in peace. But it also had to be a location where France could conquer "the king of Spain's lands and discover others." Was this going to be the Admiral of France's new strategy?[75]

Why the Punta Santa Elena?

Gaspar Coligny's strategy soon appeared to be more than just locating French Huguenots on Spanish soil in the New World. It was beginning to look as if Coligny wanted to start a war with Spain. Coligny's first target would be Spain's Punta Santa Elena (the area of today's Hilton Head Island and the deep harbor of Port Royal Sound behind it.) The Punta was discovered by Spanish slavers in 1526, and soon became recognized as having the best harbor in the southeast of North America. When the French privateers began to attack the weak spots in Spain's Treasure Fleet route, however, it took on a special importance.

Both Spain and France knew that there was one harbor that could anchor large ships intent on ambushing a returning Treasure Armada . . . the Punta Santa Elena. Location: 32.3 degrees north latitude.[†] Spain and France were now on a collision course. Spain not only saw North America as their colony, they wanted their first settlement to be located

---

† In the 16th century, ship pilots could only measure latitude, or the angular distance of a ship or port to the equator, as measured in degrees or nautical miles. The discovery of how to measure longitude would come later. With this handicap, the ship's pilot or navigator became the most despised officer on the ship. He was almost always wrong in his estimates of when they would "arrive" at a destination.

at the Punta Santa Elena. If there was any doubt about that, Philip II clearly answered that question in his 1557 letter to the viceroy of New Spain. *"I order you to make our first settlement at the Punta Santa Elena."* Then he followed up on that order in December of 1559, when he said, *"I don't care where you want to place the first North American settlement. I want it placed at the Punta Santa Elena."*

CHAPTER V

How to Start a War in North America

here was a simple recipe for war in the 16th century. Just establish a new settlement at a location that has been claimed by your enemy. That appeared to be exactly what the Admiral of France had in mind. Gaspard Coligny could argue all day long that the Pope had no authority to give North America to Spain, but the reality was that, since 1521, Spain had been actively "working" its Papal claim. In five attempts, however, Spain was unable to establish a permanent settlement. They all failed. **One thing was clear. Spain had been working its Papal Claim for almost one hundred years before England landed on Plymouth Rock in 1620.**

GASPARD COLIGNY'S FIRST MOVE

In 1562, Coligny chose the Huguenot admiral Jean Ribault to lead that first expedition into Spain's new North American territory. He had the reputation of being France's best admiral: a solid and trusted mariner, an effective leader, a man who found exploration a hobby, and a Huguenot.

Ribault was not necessarily a leader, however, who had developed a strong sense of urgency. Within the French court, Coligny was seen as either assembling an expedition to settle or explore this new North American territory, or he was making a home where the Huguenots could practice their religion in peace. Over time, the latter became the more-popular understanding. In reality, however, that may have been a secondary goal. It soon began to appear that Coligny's primary objective was to start a war with Spain in the Americas.

COLIGNY INITIATES HIS STRATEGY

On February 18, 1562, Jean Ribault departed Havre de Grace for the Punta Santa Elena. His second-in-command was Rene Laudonniere. Before they departed, Spain's agents in Havre de Grace identified two royal roberges resembling Dutch three-masters being loaded. One was about 160 tons. The other was around 60 tons. The larger ship also carried a large sloop and two smaller ones. Philip's agents reported that the ships carried 150 men, and most of them were seasoned soldiers. They had ample provisions for at least a few months. When Spain's ambassador to France, Tomas Perrenot de Chantonne, heard of Ribault's preparations for this trip, he immediately obtained an interview with the young French king's mother, Catherine de Medici. Ambassador Chantonne reminded her that La Florida belonged to Spain and that no Frenchman had the right to go there. Catherine, however, said that she had no knowledge of the expedition. The Spanish ambassador, however, had heard what everyone else at the French court had heard. The queen had invested 1,000 ducats of her own money to outfit the ships.[76] Now the true character of the Queen Mother surfaced. From King Philip's point of view, and that of many within the French court, Catherine de Medici was one who would do anything and say anything if it helped her make a point . . . regardless of whom it may hurt.

THE FUSE IS LIT

While Gaspard Coligny dispatched Admiral Jean Ribault to the Punta Santa Elena, the Duke of Guise was about to start a French civil war. On March 1, 1562, Francois, the Duke of Guise, was traveling with his wife and two sons to visit his mother at Donmartin-le-Franc. Accompanying the Duke were two hundred arquebusiers and a company of archers.[*] When the group came within a mile of the town of Vassy, they heard a bell ringing. The Duke of Guise asked what it was. He was informed that it was the bell calling members of the Reformed Church to service.

What followed was told in great detail by Eugene Bersier.[77] *"After the Duke asked about the nature of the church bell, he immediately ordered, 'March, march! We must have a look at these people while they are gathered together.' On reaching Vassy, the Duke ordered his people to march to the preaching, which was held in a barn. In the barn were assembled about twelve hundred Huguenots, some of whom were seated on the window-ledges. Two or three of the Duke's people entered; they were invited to sit down. They replied with an oath, 'Death to you all!' At the same time, the windows were fired at from without. The unhappy Protestants, totally unarmed, would have closed the doors, but the soldiers pressed in, crying, 'Kill, kill!' A veritable slaughter began. Those who attempted to escape by the roof were riddled with balls. The massacre lasted for an hour. There were sixty dead and two hundred and fifty wounded, but not one victim on the Catholic side."*

THE MASSACRE OF HUGUENOTS AT VASSY

"The minister, Leonard Morel, was on his knees in the pulpit. They fired at him. He tried to come down, stumbled over a corpse, fell, and received several sword-trusts. 'Lord,' he exclaimed, 'I commit my soul into Thy hands.' They raised him up, for he could not stand, and carried him to the Duke of Guise.

---

[*] The Duke of Guise had a staff of a true grandee noble. He had a household of 159 persons. In wartime he could muster 100 lances or 250men. See William Beik, *A Social and Cultural History of Early Modern France*, 90.

'Minister, come hither,' said the Duke. 'Art thou the minister? What makes thee so bold to teach these people sedition? 'I am no teacher of sedition,' replied Morel. 'I have preached to them the Gospel of Christ.' 'Does the Gospel preach sedition then?' exclaimed the Duke. Thou art the cause of the death of all these people; thou shalt be hanged by and bye.'"[78]

The massacre of Protestants at Vassy, France

Almost immediately, the massacre threw all of France into a firestorm. Protestants everywhere called for **"VENGEANCE."** Within each town, Protestants fought Catholics. Within many families, sons fought fathers. Brothers took up arms against brothers. The senior Bourbon, Antoine, did an about-face and declared himself a Catholic. He would fight his brother, Louis, the Prince of Conde. Gaspard and Andelot Coligny would soon face their beloved uncle Anne de Montmorency in battle. France was at war with itself. Bersier described the situation this way. *"In a few weeks the explosion of fanaticism spread over the whole country. At Sens, more than a hundred corpses were thrown into the river. At Amiens, at*

Epernay, at Chatillon-sur-Loire, at Moulins, at Blois, at Angers, at Tours. In the south, where the Protestants were unable to defend themselves, they were exterminated one by one with the utmost refinements of cruelty. Never was the soil of France reddened with so much Protestant blood."[79]

RIBAULT AND MENENDEZ ARE UNAWARE THAT FRANCE IS AT WAR
Jean Ribault departed for Charlesfort on February 18, 1562. His orders were simple. "*Determine if the Punta Santa Elena would be a good location for ambushing the Spanish Treasure Armada as it returns to Spain.*" These orders certainly seemed to confirm Coligny's intent. "Make war with Spain in North America, but first decide the best location to start an ambush." Interestingly, when Ribault departed France, he had no idea that his country would soon be in a religious civil war.[80] By the end of 1562, Coligny put more fuel on the fire. He ordered a higher level of privateer attacks on the Indies. England's Queen Elizabeth joined the threat. She quietly encouraged her privateers to participate in these illegal raids. As expected, Philip II became more and more concerned. He ordered Pedro Menendez to depart for the Indies to secure the next delivery of silver bullion. That was just 30 days after Ribault left for the Punta Santa Elena. As Menendez was sailing due West to collect that bullion, he was in the same position as Ribault. He had no idea that France was about to start a civil war.

On this 1562 crossing of the Atlantic, he had to feel an increased level of anxiety. Would this trip give the CASA another opportunity to strike back at him? How could he forget the day when he returned to Seville in 1561? His business partner, Pedro del Castillo, was arrested and charged with smuggling unregistered goods from Pedro Menendez's ship.[81]

During this trip in 1562, the CASA changed Menendez's orders once he arrived in the Indies. Menendez's brother, Bartolome, was ordered to return in April of 1563 with his bullion from South America.

Then, Pedro Menendez was ordered to delay his departure with the Mexican bullion until May or June of 1563. But bad weather, combined with leaking ships, can change orders. Bartolome discovered that his lead ships were in no condition to sail once he left Panama. Menendez decided to fill the void by giving his brother some of his New Spain (Mexican) ships. He would also help by sailing with his brother when they departed. The captain-general's son, Juan, was ordered to return later with the New Spain (Mexican) ships that his father had left behind. The captain-general gave his son only one order before he departed: "*Only leave after the hurricane season.*"

On June 14, 1563, Pedro Menendez and his brother, Bartolome, arrived at the ocean port of the Guadalquivir River that leads to Seville. Once they landed, they were arrested by the CASA and charged with carrying contraband into Spain. The CASA was intent on getting their "pound of flesh." Menendez responded to the charge by saying that only the king had jurisdiction over him. The CASA refused to listen. They quickly placed Pedro Menendez and his brother in prison for the next 18 months. During his imprisonment, Menendez would hear that his son, Juan, had disobeyed his orders. He returned during the fall hurricane season. It was bad luck for young Juan. A hurricane slammed into his ships off of the Bahama Islands. Menendez's only son was never found.[82]

RIBAULT LANDS AT SPAIN'S PUNTA SANTA ELENA

Once Jean Ribault reached the Canaries in 1562, he was at the starting point for the cross-Atlantic route to La Florida. The westerly winds pushed his two royal roberges from 3.5 to 4.5 nautical miles per hour across the Atlantic. With these trade winds, he reached the St. Johns River by May 1. On May 22, Ribault entered the great harbor at 32.2 degrees north latitude after passing the Punta Santa Elena (or Hilton Head Island) on his port side. As his ship sailed up the Spanish-named

River of Santa Elena, he made this comment: *"This is the fairest and greatest haven in the world. All the ships in the world could harbor here."* By the time he reached Parris Island, he had renamed the harbor Port Royal Sound. His mission was to determine if this site on today's Parris Island was a good location to ambush the returning Spanish Treasure Armada. When he landed with his 150 men, his first task was to build a fort. He would call this outpost "Charlesfort."[83] Then, on June 11, after helping his men build their fort, he and his junior officer, Rene Laudonniere, departed for France with 120 men. But Ribault only left after promising the 30 men who would remain on Charlesfort that he would return within six months with additional supplies.[84]

When Ribault landed at Dieppe on July 20, 1562, he was shocked. The Duke of Guise had triggered a French religious war. Dieppe was under attack by the French Catholic army.

They were at war with Coligny's Huguenot forces and their English allies. Ribault immediately went to the side of the Huguenots until they became overpowered. Then he fled to England with his Protestant allies.[85]

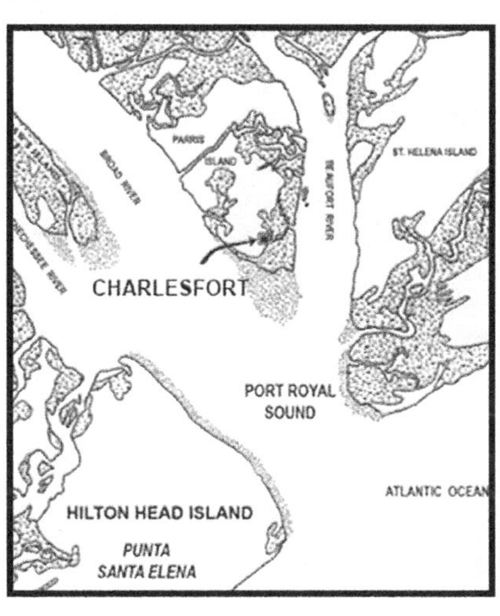

Entrance to the Punta

Soon after Jean Ribault reached England in the fall of 1562, he began to write a book on his experiences at Charlesfort. The book, *The Whole & True Discouerye of Terra Florida* was published quickly and almost immediately came to the attention of the Queen of England. Upon reading the book, Queen Elizabeth and a shady adventurer, Thomas Stukeley, proposed to Ribault that they form a partnership to resupply Charlesfort. Ribault, however, questioned their real motives. His retreat from their offer landed him in the Tower of London. He was there until the summer of 1564. In the meantime, the one question that had to be on the mind of Jean Ribault was, *"How am I going to resupply the 30 men I left behind at Charlesfort?"*

By February of 1563, Spain's ambassador to France informed King Philip II that France's Jean Ribault had made an attempt to settle Charlesfort on the Punta Santa Elena during the previous year. The ambassador also informed the king that the expedition leader, Jean Ribault, had returned to France and was imprisoned in England. But Philip did not know at that time if Charlesfort was still controlled by the French. He and his counselors had to have asked themselves, "What is France's motive for landing on the Punta Santa Elena? Who is behind this plan? Do they have something bigger in mind? And are the French still at the Punta?"

ARE THE FRENCH STILL AT THE PUNTA SANTA ELENA?

To answer that question, Philip II sent a message in mid-February of 1563 to both the governor of Cuba and to Pedro Menendez, informing them of the French fort in the Punta Santa Elena area. He ordered the two of them to investigate and take immediate action to expel the intruders.[86] It is highly doubtful, however, that Menendez ever received the message. He was returning from the Indies with his Treasure Armada. The governor of Cuba did receive the king's message, but he waited one year before he dispatched a ship to the Punta.

On May 31, 1564, the Spanish captain Hernando Manrique de Rojas departed Havana with a fragata and fifty men. He was ordered to destroy the French fort and capture any Frenchmen who were alive. He reached the Punta Santa Elena's harbor on June 11, 1564. On the very next day, the Indians escorted the captain to meet a 17-year-old French soldier dressed in Indian apparel. His name was Guillaume Rufin, the one remaining French soldier from Jean Ribault's expedition.[87]

Under sworn testimony, young 17-year-old Guillaume Rufin was asked two key questions. Question number one: *"Under whose command and at whose cost was the Ribault expedition arranged?"* Guillaume Rufin's answer: *"I understand that the expedition had been arranged and ordered to come here at the command and cost of the Queen Mother of France, the Admiral (Gaspard Coligny), and Monsieur de Vendome, and that each one gave one thousand ducats to equip the expedition; and that it was to come directly to this coast of Florida to settle on the Punta and River of St. Helena."*

Question number two: *"What was your mission?"* Young Rufin: *"Our mission was to discover whether Charlesfort was a good location for going out into the Bahama channel to capture the Spanish Treasure Fleets from the Indies. This I know because I heard it said by everyone, and it was common knowledge."*[88] (The French located Charlesfort on the western end of Port Royal Sound (today's Parris Island). As they built their fort, the French could see the Punta's large oceanfront island, today's Hilton Head Island, when they glanced to the East.

Once Captain Hernando Manrique received this information, he quickly returned to Havana. But it would not be until March of 1565 that Philip II received the report. When Philip received it, he had to be both angry and puzzled. Was the Admiral of France really trying to start a war with him on Spanish soil?

AN ASSASSIN ADDS FUEL TO THE FIRE

As the religious war was raging, a Huguenot assassin put three lead balls into the shoulder of the infamous Duke of Guise on February 18, 1563. Six days later, he died. The impact was almost instantaneous. Sir Walter Besant summarized it this way: *"Consider what an event this death was. There was no man in France like Guise. He was a better general than Coligny; he was on the stronger side; he was utterly without restraint of law, religion, or morality; he was personally idolized by his followers; he was the one man who seemed to stand between the Huguenots and the peace which they desired.*[89] *With Guise out of the way, there was no single man whom the Catholics could put forward with any chance of his taking the place of that great soldier."*

On the very next day after Guise was shot, Catherine de Medici signed the Peace Treaty of Amboise . . . the document that would end France's first religious civil war. The Prince of Conde signed for the Huguenots. Coligny was not available when the terms of the treaty were negotiated. When he read the peace treaty, he openly showed his dissatisfaction. *"With this stroke of the pen, they have ruined more churches than what the enemy could have razed in ten years."*[90]

Coligny was right! When he examined the details of the treaty, he saw the complete destruction of the Huguenots. Although the Huguenots were given the right to worship, they were forbidden to build any place of worship. They were compelled to hold their services either in the open air or in a private home. Furthermore, they were required to restore all the churches that were damaged. And they had to return all ecclesiastical revenues which they had captured. Coligny quickly saw the likely outcome of this order. The Huguenots would die, because the Church could not grow.[91]

The Admiral of France Takes the Next Step

Gaspard Coligny was still the Admiral of France at the end of 1563. He had used his time to gain his acquittal as one of the conspirators in the assassination of Guise. But he also used his time to plan the next step in his strategy . . . *"start a conflict with Catholic Spain in the Americas to weaken the Catholic influence in France."* At that time, Jean Ribault was still in the Tower of London. But his second-in-command of the Charlesfort expedition, Rene Laudonniere, was available. Historian Charles Bennett gives us this brief description of the new commander: *"Because of his 'prudence and blameless life,' the 'very religious' Laudonniere was authorized to choose 'brave, upright, and intelligent men' for the colonial enterprise.*" And Laudonniere did just that. Of the 300 men that were recruited, some came from France's leading families. Others, however, came from France's worst.[92]

What we must remember is this: Young Frenchmen, like young Spaniards, saw the Indies as a place where there were few rules and the opportunity of great wealth. Richard Dunn put it his way: "*The Indies was a region where they flouted European social conventions, acting violently and behaving viciously.*"[93] In other words, the Indies was Las Vegas on steroids. Anything goes! It was an area where soldiers, sailors, ship captains, traders, and settlers could act in ways that were completely unacceptable in Europe. Some called it Gold Fever. There was little doubt that a substantial number of Laudonniere's men joined him . . . not to colonize Fort Caroline, but to be part of that search for silver and gold.

Most of Laudonniere's men were Huguenots, but there were a few Catholics. Laudonniere, in his own words, set the scene this way. "*After the Peace was declared in France (The Treaty of Amboise which was signed in March of 1563), Gaspard Coligny remonstrated with the king that there had been no news of the men whom Captain Jean Ribault had left in Florida (i.e., Charlesfort) and that it would be a great pity to lose them.*" Because of this, the king gave him permission to equip three ships—one of 100 tons, one of 120 tons, and a third of 60 tons."[94]

What apparently happened was that Coligny got authorization for this second expedition based on the argument that "We should check to see if there are survivors at Charlesfort." However, Coligny received news the month before departure that the men who'd escaped from Charlesfort on a homemade boat had landed in France. Coligny would have been informed that only one Frenchman remained at Charlesfort. And he chose to stay there.[95]

Thus, the Admiral of France must have changed Laudonniere's orders at the last minute to give him the option either to return to Charlesfort or to choose another location for a settlement . . . a location such as Fort

Caroline, located a few miles inside the St. Johns River, near today's Jacksonville, Florida.

Clearly, Gaspard Coligny was intent on initiating that second settlement. And Catherine de Medici was equally prepared to spin a web of deception around his planned trip. Before Laudonniere departed, she sent him a letter that said, *"I charge you to doe no kind of wrong to the Kinge of Spaines subjects, nor anything whereof he might conceive any jalousie."*[96] This appears to be a message from Catherine de Medici that says, *"Okay, let's make a second attempt to colonize North America in Spanish-claimed territory, but let's do it carefully."*

We do know one other fact. The Admiral of France was about to send three ships into the southeast coast of North America, a land that had been claimed by Spain for more than 90 years. On April 22, 1564, three ships departed Havre de Grace for Spain's colony of La Florida.[97]

Now, however, the French privateers were also attacking the ports of the Indies and not just their ships. And the "pirates" were coming from both England and France. With the Protestant Queen Elizabeth I on the English throne, she authorized more of her privateers to enter the game. That included Drake and Hawkins.[98]

Chapter VI

The Pressure of Jaws Biting Down

By the dawn of 1565, King Philip II felt the pressure of three jaws biting down on his neck. Philip II's overall demeanor could best be described as tense, frustrated, and on edge. He was being constantly hit by reports of growing privateer attacks. With about two million pounds of silver being shipped to Seville every year, Philip could not afford to lose one ship.[99]

Then there was the constant rumor that France might next attack the Punta Santa Elena in force. Spain's new ambassador to France, Don Frances de Alava, was also sending Philip repeated messages that France's Queen Mother, Catherine de Medici, was showing that she could not be trusted. She was developing a new religious strategy of "moderation." France would give the Huguenots some crumbs to quell the unrest. That would be entirely unacceptable to Philip II. If that did not cause King Philip's blood pressure to rise, he then heard that his mother-in-law, Catherine de Medici, was planning to invite him to a June meeting at the border town of Bayonne, France. The intent of that get-together was to soothe feelings and agree on certain areas of concern . . . like their mutual policies against heretics. But in the mind of King Philip II, the question had to be "WHY? Why would she do that when she knows that her admiral is preparing to go to war with Spain in La Florida? Why?"

More than ever, the King was concerned that France, or the French Huguenots, may be preparing to develop a second settlement in his North American colony. Rumors were everywhere. France may still be in control of the Punta or, as the French call it . . . Charlesfort. This situation had to remind the king that, as early as 1557, he ordered the Viceroy of New Spain (Mexico) to find the Punta Santa Elena and make it Spain's first settlement. But that did not happen. The Punta remained untouched and vulnerable. Very vulnerable.

In Philip's mind, the risk was HIGH in the Indies. He badly needed the flow of bullion that annually arrived from the Indies. It may only represent 10–15% of his annual revenue, but it was fluid cash. When he received it, he could immediately apply it to his war debt. It also irritated Philip that he was receiving reports of increased pirate activity coming from both France and England. He may have been at peace with France, but there were increasing corsair attacks from Huguenot ships leaving La Rochelle. Now for many in Spain, the enemy was not so much France as it was the Protestant French Huguenots and the English.

Philip was also concerned with the Netherlands. The king was trying to solidify control of his seventeen Low Country provinces. They were pushing for open religious freedom. And Protestant England was becoming the belligerent supporter of those Low Country renegades. Then there was Malta. Malta was the home of the last of the three military orders that sprang out of the Crusades. The Knights of St. John began as a knighthood dedicated to nursing and the defense of pilgrims going to and from Jerusalem. By 1310, they established a home base on the Island of Rhodes and quickly developed into the finest maritime fighting force in the Mediterranean. But the aggressive Muslim leader Suleiman the Magnificent reacted to that threat. He expelled the religious order from Rhodes in 1522, however, Charles V came to their rescue in 1530. He gave them a new home . . . the Island of Malta. In the meantime, Spain's new dependency became the home of the most skilled mariners in the Mediterranean. That meant one thing to Suleiman the Magnificent. Unless he could conquer Malta, he had no path to control the western Mediterranean.[100]

In October of 1564, Jean Parisot de la Valette, the Grand Master of the Order, received information from his agents in Constantinople that the Muslim sultan planned to attack Malta in either May or June of 1565. And it would be some attack. Suleiman would attack with 180 ships and no less than 30,000 men. La Valette did not wait long to assemble his defenses. He immediately sent a letter to Philip II asking for 25,000 Spanish soldiers.[101]

In Philip's mind, the Netherlands issue was important, but it was not as critical as either the Indies or Malta. Philip II did not have a good record for making timely decisions. But he was up against two real risks. If Suleiman were to conquer Malta, the Muslim world would have an open door to attack Sicily and Spain. The Muslim control of Malta would also give the Turks control of the Mediterranean.

Philip knew two things. Nothing would stop the 70-year-old Suleiman the Magnificent from making his planned attack in May or June of 1565. On the other hand, there was every indication that the French Huguenots were planning another attack on Spanish soil in North America. If they were successful, that could lead to a significant loss of his returning treasure. To assess the French threat to the Indies, Philip needed the input of someone who had the broadest experience. He needed the advice of Pedro Menendez de Aviles. But first he needed to get Menendez out of prison. He needed to settle Menendez's dispute with the CASA. Pedro had already been imprisoned for 18 months.[102]

On February 3, 1565, Pedro Menendez gained his freedom. The Council of the Indies terminated the two cases that the CASA had against Pedro Menendez de Aviles . . . and in his favor. Now Spain's king could seek his advice. He contacted him by courier and asked him to answer these questions: *"With your experience in the Americas and your experience in fighting the French privateers, what are our problems in defending our new colony? Where are we most vulnerable? What should we do to settle this colony? What action should we take if we discover that either France or England has already established a base in our colony?"*[103]

These may seem like questions that any king would ask. But they were not. Menendez's answers actually formed the basis of how Spain would proceed to push France off of the American continent.

PEDRO MENENDEZ'S ASSESSMENT OF SPAIN'S NEW WORLD RISK
By mid-February of 1565, Philip II received his report, or memorial, from Pedro Menendez. The core of this exceptional report became the strategy that Spain would use to both defend and settle its new colony. Up to this point, Pedro Menendez had to use his tactical skills. Now his king was testing his strategic abilities. Appendix I contains the entire translated report (or memorial) that Menendez sent Philip. However, in a condensed format, this is what Pedro Menendez de Aviles said when Philip II asked him, *"What is our situation in North America?"*

♛ "I heard reports that English and French corsairs have recently been in our Indies. If this continues, we can expect them to build their own settlements in our colony.

"When they do build their first settlements, we can expect them to be most interested in locating near the Bahama Channel, where they can attack our returning Treasure Fleet.

"I believe that the French or English probably landed on La Florida last summer. If they did, they will be very difficult to remove. By the time we can identify where they settled, they will have had one year to develop a good relationship with the Indians. Thus, we will be facing both the invaders and their Indian allies."

"The blacks now represent at least 30 times our Spanish population in the Indies. They want more freedom. **If the French or English were to offer them their freedom, they could quickly seize our forts and settlements in the Americas. That could be a French 'strategy.'"**

"We have another threat, which is also a big opportunity, in North America. I met a man while returning to Spain who said that he had heard that a French ship had discovered a "northwest passage" that led from Newfoundland to an area near the Spanish mines in northern New Spain (Mexico). This man informed him that the French believe that this route may also lead to the South Sea. In other words, it may be that shortcut to the Orient that we have been looking for. Apparently, the French ship that made this discovery sank before it returned to France. But if this story is true, our mines in Mexico would be threatened. And France would have discovered that shortcut to Asia."

"With this review of our situation, I (Pedro Menendez de Aviles) recommend that we do the following: *First, we go to the Punta Santa Elena and make it our first settlement. We make it our first priority because it can help us protect our returning Treasure Fleet. We can also use it as a hub for exploring everything west and north.*"

"We settle the Punta Santa Elena as a complete, fully functioning community. It should have at least 500 soldiers, sailors, farmers, and craftsmen. In other words, it should be self-sustaining. Once we settle the Punta, we expand and establish at least one or two additional settlements."

⚜ "This endeavor will be expensive. It should cost about 80,000 ducats for one year. Because we need to act quickly, the Crown should pick up this initial expense."

⚜ Finally, Menendez made one more important point that would later rise to be part of Spain's war plan. "If we find that the Frenchmen have again landed in our colony to establish a settlement, we will need to remove them with an armada that includes an additional four galleons with a thousand sailors and soldiers."

If one had to condense Menendez's report, it clearly emphasized these points: *"We don't have any more time. We need to settle North America now, before the French do. And we need to establish that first settlement at the Punta Santa Elena. Furthermore, forget about our past claim that the Pope gave it to us. Let's claim North America using the French guideline . . . We will claim it based on developing two or three self-sufficient settlements."*

King Philip II hated meetings. He almost always preferred written correspondence. However, when he faced a critical issue, he often insisted on meeting with the author of an important report. There is no evidence that he personally met with Pedro Menendez after he received his Memorial. However, it is highly likely that he did. Philip admired Menendez, much like any king would admire a national hero.

Philip did not waste any time in making a decision. After receiving Pedro Menendez's report, the king took his recommendation to the Council of the Indies.[104] It was a hard choice. With a Treasury that was almost empty, he had to decide if he wanted to defend Malta or the Indies or both. If Malta were lost, the Muslim Turks would only be a short hop away from either Sicily or Spain. If Santa Elena was not settled, the returning Spanish Treasure Fleet would be at risk. Philip made the hard decision. Spain would focus its attention on protecting the Indies. Philip II would give limited help in the defense of Malta.

He would hold the Viceroy of Sicily, Don Garcia de Toledo, responsible for assisting the defense of the Islands. Philip would acquire control of North America using France's definition of "selective control." Instead of justifying North America as Spain's because the Pope gave it to them, Philip justified it using France's definition. Spain would create two or three continental-style settlements. Each would have a garrison, a fort, soldiers, a church, artisans, men and women, families, and farms.

On March 15, 1565, Philip II signed a contract with Pedro Menendez de Aviles that made him responsible for settling at least two North American towns for Spain. In other words, Menendez would settle, pacify, and then defend settlements that would qualify under France's own words as *"necessary to lay claim to North America."*

There was a lot at stake. In 1565, Europe had limited geographic knowledge of North America. Philip II showed his understanding of the extent of the area by early 1540, when he labeled North America "La Florida." In his mind, his North American colony extended from the Maritime Islands of Newfoundland to the Florida Keys, and from the Atlantic to a little west of the Mississippi River. **In other words, in the eyes of Spain, La Florida was North America, and it included a territory that extended as far as they had ventured.**

1584 map by Jeronimo Chaves

No one knew what was above the border that separated today's United States from Canada. Most cartographers and mariners believed that China and Russia were probably north of that border. Even Japan, or what they called "Zipanga" was believed to be somewhat west of the Rocky Mountains.[105]

As part of the King's contract with Menendez, he would carry the rare title of Adelantado. That title would give him the broad authority he would need to bring a newfound territory under Spain's control. For example, he would have all civil, judicial, and military authority over Spain's new North American colony. He would be governor of the territory and report directly to King Philip II. With the title of Adelantado, there would be no question about his social standing in Spain. He would be considered one of only a few who rose from being a hidalgo (a peasant with honor) to become a genuine noble. His benefits would be huge. (*See Appendix VI*)

Pedro Menendez had to be more than thrilled at the offer of being made an Adelantado. There was, however, a hitch. With the amount of war debt that Spain needed to repay, Menendez would have to pay for the entire conquest, estimated to be 80,000 ducats for the first year.[106]

MENENDEZ'S REPORT TURNS INTO AN EMPLOYMENT CONTRACT

The bargaining behind Menendez's employment contract ended on March 15, 1565. Interestingly, the very first cover page of Menendez's contract acknowledged that, before 1565, Spain had made five failed attempts to establish a settlement in North America.

". . . never up to now has this land been colonized; nor what we desire has been accomplished."[107]

Philip did not forget the current threat to the Knights of the Order of St. John on Malta, but it would not be his first priority. He immediately informed Malta's Grand Master that he would ask his viceroy of Sicily to do everything possible to provide troops and ships for the defense of Malta. Philip II knew, however, that he had to protect his claim on North America before France took it away from him.

Chapter VII

All Hell Breaks Loose

On March 30, 1565, all hell broke loose in the office of King Philip II. On March 26, the Cuban merchant ship *La Vera Cruz* landed at Sanlucar de Barrameda, the deepwater ocean port that is linked to Seville by the Guadaquivir River. As soon as the ship landed, a mounted courier raced a message to Philip II. On March 30, Philip received the coded message in his Madrid office. The scene was one of an emotional explosion.[108]

Philip II got more than a message from the Governor of Cuba, Diego de Madzariegos. Along with the message were three French deserters who would add fuel to the fire. The message?

A second French Fort exists in his North American colony. France's Fort Caroline is located a few miles inside the St. Johns River, just west of today's Jacksonville, Florida.

The French deserters had an even more alarming message. *"France intends to send a large re-enforcement armada to Ft. Caroline sometime in the spring or summer of 1565."* In Philip's mind, Spain was under attack. For the first time, France and Gaspard Coligny had sent a clear signal of their intentions. They appeared to be doing much more than planning to locate a future settlement on Spain's North American colony. France appeared to be sending a message that they intended to push Spain out of the Americas. For a monarch known as one who was slow in making decisions and poor at delegating, he made a complete about-face. Philip II immediately shifted gears. Fort Caroline was not just a surprise to him. It was inherently more threatening than even Charlesfort. If France held onto Fort Caroline, it would be a near-perfect location from which to ambush Spain's returning Treasure Fleet. Fort Caroline was located at the end of the Bahama Channel, at 30 degrees, 19 minutes north latitude. The ship pilots on Spain's Treasure Fleets considered the northern end of the Bahama Channel their Achilles heel. It was narrow, full of unknown shoals, and frequently threatened by hurricanes. To meet this challenge, Spain's ships slowed down, making them very vulnerable to an attack.[109]

"A second French fort is located in our colony."
(Jacques Lemoyne map of 1564–1565)

Philip II acted! He immediately sent a letter to Menendez informing him of the situation.* His message noted the inevitable. *"Put your current contract on 'hold.' Your first assignment has to be to get rid of the French in the Americas. Leave as soon as possible. And keep your mission a secret."* Then he sent a second message to him on the same day. *"Try to depart by May 1."* [110]

Spain's Achilles heel: The Bahama Channel

Philip acted if he were in the middle of a firefight. He immediately contacted his top government ministers and informed them of the news. The Duke of Alba immediately responded, *"Issue an order that an armada be immediately sent to repel the French. Drive them out of the Americas."* Another counselor, Juan Rodriguez Noriega, was equally blunt. *"France has put the Indies in a crucible. We are compelled to pass in front of their port, and with the greatest ease they can sally out with their armadas to seek us, and easily return home when it suits them. Act promptly before the Admiral of France (Coligny) can forestall you."* The ambassador to France quickly responded to Philip that he had heard nothing from his agents. However, he promised to immediately send his top French spy, Dr. Gabriel de Enveja, to Dieppe and conduct a special surveillance.

The king and Pedro Menendez had not yet had the time to develop either a formal or informal plan of attack. In fact, they had no idea at

---

* When Philip II sent an important letter to someone in Europe, he would dispatch two or three different messengers at the same time. Each of them would take a different route. With this approach, Philip II believed that one of his messages would "get through." Parker, *The Grand Strategy of Philip II* (New Haven, Yale University Press, 1998), 55.

this time when and from where the French armada would depart. Nor did they know the size of their armada. Philip simply knew that he had to have an armada that would reach Fort Caroline before the French. He simply did not have the information he needed to develop a plan. Pedro Menendez de Aviles, however, had heard something when he recently visited the Bay of Biscay port of Vizcaya. *"I heard that sixteen French ships, with two thousand men, were being outfitted in Le Havre for the reinforcement journey."*[111] But neither Menendez nor King Philip II had received any official intelligence on the size of France's planned reinforcement armada. That would not delay them from preparing an armada to sail.

Impulsively, the king sent a message to Pedro Menendez that the Crown would pay for an additional 500 men and three ships. Then he ordered Cuba, Hispaniola, and the captain-general of the Treasure Armada to give him an additional three ships and 550 men once he reached the Indies. That would increase Spain's attack force so that he should be able to leave the Canary Islands starting point with 1,364 men and arrive at the mouth of the St. Johns River with 16 ships and 1,914 men.*[112]

See page 251 in Appendix VIII for discussion of ships and manpower promised vs. delivered.

Chapter VIII

The Race is "ON!"

hilip II rang the bell. And he rang it hard and long. There was no question that both Spain and France understood that they were about to be in a cross-Atlantic race . . . a race that would determine which country would first control North America. Gaspard Coligny, the Admiral of France, took the first step. His strategy was beginning to be seen by some as a move to start a war with Spain in La Florida. Why? Possibly to diminish the role of France's dominant Catholic party. In other words, if France saw Catholic Spain attacking them in North America, that should transfer their anger to the French Catholic party, which was already promoting a close relationship with Spain. If that was Coligny's strategy, it could improve the position of Protestants in France.

Coligny set the stage by sending Jean Ribault to the Punta Santa Elena in 1562 to assess the area as a launching site for ambushes. Then, he authorized Rene Laudonniere to settle at Fort Caroline in 1564 . . . an even closer location to Spain's ports in the Indies. Now, thanks to three Fort Caroline deserters, Philip II knew that France intended to launch an armada to do more than resupply their "illegal" fort in July or August of 1565. They intended to use it as a base to expand further south into the Spanish Indies. France was setting the stage for a cross-Atlantic invasion of Spanish North America. But to do that, they would have to race Spain to the peninsula of Florida. And the winner of the race would be in the strongest position to first control North America.

As soon as Spain's Philip II received the news that France had a base at Fort Carolina (near Jacksonville, Florida), he rang the bell. He immediately ordered Menendez in March to assemble an armada and attempt to beat France's Jean Ribault to Fort Caroline.

Then in April 1565, he ordered Spain's top spy in France, Dr. Gabriel Enveja, to go to Dieppe and get the facts. When do they intend to depart? How many ships? How many men are they sending? What's the size of this armada? Then both King Philip II and Pedro Menendez de Aviles broadcast one message to the officials of Spain. *"We intend to beat France's armada to La Florida and push them out of North America."* More than likely Philip would have parceled his words in more colorful terms.[113]

The king did not forget the CASA. He immediately ordered them to help Menendez dispatch his armada as soon as possible. And he reminded them that they needed to immediately pay Pedro Menendez the 20,000 ducats they owed him. To the CASA, that had to be a painful message. They had now been ordered to help the one person who had been their longtime adversary.

The CASA officials had to feel great pain when they were forced to outfit Pedro Menendez's armada. Before Philip II appointed Pedro Menendez to the position of captain-general of the armada, the CASA lined their own pockets. They had the envious job of appointing the captain-general and the fleet admiral of the expedition. They did that by selling those top two offices to the highest bidders. They, in turn, would sell their subordinate-officer positions to the highest bidders.[114]

The CASA was like any large bureaucratic organization. It had a range of camouflaged steps that they could take to delay any armada. In this case, the most effective one might be to delay paying Menendez the 20,000 ducats that the court ordered in January. They certainly knew that Pedro Menendez de Aviles could not buy the supplies he needed or pay for the sign-on wages if they did not pay him the 20,000 ducats that they owed him.

SPAIN'S "BACK-OF-THE-ENVELOPE" PLAN

It did not take long for Pedro Menendez and the king to develop a rough "back-of-the-envelope" plan. At this point, they had no solid information on the size or composition of the French armada that was about to depart Dieppe. However, their quick-response plan looked like this: Spain would line up 16 ships for their attacking armada. Menendez would leave Spain with 15 ships . . . 10 from Cadiz and 5 from Asturias.[115]

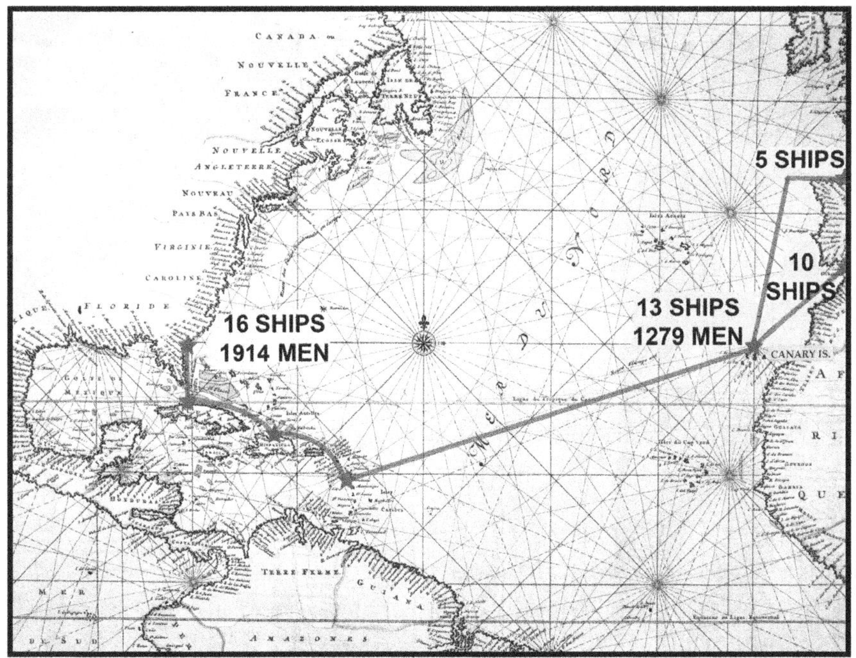

Spain's Back-of-the-Envelope Plan

Once Menendez reached the Canaries, the two shuttle ships would return to Cadiz. He would leave the Canaries with 13 ships. He would pick up three additional Crown ships in the Indies and 550 men. That would allow him to attack Fort Caroline with 16 ships and 1,914 seamen and soldiers.[116] Menendez would follow the traditional navigational track that Spain and Europe used to reach the southeast of North America. The Canary Islands were the starting point The African trade winds blow past the Canaries and sweep directly toward the Canaries. Menendez's ships would catch those winds at the 28-degree north latitude line by heading due West. In about two weeks, they would land at the Antilles islands of Dominica. They would stop, however, only long enough to pick up fresh water and wood for the cook stoves. Then they would head to San Juan and Havana. From Havana they would head north, go through the Bahama Channel, which follows the east side of the Florida peninsula, and land at the mouth of the St. Johns River. The St. Johns River is located near today's Jacksonville. That was the plan.

Once Menendez reached the mouth of the St. Johns River, he planned to make an amphibious landing on a large island located at the mouth of the river. It may have been the island that is today called Fort George Island. With this plan, Menendez believed that he could block both the French infantry from escaping to the Atlantic and the arriving Ribault armada from entering the St. Johns River.[117]

Following his plan, his infantry would then offload cannon and soldiers. By then he would be in an excellent position to attack Fort Caroline with his smaller ships. Meanwhile the *San Pelayo* and the *Sant Andres* (the admiral's flagship) would be outside of the river's entrance and facing Ribault's arriving armada. Menendez knew from the three captured deserters that Fort Caroline was still manned by about 200 men under the French commander, Rene Laudonniere.[118]

Fort Caroline. Is It still manned by 200 Frenchmen?

The fort, however, was 6–9 miles inside the mouth of the St. Johns River. Menendez also knew from the French prisoners that Laudonniere would already have either two or three ships in the river. He knew one other thing, and he communicated it to every important government decision-maker. *"Everything will rest on having the Spanish armada arrive before Ribault lands."*[119]

THE "MEN OF ASTURIAS"

Menendez's agreement with the King required him to recruit 500 men in Spain at his cost, plus 300 that the king would pay for. But first the captain-general had to assemble his "band of brothers"—the 20 to 30 men that he could count on to captain his ships and lead his 1,000-plus infantry. Menendez's sea and infantry captains would be far different, however, from the ones who'd led past expeditions. They would be men who honored their God and country above gold and silver. And they would be men who had an unusually deep respect for Pedro Menendez de Aviles. Menendez was about to assemble an unusual team of leaders. If one had to compare them to any other group, one would think of the mythical Robin Hood and his "Men of Sherwood Forest." They were motivated by the basics in life . . . a love of the common man, their family, their God, and their country. Furthermore, they had a deep respect for their leader.

When the CASA saw Pedro Menendez de Aviles recruit these key officers, they had to be shocked. Instead of selling key positions, he was offering each man the opportunity to be part of an enterprise that was bigger than himself. He didn't approach strangers who would pay for the opportunity to be in a position to smuggle bullion. He approached his longtime friends, family members, and shipmates who had common values and a similar background.

Menendez focused on recruiting Asturians or "Northerners" for good reason. He knew that most of these men would have a relationship with each other. The Asturian families were merged together like a woven blanket. More than anything, they were born into a culture of the sea . . . and they had a reputation of being unusually strong fighters. It was part of their genetic fabric.[120]

When one looks back at the great trans-Atlantic race that was about to unfold, it becomes entirely clear why Menendez was so intent on recruiting Asturians to fill his senior leadership positions. Every Spanish ship that left for the Indies had one major problem . . . discipline. Young Spaniards would use every reason possible to hire on for a round trip to the Indies and back. But a large number of them would desert once they reached the Indies. Gold fever would set in. Menendez knew, however, that his expedition would be even more difficult than any regular voyage to the Indies. More than likely, his men would also be under enemy fire. He had to have leaders who would support him even when his orders made no sense to them.

THE TEAM COMES TOGETHER

Menendez selected Diego Flores Valdes as his Almirante or second-in-command of his armada. Diego Valdes had worked under Menendez for 15 years in the most daring situations in both the Indies and Flanders. Their relationship was so strong that Valdes pawned the greater part of his estate to help Menendez finance the attack on the French.[121] Menendez had to put the five ships that would come from northern Spain under its own command. That would allow him to concentrate on assembling the larger force in Cadiz. He chose Esteban de las Alas as his admiral of the Bay of Biscay contingent. Esteban had worked under Pedro Menendez for 12 years. He also suffered as a result of that allegiance. In 1562, the CASA imprisoned him when he returned from the Indies.[122]

Menendez assigned one of his most experienced sea captains to work under Alas as his vice-admiral . . . Pedro Menendez Marquez. He was much more than the Adelantado's nephew. He had worked for 20 years as an armada ship captain under Pedro Menendez.[123]

One other Asturian would fill out the first five officers that Pedro Menendez would select to help him organize his 1565 attack armada. His brother, Bartolome, would continue to be at his side. Just as France's Gaspard Coligny's brother, Andelot, was his best friend, Pedro Menendez de Aviles' closest friend was his brother, Bartolome. He served under Pedro in every major expedition. He even went to jail with him in 1563. Pedro Menendez de Aviles was about to go to war with France with a highly integrated and disciplined armada of close friends and family. However, one element stood out as "abnormal" in his battle plan. With few exceptions, Menendez appointed only maritime or naval officers to lead his entire expedition. That is just the opposite of how the CASA had manned past expeditions. With the exception of ship captains, ship pilots, and non-commissioned marine officers, the CASA armadas were led by nobles who usually had land-based infantry experience. In other words, Menendez was giving more weight to "known leadership and loyalty" than he was to specific skills that were usually needed to conduct a land-based operation. The big question for some of the Spanish officials had to be, *"How could this possibly work?"*

THE CASA GOES TO WORK

The CASA traditionally had to manage a series of tasks before any ship could leave for the Indies. First, they had to assemble the ships that the king had ordered for the expedition. Then, they outfitted their ships with weapons and rigging and put each ship into a fighting condition. Once the captain-general gave them a list of officers and crew, they were also responsible for checking the qualifications of the men. Were they who they said they were? Were they true Christians? Then the CASA made a second visit to the ships to see if the recommended repairs had been made. Finally, they would not allow the armada to leave until they approved the final manifest. Were the ships equipped as the Adelantado had promised? Were there any unauthorized passengers, such as men trying to escape their creditors or women not accompanied by their husbands? By delaying any one of these tasks, the CASA could make life miserable for Pedro Menendez de Aviles.

The CASA made every visible effort to honor the king's request to play ball with the Adelantado. But they knew that Pedro Menendez had been ordered to depart within an unusually short period of time. During the mid-1500s, the CASA would outfit an armada in 3 to 6 months. King Philip asked the Adelantado to dispatch two armadas (the Asturias and Cadiz fleets) in two and one-half months.

The captain-general soon felt the pressure of the CASA's "unintended" delays. To counter this frustration, he sent Philip II a letter on May 18th that simply said, *"The CASA is delaying the armada. I cannot pay for my share of the supplies or the signing payment for the crew unless the CASA pays me the 20,000 ducats that they've owed me since January."*[124]

MAY, 1565: A RACE TO AMERICA IS EMERGING

France was quickly alerted to Philip's planned response. Soon after the Council of the Indies backed Philip's plan for war, Spain's newly appointed ambassador to France, Don Frances de Alava, sent this coded message to Philip: "*The French are already aware of the size and destination of our planned Spanish armada.*"[125]

This message only magnified Philip II's sense of urgency. They still did not have the intelligence they needed to "size" France's armada. Most importantly, how many ships was France planning to send to Fort Caroline? What was their tonnage? What artillery would they load? How many soldiers would they carry? And what course did Ribault intend to take once he spotted the Canary Islands?

Now the report from Spain's agent in France, Dr. Gabriel Enveja, was more important than ever. What did agent Gabriel de Enveja discover when he went to Dieppe? It did not take him long to visit the French port of Dieppe.

JUNE 10, 1565: SPAIN'S SPY DELIVERS A REMARKABLE REPORT

By June 10, Philip II had received the first "hard data" on the size of the planned French armada. In response to the request from the king to Spain's ambassador in France, Dr. Gabriel Enveja gave this report to King Philip II on June 3, 1565:

Seven ships were ready to depart for Florida, all in very good order and very well armed, of which the flagship, (ship of Jean Ribault) called the Trinite, is a galleass (has both oars and sails). It is about 150 to 160 tons. There are two others among them of the same size. The fourth is of 120 tons, the fifth is of 90, the sixth of 70, the seventh of 60 tons. Three of these ships were outfitted in Havre de Grace and the other four in Dieppe. They go very well armed with artillery, people, and munitions.

The people who go within (aboard) are first of all many good seamen picked from the coast of Normandy, and principally from Havre de Grace and Dieppe. Five hundred soldiers go, who wait there to make their entries—people to whom they affirm me (because they were already embarked when I arrived), brilliant and well treated, almost all arquebusiers, many (with) gilded helmets, most of them with beginning beards, dressed with their short skirts and breeches in the Levantine style or various colors. They tell me that among them go 100 cavaliers to see and bring gold.

There go among them also German cavaliers, very well- disposed young men, well-treated. They tell me that the Admiral Coligny sent them. There also go others sent by the Prince of Porcian. The Captain of these people on land is one named La Grange, a man of medium body plump-faced, short stretched beard, between black and chestnut. He is a man who never entered on the sea. They all wear doublet clothing, many pair of shoes. There also go in this armada all kinds of officers with the proper equipment of their offices. Many bring their wives and children, in such a manner that there go in these ships up to 900 or 1,000 people, all Lutherans. And in order not to forget their evil sect, they bring 7 or 8 ministers. All these people were embarked except some noble ex-cadets who had gone on land. They also carry animals in one ship . . . horses, mares, bulls, cows, sheep, ewes, pigs of both sexes, even asses and female asses.

The munitions they carry are very great, because they tell me that they carry a lot of gunpowder and shot—200 reinforced canon which go unmounted to put in the said fort which they have made there. They carry many hatchets, hammers and dies—victuals for sea and victuals for land, for going and coming, for land, provision for one year.

The Captain-General of this armada and leader on land as well as on sea is a man named Jean Ribault, native of Dieppe, married there, a man of good form, of long red beard, skin of his head reddish and somewhat bald, countenance of a little small, eyes medium white, of an age between 45 and 50 years, even though he does not seem of such an age. He is reputed to be a good man and valiant, but he is a very great Lutheran, and to him is attributed the discovery of Florida, where he has been twice. He is a very good sailor in those parts. The King (of France) has given him the title of

Lt. General of Florida for two years. His son, Jacques Ribault, goes as his Lieutenant, who will return with this armada.

The course they observe is to seek the Canary Islands and take the course outside the islands, which they call the Antilles, without touching any cape whatever until they enter the river they have given the name The River of May (St. Johns River).

The intention which these people have is to conquer the land, populate and fortify it and plant what they call the evangel. They do not permit that another book be carried except the Lutheran.

The people that are now in La Florida (at Fort Caroline) are about 190 up to 200 men. Because of the three ships they would have there, two returned the past day of San Miguel. The captain who is there; he is one called Laudonniere. He has made a fort next to the said river (St. Johns). They say it is strong enough. I understand that those who are there have very few provisions and that they have suffered great hunger.

It is understood that the King of France issued from his Rouen profits 200,000 francs for this enterprise. It is feared that our ships will encounter Spain's armada, because they would have understood that His Majesty had named as Marquis of Florida, Pedro Menendez, and that he went with an armada (to counter our reinforcement armada).

They tell me in Dieppe that next year another four or five ships will go, and that from there onward there would go two fleets—one in May and another in September.

Signed June 3, 1565 by Dr. Gabriel Enveja[126]

WERE THE FRENCH REALLY READY TO DEPART?

Dr. Enveja's report shocked King Philip II. This was not just another threat. The French armada was about ready to depart. Both King Philip II and Pedro Menendez had to have had these thoughts: *"What did Enveja mean when he said, 'They come to conquer our land?'"* They must have had a longer-range plan than to resupply Ft. Caroline. Otherwise, why would they be planning annual relief armadas? If they were to depart in a couple of weeks, they could be at the Canary Islands by mid- June.* If they took seven ships, they could greet the French at Fort Caroline with 9–10 ships. The French prisoners had already told the Spanish that they had 3 ships in the St. Johns River. If Ribault carried 800 soldiers and sailors on his relief armada, he would have another 200 men at Ft. Caroline. That's 1,000 men that Menendez would have to face. *And why would they be loading 200 cannons for one fort?* That would be enough to equip three to four forts. They already knew that Menendez was preparing to meet and attack them. Clearly, this was a race. And Menendez was behind.

Phillip II would certainly have wondered, *"How in God's name can Catherine be planning to attack us and at the same time initiating a June peace conference at Bayonne?"* The Enveja report now gave Menendez two additional insights into Ribault's plans and a better idea of the size of Ribault's armada. He would leave with seven ships and probably add up to three more once he reached Ft. Caroline. Ribault would probably have an available armada of 9 to 10 ships. Furthermore, it appears that he would have to turn west before reaching the Canaries to avoid any contact with Menendez. That may be a shorter route, but it would also take him out of the direct African trade winds.

MAY 10, 1565: DELAY AT DIEPPE

While Pedro Menendez assembled senior officers who were used to working together, the same was apparently not true for Jean Ribault. When Spain's French spy, Dr. Gabriel Enveja, interviewed the French admiral, he shared some frustration as to why he'd decided to delay his departure. Ribault's infantry captain, Francois Leger de la Grange, had questions about the extent of his authority. Admiral Ribault decided that he would not leave

---

* The starting point for any European trip destined for the Indies was the Canary Islands. At that point the trade winds blow east to west and carry any ship, or hurricane, on a direct route to the Indies.

port until Gaspard Coligny had clarified the captain's role and authority. Among his peers, la Grange was referred to as "Corsette." Ribault's differences with Francois la Grange did not end at Dieppe. Once Ribault's ships landed at Ft. Caroline, he would find himself at odds with la Grange on a more critical matter.[127] Ribault clearly knew that his mission was much more than resupplying Fort Caroline. The Admiral of France had also ordered him to replace Rene Laudonniere as the commander of Fort Caroline. But that was just the first step. Coligny had more expansive plans for his admiral once he resupplied the fort. And Pedro Menendez would discover those plans once he attacked Fort Caroline.[128]

Before Jean Ribault got underway on May 10, 1565, the Admiral of France arrived to discuss some "open" issues with Admiral Ribault. When Coligny's carriage stopped at the waterfront, he saw seven French ships anchored in Dieppe's harbor.

As soon as Coligny stepped onto the French flagship, the *Triniti*, he handed the Admiral this letter:

"Captain Jean Ribault, As I was closing up this letter, I received advice that Don Pedro Menendez has departed from Spain to go to the coast of New France. See that he does not encroach upon us any more than he would encroach upon you." Signed Gaspard Coligny, Admiral of France

The letter could not have been clearer. He was telling Jean Ribault, *"We have the intelligence to know that Spain (i.e., Menendez) is also headed for Fort Carolina. If you encounter him, attack and destroy him and his armada."*[129] When Coligny handed Jean Ribault the letter, Ribault had to know approximately when Menendez would leave Cadiz, the size of his armada, the number of seamen and soldiers, and their mission. France's spies were at every major Spanish port. More than likely, France's spies would also have known the navigational track that Menendez planned to take. **The race was "on."**

FRENCH SHIPS READY TO DEPART FROM DIEPPE[130]

- *La Trinite*, 32-gun flagship of Admiral Ribault, powered by sails and oars. 150–160 tons Roberge design with rounded bow with a square-tucked stern. Driven aground south of St. Augustine.

- *L'Emerillon*, 29-gun vice-admiral flagship. The vice-admiral's ship, Nicolas d'Ornano of Corsica, known as Corsette. A Roberge. 150–160 tons. Had both oars and sails. Carried iron weapons: 18 cannon, 7 iron carriages for bronze guns, 380 cannon balls and 7 iron pikes. Driven aground south of St. Augustine.

- *La Perle*, 80 tons. Captained by Jacques Ribaut, the Admiral's son. Returned safely to France.

- *La Levriere*, 70 tons. Captained by Vivien Maillard. Returned safely to France.

- *L'Epaule de Mouton*, 60 tons. Captained by Machonville. Sunk with the fall of St. Augustine.

- *La Truite*, Roberge, 150–160 tons. Roberge design. Driven aground south of St. Augustine.

- *L'Emerillon II*, Roberge, 120 tons. Privately owned and contracted by the Crown. Captain: Vincent Collas. Driven aground south of St. Augustine.

CHAPTER IX

Underway

ith Dr. Enveja's report, King Philip II and Pedro Menendez de Aviles had a clearer picture. Forensic navigators Heckrotte and Nelson believe that it was probably Ribault's intention to leave France no later than June 7th. They also believe that it would have taken Ribault about 21 days to sail from Dieppe to the Canary Islands.[131] If a few problems surfaced, Ribault would not be able to reach the Canaries (the cross-Atlantic starting point) before the June 20 to June 30 period. And with a little bad weather, Ribault might not reach the Canaries until July. That had to tell Menendez that his armada must depart Cadiz between June 15 and June 30. It would then take him 7–10 days to go from Cadiz to the Canaries.

Ribault had to assume that he had nine to ten ships available to him . . . seven from Dieppe and two or three in the river near the mouth of the St. Johns River. With approximately 200 French troops already at Ft. Caroline, Ribault probably estimated that he would have at least 1,000–1,200 seamen and soldiers available to him once he reached the mouth of the St. Johns River. More importantly, he would also have a sizable "defensive" advantage . . . if he could arrive before Spain's Pedro Menendez de Aviles.

THE SPANISH PLAN GETS FINE-TUNED

Knowing this situation, Menendez planned to depart Cadiz and the Bay of Biscay with a total of 15 ships and 1,424 seamen and soldiers between June 15 and July 1. Ten ships would depart from Cadiz under the command of Pedro Menendez. Another five would depart from Asturias, in northern Spain, under the command of Esteban de las Alas. Once Alas and Pedro Menendez met at the Canaries, they would depart together for the Indies with 13 ships and 1,364 soldiers and mariners.[132] Once Menendez reached Havana and collected the additional three ships and 550 men, he would arrive at the mouth of the St. Johns with 16 ships and about 1,914 fighting men.* In Menendez's mind, that would be a force that should be able to defeat the French, **if he could arrive before Ribault**. But for this plan to work, everything had to fall in place at the right time, with few interruptions. The CASA could not be the tormentor. They would have to do their inspections exactly when needed. To stop the French attack on Spanish America, everything would have to change. No longer could the King expect to hold Pedro Menendez to a contract in which he would have to pay for everything. This would now be more like a 50–50 proposition.

But both Menendez and King Philip II knew two things. France's armada was about to depart. And if they arrived at the mouth of Fort Caroline before Menendez, they would have an almost-overwhelming advantage. King Philip II knew what he had to do, and he did it in a very uncharacteristic fashion. He maintained a "sense of urgency." Unexpectedly, he pushed and shoved. Philip sent a message to Jean Parisot de la Valette, the Grand Master of the Order of St. John on Malta. He

---

* This is the author's estimate. Others have estimates which range from 1900 to more than 2,000. See Appendix VIII.

emphasized that Spain would do everything possible to help the Order defend itself from the anticipated Muslim invasion. But he also told Malta's grand master that he'd delegated the major responsibility to his Viceroy of Sicily, Don Garcia.

The king ordered the CASA to support Pedro Menendez in every way possible. And he was not naïve. He knew that the CASA would be tempted to get too involved in Menendez's preparation. His letter to the CASA sent a clear message. *"I forbid you from intruding into anything dealing with the Menendez armada, including visiting the fleet, unless you have my written approval."*[133] He knew that Menendez could not pay for his ships or men until the CASA paid what they owed him from his recent court settlement. But he also knew that that was the last thing that the CASA wanted to do for their long-time adversary.

PHILIP'S COMMITMENT

Philip knew that he had to find the funds to pay for the Crown's commitment of men, ships, and supplies. The Treasury, however, was empty. He ordered the CASA to find the money to pay for the Crown's offer of men. Philip knew that neither the New Spain nor the Tierra Firme Treasure Armadas were due to arrive in Seville.† But maybe there was a fund available from the taxes that the merchants paid for the protection of their outgoing ships. Could the merchants help fund this armada? If Menendez's expedition was successful, it would certainly make their investment safer.

The Adelantado knew what he had to do . . . depart Cadiz by the end of June. But to do that, he needed the help from every influential department that reported to the king. Menendez had enough political

---

† If Philip II was short on cash, his household budget did not help. By 1560, Philip employed approximately 1,500 people on his household staff . . . 800 servants for his personal staff; 200 for his stables; 100 for his chapel; and 400 for such miscellaneous duties as "special police." Geoffrey Parker, *The Grand Strategy*, p. 17.

savvy to know that he could not do this on his own. He needed help. He needed to put pressure on the CASA. Throughout April, he met with the Council of War, the Council of the Indies, and the Royal Council of Castile.‡ His message was simple. *"If we do not depart by June, we will have to wait until next year. If we are late, we will be facing a very large entrenched French army next year . . . an army that has had the time to use their Indian allies as part of their defense."*[134]

A TROUBLESOME MOTHER-IN-LAW

Philip II was in the center of a whirlpool, and he knew it. On top of these headaches, the king had one irritant that ate at him. Catherine de Medici, the de facto leader of France, may have been his mother-in-law, but he clearly did not trust her. And now that he knew that France was about to launch an armada to reinforce their secret base in Spain's new colony, Philip was enraged. Philip strongly disapproved of Catherine's policy of religious moderation. How could that possibly work? To Philip II, she spoke out of both sides of her mouth. She had organized a June "peace" conference between the two governments at the very time her ships were preparing to attack him in La Florida. The meeting was to take place at the border town of Bayonne, France. That raised two questions. Should he immediately contact France's Queen Mother and confront her with his knowledge of her war plans? Or . . . if Ribault's ships had already departed, should he have that discussion after Spain had removed them from the Americas? Philip chose the latter approach. It had more "sting" to it.

---

‡ Traveling from town to town in Spain in 1565 was not easy. Unlike France and Italy, Spanish inns did not offer both board and lodging. The country taxed the inns so much that it forced the travelers to buy their meat in advance and ask the innkeeper to cook it. Prices for lodging were moderate. Some inns had beds. Others offered straw-filled sacks. In 1565, it cost the traveler one *"real"* for a bed; another *"real"* to cook the traveler's meat and serve it; and one *"real"* for a candle. Defourneaux, *Daily Life in Spain in the Golden Age,* 16.

Menendez had a gigantic task ahead of him. He not only had to assemble an armada, but he also had to assemble one that could beat France's reinforcement armada to Ft. Caroline. He now found himself in a race that would most likely determine whether France or Spain would first control North America. Speed was everything, but so was the quality of the men he selected and the ships he needed.

Fifteen ships would have to be collected before he could leave . . . ten from Cadiz and five from Asturias. One thousand men would have to be recruited. The CASA would have to do its inspections without slowing down the process. And those 15 ships leaving from Spain would have to be loaded. That would take weeks.

EARLY MAY 1565: THE SITUATION WAS NOT GOOD FOR MENENDEZ

It did not take long for Pedro Menendez to forward the CASA a list of the ship-types that he needed. Menendez knew that he needed a few larger ships to balance the men and provisions that would be on the expedition. But that was not possible. The king had a "hold" on the larger available ships so that they could be used to support the expected Muslim attack on Malta.

Now it was the CASA's job to inspect Menendez's ships, order the needed changes to the ships . . . and place artillery on them. Pedro Menendez, however, would have to pay for most of the ships and men that departed from Spain.[§] And the CASA had yet to forward him the 20,000 ducats that they had been ordered to pay him. When he reviewed the final ships that the CASA had collected, it looked like this.

---

§ Of the 13 ships that would leave Spain and continue to La Florida, the Crown committed to pay for only the lease cost of the *San Pelayo* and 300 men. However, Philip II agreed to give Menendez three additional ships and 550 men once he reached the Indies.

SPAIN'S ARMADA[135]

- *San Pelayo*

  Pedro Menendez's flagship galleon of 906 tons. 490 sailors and soldiers, and 100 settlers. The ship would play the important role of being the armada's floating warehouse. But it could also be an effective gun platform. The cost of leasing this ship would be paid for by the Crown. It was one of four ships that Philip II agreed to underwrite during the 1565 race to push France out of its colony. The other three would come from Hispaniola and Cuba.

- *Magdalena*

  A chalupa of 75 tons. A double-ended ship with a shallow draft propelled by both oars and sails. She had two masts and sails. She would carry 14 mariners and 70 soldiers.

- *San Miguel*

  A chalupa of 60 tons. She would carry 9 mariners and 51 soldiers. Loaded with provisions and munitions.

- *San Andres*

  Flagship of Admiral Diego Flores Valdes. A chalupa of 70 tons. Carried 15 mariners and 83 soldiers.

- *Concepcion*

  A chalupa of 60 gross tons. She would carry 12 mariners and 64 soldiers.

- *Vitoria*

  A galeota with 17 benches. Propelled by both sails and oars. Carries 17 mariners. A ship of about 80 tons.

Esperanza

A bergantine. Small ship. About 66 feet length on deck. Has both sails and oars. Has 11 benches and six mariners.

Sant Antonio

A caravel of 150 tons. Medium-sized ship. Estimated length: 70–90 feet. Has a sharp prow and a flat stern. One covered deck. Carried 114 soldiers and unknown number of mariners. Being loaded with provisions and munitions.

Concepcion #2

A caravel. A shuttle ship that would carry 96 soldiers to the Canaries and then return to Cadiz. Cargo: soldiers and provisions.

At this point, Pedro Menendez had selected the "admirals" of his armada—Esteban de las Alas, Pedro Menendez Marquis, and Diego Flores Valdes. Then he had to recruit 1,100 soldiers and seamen before he could depart. There was, however, a shortage of seamen, and gunners were hard to find. But what Pedro Menendez de Aviles did have was a family of connections. Spain had always been a country where men developed careers through relationships . . . both family and friends. Today we call it nepotism, and it is frowned upon. But in 16th-century Spain, it was an employment standard. There was, in fact, no greater opportunity for a young lower-class hidalgo than to work for a well-known captain-general of a Spanish armada. As the conquistador soared in prominence, so would the careers of the young men who worked for him. Now Pedro Menendez leveraged that recruiting advantage. For his top and intermediate positions, he focused on recruiting men who had three characteristics. They had to be Asturians, or men from the Bay of Biscay. They had to be hidalgos. Poor perhaps, but they had "honor." And, if possible, they had to have had some "fighting" experience. With that in mind, Menendez focused on hiring men from 15 families that he was close to.[136] Naturally, these families would recruit their friends.

MAY 26, 1565: RIBAULT DEPARTS

While the French armada was anchored at Dieppe on May 22, a huge channel storm literally swept the ships to Le Havre. On May 26, 1565, Jean Ribault raised his anchors and set a course for Spain's colony of La Florida.[137] Once Ribault departed Le Havre, the French armada was once again attacked by a channel storm.

They quickly sought refuge at England's coastal Isle of Wight. Ribault landed there on May 28 and was warmly received.

Menendez, on the other hand, would only have known from his Spanish spies that Admiral Ribault had departed Le Havre on May 26. He would have had no knowledge of Ribault's two-week delay on England's Isle of Wight. It would not have taken Pedro Menendez and his ship captains long to know what that meant. They would have quickly calculated that, at an average speed of 3.1–4.0 knots, Ribault would reach the Canary Islands cross-Atlantic starting point in three

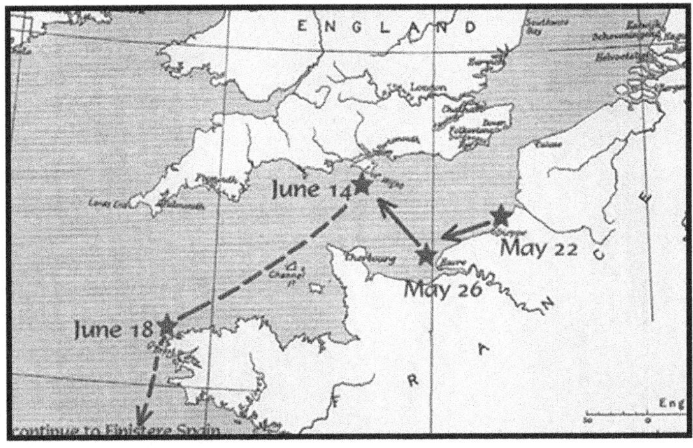

A channel storm gives Ribault a two-week delay

weeks. He would arrive at the Canaries around June 20th.[138] If he ran into some bad weather, it might take him until July 1. It would be easy to visualize Pedro Menendez de Aviles turning to one of his lieutenants and saying, *"We have to be at the Canary Islands no later than the first of July."*

The ambassador's report on Ribault's departure had to have only raised Menendez's anxiety . . . and his questions. How many ships are in Ribault's armada? How many soldiers are they taking? How much artillery are they taking? What's the size of their ships? Menendez will get his answers to those questions on June 10 when Dr. Enveja gives the King a report on his undercover visit to Dieppe, France.

JUNE 14: RIBAULT DEPARTED FROM ENGLAND'S ISLE OF WIGHT

On June 14, the wind quickly turned to the northeast. Jean Ribault weighed anchor and departed England's Isle of Wight. France had now lost two weeks in its race to the Florida peninsula.[139] When put together, the intended navigational plans of both France and Spain looked like this.

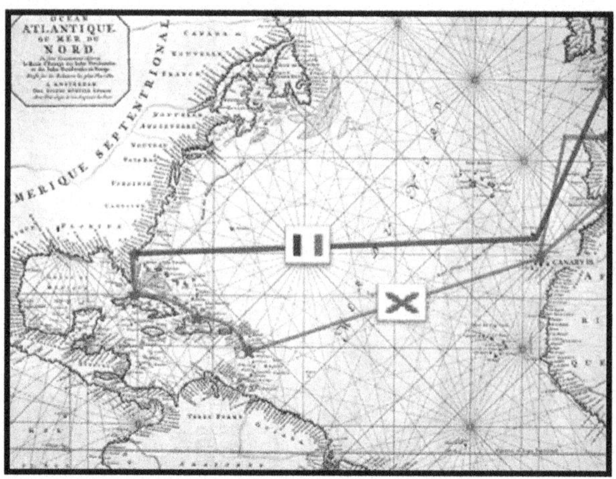

Planned Race Track of France and Spain.

THE BATTLE PLAN EMERGES

But intent rarely matched reality in the 16th century. Now the big question was which country would be the first to reach the starting point of the race, the Canary Islands?

Jean Ribault departed Le Havre on May 26, 1565. Destination? Fort Caroline on the St. Johns River, near today's Jacksonville, Florida. However, once he turned his prow west to reach the northern coastline of France, his armada was swept to England's Isle of Wight. He stayed there for two weeks and departed on June 14, 1565.

But when did Ribault's ship spot the Canaries and start the race by turning due west? And what key events happened during the race? Who led the race? Who lagged? Did they make contact with each other? We know that Menendez's armada was hit by a violent storm. Did they lose any ships? And who crossed the finish line first? Remember, Menendez frequently noted that he could push France out of North America only if his armada arrived first.

Four-hundred-fifty-year-old documents gave the author the starting and ending dates for the race . . . and some intermediate points.

They also provided the dates when a hurricane hit the Spanish armada. However, there were no documents that informed him of where each armada was each day as they crossed the Atlantic. If we could obtain that data, we could begin to see who had the best chance to be the first to reach Fort Caroline. In the author's mind, there was only one possible way to get a more detailed picture of the Spanish-French race to North America . . . find a forensic ocean navigator who specializes in uncovering such information.

In 2015, the author got lucky. He located two forensic ocean navigators who work together as a team. Both Douglas Nelson and Howard Heckrotte had been teaching advanced ocean navigation for years within the U.S. Power Squadron. Their navigation experiences cover both sides of the Atlantic Ocean and the Caribbean. Nelson was considered a master navigator. His partner, Howard Heckrotte, has almost the same pedigree. Heckrotte, however, was quick to say that his partner is the best of the best. If anyone could solve this problem, it would have to be someone like Nelson and Heckrotte.

The author approached these two navigators with this challenge. *"I have strong documentary evidence that Spain and France entered into a race in the summer of 1565, to see who would be the first to reach the mouth of the St. Johns River near today's Jacksonville, Florida. This race was unusually important. The winner would put his country in the best position to be the first European nation to control North America.* My question to you is this: *"Is it possible to identify the navigational track that Spain and France took during this race and with a high level of statistical confidence?"*

After several months of research, Nelson and Heckrotte provided a hint of good news. *"We found North Atlantic pilot charts that go back to the early 1800s. They should be able to give us the historic winds, currents, and calms for every three hundred square miles of the Atlantic Ocean. If we can piece this data together, we might be able to identify the most-likely tracks for both countries."* Three years later, these forensic scientists gave the author the news. *"With a confidence of at least 90%, we believe that we can show you the 'most likely' track that each country took when they raced across the Atlantic in the summer of 1565."* After taking several weeks to examine their work, the author gave them one message along with a glass of bourbon*: "Gentlemen, you just became part of American history."*

RIBAULT'S TRACK IS UNVEILED

Heckrotte and Nelson believe that Ribault's navigational track to the Canary Islands was simple. From the Isle of Wight, he headed west to the northwest corner of France. Once Ribault sighted the town of Brest, he turned "South to Southwest" (about 214 degrees on today's compass).

On this track, Ribault would have been expected to be off the Spanish town of Finisterre in ten days. Then he would have continued another eleven days until he saw Mount Teide on top of Tenerife in the Canary Islands.[140] It can be seen 100 miles away when at sea. The forensic navigators believe that Ribault would have followed the guidance that the Spanish spy, Gabriel Enveja, discovered in his June report to Philip II.

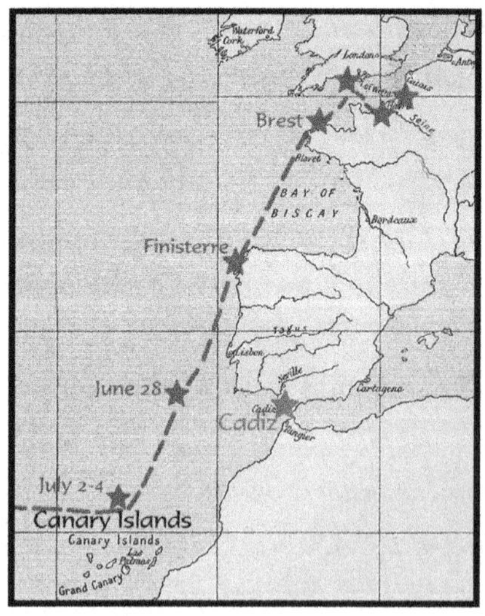

On the way to the Canary Islands.

"The course they intend to take is to first spot the Canary Islands and then set a course that will not touch the Antilles or any cape until they reach the St. Johns River."

To our forensic navigators, that comment meant one thing. Once Ribault spotted Mount Teide on the Canary Island of Tenerife, he would have continued to sail south for one more day. Then he would have turned west at 29 degrees, not the traditional 28 degree north latitude mark. At that latitude line, Ribault's armada would not have been spotted by anyone on the Canary Islands, the Antillies, Puerto Rico, Hispaniola, or Cuba. He would also be taking a course that was 60 miles north of the traditional Spanish track. And if he stayed on that track, he would land near Cape Canaveral. But we can also hear Menendez say, *"If he turns West at 29 degrees, he will be out of the main African trade winds. That may be a shorter track, but ships can be in "calms" that last for weeks."*[141]

Yet, when the forensic navigators lined up the date that Ribault turned west at 29 degrees to the time and date that he landed near Cape Canaveral, it tells one story. Ribault turned west 60 miles before he reached the Canary Islands.[142]

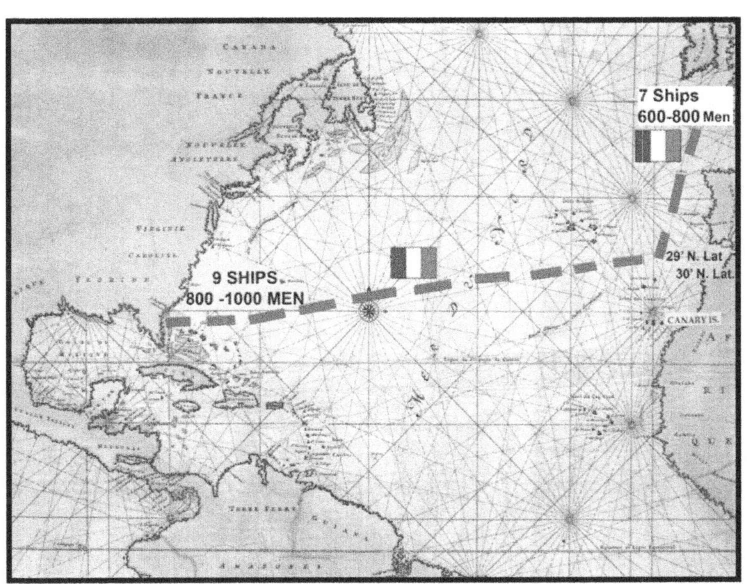

A Route to Avoid the Spanish

KING PHILIP II FEELS THE HEAT.

At this point, neither King Philip II nor Pedro Menendez knew that Ribault had run into a channel storm that delayed his armada for two weeks. Menendez could only have guessed that the French admiral would probably reach the Canaries during the last two weeks of June. Everything could change, however, if the French admiral ran into a storm. And that was often the case in the 1500s. Without any doubt, both King Philip II and the Adelantado felt the heat. They did not want Ribault to be too far ahead of them. And they were worried.

On June 15, Menendez was at the port of Cadiz and loading his ten ships under a cloud of high anxiety. When he scanned the Bay of Cadiz, he would have seen ten ships. Nine of them were much smaller than his *San Pelayo*. At 906 tons, it could carry the equivalent load of six average-sized ships. Historian Carla Rahn Phillips gives us a very good idea of how Menendez would have loaded his ships and gotten underway.[143]

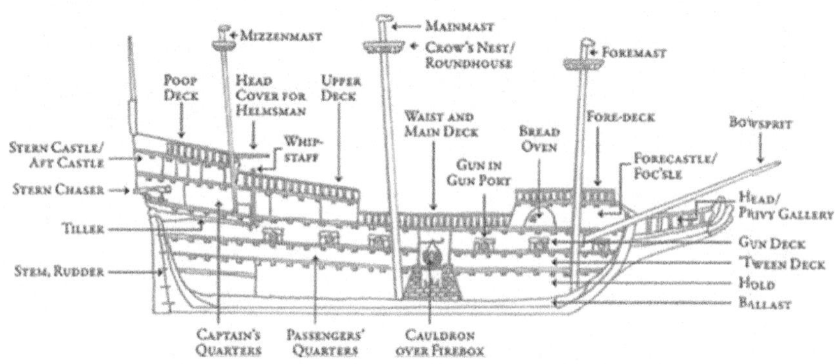

A Galleon similar to the San Pelayo

By June 15, the loading would have been progressing for at least six weeks. As in any mid-16th-century departure, the entire town would have been on the edge of the bay, watching the event. Picture ten Spanish ships anchored in a circle a short distance away from the port's landing, with sail and oared boats of all sizes going back and forth between the landing and ships.

This scene had to look very similar to the situation in the Allied war room in England, the day before "D" Day. Voices were issuing

commands from every cor-
ner of the loading dock. Yet
there was one person who was
overseeing the entire commo-
tion . . . the *Pelayo's* chief boatswain. He was at the loading
site directing traffic.¶ At each
end of the ship landing, the
CASA's police were checking
the manifest of every mule- or
ox-driven wagon that asked

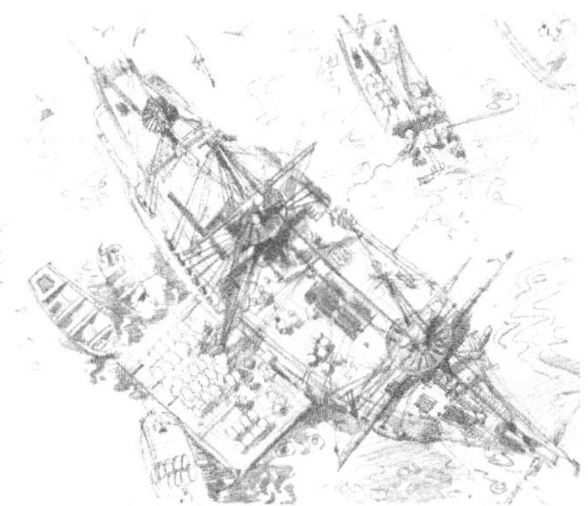

Loading at Cadiz.

permission to unload their supplies. It took a while for the CASA's
men to check out each wagon. Off to the side were a couple of wagons
that had been delayed. They didn't have the right papers. All around
the boatswain were dozens of young apprentice seamen loading barrels,
boxes, and crates of food, supplies, and munitions.

¶ The boatswain had one of the most important positions on a 16th-century ship.
He was the one officer who directly transmitted all orders from the ship's captain
and pilot to the crew. His orders focused on loading the ship, storing the cargo, and
taking the critical steps to "get underway." He was the crew's orchestra conductor.
He passed on all orders that directed the crew to raise anchors, release the sails,
and move the yardarms to grab the winds. Pablo E. Perez-Mallaina, *Spain's Men
of the Sea*, trans. Carla Rahn Phillips.

But beyond them was a stretch of quickly thrown together merchant stalls and pushcarts selling fish, melons, bricks, perfume, and all sorts of trifles . . . like the figa, a miniature hand suspended by a necklace. The seamen believed that it would ward off arrows, lead balls from an arquebus, and infection.** Another vendor was selling a wood carving of a small unicorn. Many Spanish seamen believed that unicorns roamed the colony of La Florida.[144] This was a scene filled with loud and raucous bargaining. The soldiers who eventually would be boarded had plenty of time on their hands and plenty of money to spend. They had just received a cash advance of two months' pay.

Until the final June 25th muster, they would remain onshore. The sailors would be doing double duty . . . loading supplies onto small boats and barges and, on ship, stowing them away. They would sleep aboard their ships. The soldiers, however, roomed in nearby homes and inns.

Before these sailors could board their ship, however, the CASA would check to see if the men matched the ship's register. Every seaman and soldier was identified by his key features, such as this name that was recorded in a 16th century ship's boarding register: *"Francisco Martin, Portuguese, 25 years old; medium build, black beard, and dark. Has one eye and a scar next to his left eye from a knife wound."*[††]

When Menendez picked up the ship's inventory sheets, he undoubtedly paused. One point had to hit him. He would be transferring an entire Spanish culture to North America. His ships would be carrying two rope-makers, eight blacksmiths, two surgeons, three sword-makers, one crossbow maker, one trumpeter, six priests, and 100 farmers. The

---

** In 1565, the arquebus was the dominant weapon of the infantry. It was gradually replacing the crossbow throughout Europe. Thus, Menendez carried more arquebuses than crossbows on his ships. He would soon discover that that was a mistake.

†† From the La Florida Interactive Digital Archive for Colonial Florida History. Actual description provided by Dr. J. Michael Francis (St. Petersburg, University of South Florida, August 2020). Dr. Francis led the development of this important national archive.

inventory of Menendez's flagship, the *San Pelayo*, included 3,000 pounds of ordinary ship-biscuits; 2,500 pounds of bacon; 150 pipes of wine (a pipe holds 126 gallons); 1,080 gallons of olive oil; 2,600 pounds of match cord (used for firing arquebuses); 6,900 pounds of oakum (used to patch holes in ships); 250 arquebuses; 100 lances; and 30 crossbows.[145]

In the center of the loading area, the boatswain was directing his seamen like an auctioneer accepting bids. Loud sounds enveloped the entire area. *"Put that crate over there." "Don't jostle the wine jugs." "Let's load the millstones next." "Where is the sergeant for this group of new soldiers?" Move that barkentine to this spot." "Load it with those millstones." "Hey, don't let those young scoundrels steal that box of candles."*

The boatswain's first job was to load the heaviest, and least important items, onto the anchored ships. They were loaded first because they went to the bottom of the ship's hold. They would act as ballast. Soon three large shuttle boats were heading for the ships and carrying 950 pounds of steel, 6,900 pounds of oakum (used to seal cracks in the hull), 10 milestones, and 2,500 Peruvian jugs.[146] Some of the young seamen were emptying the water barrels that had been filled with salt water for three months. Then they refilled them with fresh water from the town's fountain. That helped tighten the barrel staves so that they could be filled with clear water today. Two coopers were constructing large barrels. They would soon be loaded with smaller items . . . horse shoes, bridles, and stirrups. The chief gunner was directing his men to be sure to load the vinegar bottles. They would be used by his gunners to cool down the cannon barrels after every three shots.

Near the artillery men on the dock was the *Pelayo's* surgeon. He was checking the medical box that contained all the pharmaceutical drugs. He soon spotted a missing drug . . . Unguento Apostolorum, an ointment composed of 12 ingredients, including lead oxide. It contained senna, rhubarb root, and tamarind pulp and was used to consume dead flesh and ulcers.[147]

A large group of the young men were at the waterfront studying how to move the *Pelayo's* artillery onto the barge in front of them. The ship's chief gunner was barking the orders. With the help of a fairly tall tripod and two pulleys, they attempted to move several medias, medias sakers, and salvades (all cannon or heavy guns) onto the barge headed for the *San Pelayo.*

On June 18, two hundred of the needed Crown-paid soldiers arrived at the landing. Another 99 arrived two days later.[148] They were housed in nearby homes and inns until they passed the June 25th dockside muster. Their sergeant quickly examined the new arquebuses that had been crated. He decided where to store them on each ship. By June 26, Menendez's team was loading the last of the smaller and more valuable items. They would be stored as close to the main deck as possible. The steward loaded the wine and food provisions in a locked room on the galleon. The last to be loaded were the 250 arquebuses, 2,600 pounds of match cord (for firing arquebuses), 30 crossbows, one bale of Rouen linen, one piece of Holland linen, and 120 English shirts.[149]

While the soldiers and crew were being loaded, two new volunteers arrived at the dockside with a letter of recommendation in hand. Juan de San Vicente and his friend, Fernan Perez, had just come from Italy where they were soldiers in His Majesty's infantry. The name "San Vicente" rang a bell with the Adelantado when he met them. He had already recruited a "San Vicente" from Medino del Campo, a town in central Spain. Menendez took the advice of his friend and hired them. Juan de San Vicente would later be named only one of two infantry captains that made up his "men of Asturias." The only concern that he had with this new volunteer was his attitude. Vicente immediately started to challenge the daily rations that the Adelantado intended to give his infantry. This was not something a new infantry captain would normally comment on when he first met the captain-general of the armada.

By June 25, the Cadiz armada had been loaded. The soldiers and seamen were now on their ships. That would include 211 sailors, 812 soldiers, 100 settlers, one fleet pilot, and two priests. Pedro Menendez was ready to move from ship to ship to take that final muster. Surprisingly, the CASA's factor, Francisco Duarte, insisted on participating in that same muster. In the past, he had that right. However, under the king's current order, any CASA employee who desired to be involved with the armada must first have the king's approval. Duarte did not. Even without the proper papers, Francisco Duarte insisted on being part of the muster. Menendez knew that he could exclude Duarte. However, he chose to restrain his feeling of vengeance. He invited Duarte to join him.[150] Together they rowed from ship to ship and made the last muster together. This was just one of many times when Pedro Menendez showed a character that included choosing restraint in the face of a slap in the face.

Once Duarte boarded each ship, he asked the ship's captain to give him a list of the cargo that had been loaded. Then they opened the hatches and inspected that cargo. Was everything on the ship's manifest onboard this ship? Which men will crew this ship? Was this ship ready to depart? And are there any unauthorized religious books on this ship? At the end of the day on June 25, the CASA's Francisco Duarte wrote his report: "*The Cadiz armada includes 211 mariners, 812 soldiers, 100 settlers, six priests, and one fleet pilot.*" His concluding remarks were surprising. "*Pedro Menendez de Aviles has complied with the asiento (his personal contract with the king) more completely and in greater quantity than he was obliged to do.*"[151]

Knowing the leadership style of Pedro Menendez de Aviles, it is almost certain that he would have made that same inspection the day before. Pedro Menendez was a "detail man." He would have looked, for example, for the two white horizontal chalk lines that are always on the inside of each ship's hull . . . on both the starboard and port side, about half way from the bottom of the hull to the first deck. In the mid-16th century, ship captains painted these chalk lines to let them know when the water reached that point. When it did, the captain would immediately order "abandon ship."

Menendez had to be both pleased and worried. His biggest worry had to be, "*Where is the French armada . . . today?*" Menendez was still not aware that Ribault had suffered a two-week storm delay. He had to

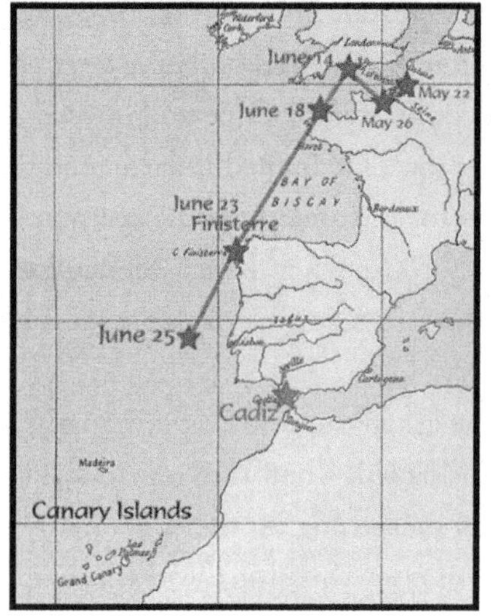

Where are they?

be thinking on June 25, "*Is he within sight of Mount Teide on the Canary Islands today?*" In reality, the forensic navigators believe that Admiral Ribault's armada was directly west of Lisbon, Portugal, at 40 degrees, 30 minutes north latitude.[152]

At the end of the day on June 25, Pedro Menendez de Aviles and the CASA had literally done the impossible. In two and one-half months, they had acquired the ships and men, modified the ships, and equipped them with cannon from the Crown's armory. This normally would have taken three to six months. In fact, the Cadiz ships' combined tonnage equaled that of the entire French armada that they expected to meet. But, of course, that comparison could quickly change if the armada were to face a storm along the way. And who really knew how many French ships were already in the St. Johns River near Fort Caroline? Before the sun set on the 25th, Menendez would have followed his typical practice. He would have met with all of his ship captains and his key "men of Asturias." He would have thanked them for their hard work. No doubt, he would also have done the unthinkable and thanked the CASA. Then, he would have again reviewed the planned route that he intended to take to Fort Caroline. We can almost hear him say something like this.:

"Let's review our plan. We have to beat Jean Ribault's resupply armada to Fort Caroline. He will have nine to ten ships available to him . . . seven from France and two to three that are already at Fort Caroline. We believe that he is ahead of us by a few days. But with a little luck and God's grace, we should be able to get there before he does. If we don't, we will be facing 1000 soldiers and mariners, plus their Indian friends.[‡‡] And they will have a huge defensive advantage.

Weather permitting, we will depart in two days . . . June 27th. Admiral Alas will, hopefully, meet us when we arrive at the Canaries around July 2 to 4. He will arrive with five ships. We will arrive with ten. But we will send two of our shuttle ships back to Cadiz once we reach the Canaries.

After we refuel with wood and water, we will head for the Indies with 13 ships. We will pick up three additional Crown ships and another 550 men once we reach Puerto Rico, Hispaniola, and Havana. With a little luck and the Grace of God, we will reach the mouth of the St. Johns River with 16 ships and more than 1,900 men."[153]

Menendez would have certainly been asked one question when he visited each of his ships on June 25: *"Sir, where do you believe Ribault, and his armada, are right now?"* We can almost hear his answer. *"They may be very close to the Canaries. But do not worry, we will overtake them."* Our forensic navigators would have disagreed with that statement. Using their calculations, they

---

[‡‡] Best estimate at the time was that Ribault would have departed Dieppe with 800 men from Dieppe, plus 200 more already stationed at Ft. Caroline. See Appendix VIII.

believe that Ribault still had 600 miles to go before he sighted the Canaries.[154] His two weeks at the Isle of Wight had caused the delay.

At this pace, Jean Ribault would not see Mount Teide on Tenerife Island until July 3 or 4—about the same time that Menendez expected to anchor off of the island. But once Ribault spotted the mountain and turned due "West," he could possibly have a built-in lead of about eight days . . . unless he was hit by a storm or too many "calms."

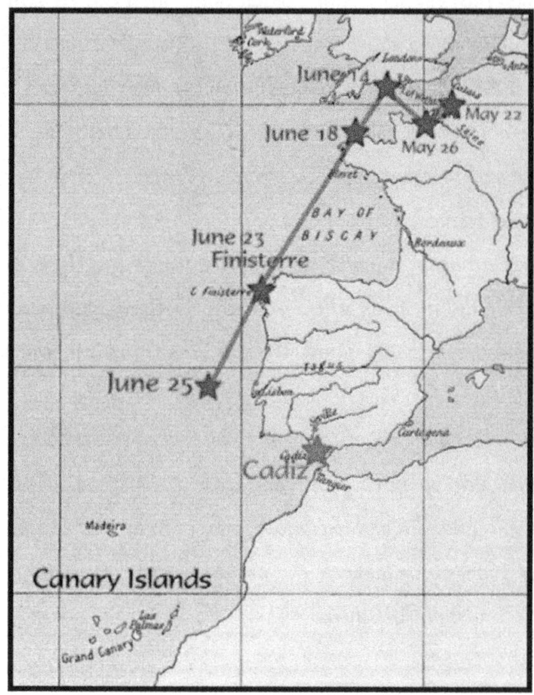

Ribault has 600 miles to go.

SPAIN'S ARMADA GETS READY TO SAIL

When Menendez and his "Men of Asturias" departed from their June 25, 1565 meeting, they returned to almost totally darkened ships. Once the sun set, Spanish ships extinguished every candle and light except the large lantern on the stern of the ship and the lone candle that lit the ship's compass. Except for the one-third of the crew that was always on watch, the ship's crew would go to bed. For most of the men, that meant sleeping somewhere on the main deck in a sack filled with straw. Historian Carla Rahn Phillips describes the scene:

> *"At nightfall after the evening meal, those on board heard the 'buenas noches' of the ship's page bringing candle light to the compass box for the night: 'Amen, and God give us good night; good voyage, good passage for the ship, sir captain and master and good company."*

Then two pages recited the evening prayers: Pater Noster, Ave Maria, Credo, and Salve Regina.[155]

Once finished, the ship's pages turned the watch glass, which presumably had been running as usual while the prayers were being said aloud. Then they recited the nightly blessing:

> *Blessed be the hour God came to earth.*
> *Holy Mary who gave him birth.*
> *And Saint John who saw his worth.*
> *The guard is posted.*
> *The watch glass filling.*
> *We'll have a good voyage.*
> *If God be willing.*

Menendez tried to get his armada underway on June 27, but as soon as he cleared the harbor, a dangerous storm descended on him. He returned to the harbor to wait for the next best day. On the morning of June 29, the skies were clear. It was a good day to get underway.

The Adelantado would have awakened on a cheerful note. At first, he would have heard the sounds of the infantry's fife and drum. A moment later a page would start chanting . . .[156]

Blessed be the light of day and the Holy Cross we say;
And the Lord of Verite.
And the Holy Trinity.
Blessed be the Immortal Soul.
And the Lord who keeps it whole,
Blessed be the light of day.
And He who sends the night away.

With the exception of the men who were "on watch," the crew would have quickly assembled on the main deck for morning prayer. At the close of the prayer, a priest on the *San Pelayo* (and a ship's captain on the smaller vessels) would call out . . .

"God, give us good days, good voyage, good passage of the ship, Sir Captain and master, and good company. So let there be a good voyage, and many good days, and may God grant your graces."

Then, the men would disperse and prepare for getting underway. When Pedro Menendez scanned the harbor, he would have seen ten ships in a circle with the *San Pelayo* closest to the harbor entrance. The *San Pelayo* would lead the armada out of the Cadiz harbor. Menendez would always keep his galleon in front of all others. The admiral's ship, the *San Andrea*, would be the last ship to leave the harbor.[§§] Each of the ten ship captains knew approximately when they would depart. Six hours before Menendez was ready to depart, he would fire one cannon shot to inform the crew that he was preparing to get underway. All eyes would now be on the Pelayo.[157]

At this point, the entire crew of the armada was boarding their ships and going to their work location. Menendez and his chief pilot,

---

§§ Note: Spain called the admiral's ship the "Almirante."

Gonzalo Gayon, were on the upper deck of the stern poop deck. Gayon was a highly skilled Asturian pilot. He would guide the armada to Fort Caroline. Next to Pedro Menendez and the armada's pilot was a young ship's page. He watched the sand glass, making sure that it was turned every thirty minutes. Immediately below the captain-general and the pilot was a room with an open view to the bow and the ship's masts. Inside this small room were two to four robust young seamen who were literally steering the ship by a whipstaff. This was before the time when a ship's wheel was used to change directions. Instead, ships used a whipstaff, or a long vertical post that, if moved left or right, would turn the rudder left or right . . . or as the sailors would say, to starboard or port. Once the pilot wanted to turn in a different direction, he would yell to the men below him on the whipstaff: *"Come right to "south by southwest."* Then, the men would push the post either to the left or the right, while they were watching their compass and the sails in front of them unfurl. When each ship prepared to "get underway," the boatswain had more authority than almost any other officer. He took his orders from the captain or pilot and relayed them to the assistant boatswain, who was located near the prow (or front) of the ship. Within seconds, the entire crew acted on the "captain's" orders. The seamen who manned the ship's capstan were immediately in front of the mainsail. Once they heard the words *"Let's get underway,"* they began pushing the multi-spoked wheel of the capstan. Pushing together, they slowly raised both of the anchors.

Most of the seamen who manned the sails and rigging were located forward of the mainsail. But a small group of them were under each mast, ready to pull the lines that raise and turn the yardarms. Then, young and nimble apprentice seamen immediately climbed the masts and prepared to unfurl the sails.

Envision this scene as Pedro Menendez de Aviles was about to depart for Spain's North America.

As soon as the Adelantado alerted the armada that they should prepare to get underway, every ship knew what to do. The *Pelayo's* boatswain immediately yelled to the seaman in charge of the capstan: *"Raise all but one anchor; then attach the cable of the last anchor to the capstan."*[158] That was no easy chore. The anchors of a 400-ton ship weigh 1,300 pounds. The *Pelayo* was a 906-ton ship. It would have had an even larger anchor. As soon as the young and muscular seamen started to push the spokes on the horizontal capstan, an older seaman began a chant.

The chant had a slow meter to match the pace of each seaman's push. But it would help. Almost always the chant would follow an old verse of the Bible or the beauty of the sea, or it would foreshadow the dangers ahead. It had a slow cadence, but it was loud enough to be heard by those on the main deck. With that order, the boatswain would immediately pass a second order to the seamen who were standing below each mast. *"Prepare to unfurl the sails."* Immediately, young, nimble seamen climbed the foremast and mainmast and got into position to unfurl the sails. At the same time, the seamen on the main deck were pulling lines to turn the yardarms so that they could catch the wind. They reached above their heads and pulled the line down. Then they again reached above their heads and pulled the line down. The yardarms turned. Looking up, one could see the young seamen wrapped around the high sails and ready to unfurl them. Now two groups of cadenced chants filled the air . . . one from the men on the

Raising the anchors
By Neueste Beitrage

capstan steadily raising the anchors, and the other from seamen pulling on lines attached to the yardarms.

Then, pilot Gayon gave the final order just before the last anchor was pulled off the bottom of the bay. In a loud voice, he called to the chief boatswain, *"Ease the rope of the foresail. In the name of the Holy Trinity, Father, Son, and Holy Spirit, three persons and one true God. Be with us and guard and guide and accompany us, and give us a good and safe voyage, and carry and return us safely to our homes."*[159] That order ignited a chain reaction. Within seconds, the last 1,300-plus-pound anchor rose from the floor of the bay and reached the side of the ship. As this anchor touched the ship's hull, the apprentice seamen unfurled the sails on the foremast.

All of a sudden, the wind grabbed the armada's sails. The ships began to move. It was an incredible concert of orders, chants, and sounds mixed with a background of blossoming colorful sails. The entire town of Cadiz was on the harbor shore watching. They all had one thing in common. Their mouths were open in awe.

Departing Cadiz

On the morning of June 29, 1565, the Cadiz armada departed. They were underway for the Canaries. As soon as they cleared the harbor, *Pelayo's* pilot set a compass course of "SOUTHWEST" (or 225 degrees on today's compass) to the Canary Islands, 540 miles away. Navigators Heckrotte and Nelson believe that they continued on that course at a speed of 3.8 to 4.2 knots.[160] They also believe that on June 29, Ribault's armada was only 420 miles from the Canaries. The French had only a 200-mile lead.[161] In 1565, that was no lead at all. It could change in a few days.

Pedro Menendez de Aviles was like his French adversary, Gaspard Coligny, in many ways. One of those common characteristics was his insistence on a firm military discipline. Coligny, in fact, had made his military reputation at the Battle of Boulogne by insisting that his troops adhere to a strict discipline . . . no blasphemy, no threats of dueling, no women in camp, no looting of nearby homes, and a rigid adherence to military orders. Menendez had the same rules.[162] The first one dealt with how Spanish ships would act while traveling in a formation. For example, Menendez's ship captains knew that they should never pass the *San Pelayo* while the armada was at sea. They also knew that each ship was to come alongside the *Pelayo*, once in the morning and once in the afternoon.[163] On one of those contacts, the *San Pelayo* would give each ship the day's password. That would be used if the ship needed to approach the flagship at night.

Another one of Menendez's rules was that, if a ship needed help during the day, he would fly a flag on the main topmast and fire two cannon shots. If the danger was great, the ship's captain would fire four shots, one after another, and fly another flag on the foretopmast. On July 8, one of Menendez's ships would send that signal.[164]

The Cadiz-to-the-Canaries part of the voyage had been backed by good winds and fair days. Because Menendez's armada departed on St. Peter's Day, it would have been a day full of religious activities and some relaxation when they were not on watch. The ship's officers and the "Men of Asturias" would have attended the religious services, but not most of the seamen. The typical Spanish crew would sit on their sea chests and brag about their lack of interest in religion.[165] Instead, the seamen would play cards (which was prohibited), chat, tell stories, or read a few books. But not many read books. Most of a ship's crew were illiterate.[166] At night most of them slept on the open deck in a straw-filled sack.¶¶ With the exception of the *Pelayo*, nine of the ships had only one covered deck, and that was filled with supplies.

¶¶ With the exception of the *Pelayo*, nine of the ten Canary-bound ships had only one covered deck, and it was filled with supplies. Thus, the entire crew slept on the open deck as they sailed to North America. See Pablo E. Perez-Mallaina, *Spain's Men of the Sea*, 137.

THE START OF THE RACE

On July 4, 1565, after five days at sea, Menendez's armada spotted the 12,000-foot mountain punching the sky on the island of Tenerife, one of the major Canary Islands. He could first see the mountaintop from his ship when he was 100 miles away. According to our forensic navigators, Ribault would have been 60 miles behind him, ready to turn west at the 29 degree north latitude line.[167]

At the start of the race, one thing was clear. Menendez had the tactical seamanship skills to win the race. But he also had the leadership skills to hurdle any unforeseen barrier. Most importantly, his message was consistent: **"Everything depends upon arriving at the mouth of the St. Johns River before Ribault."** Menendez's plan was simple. His ten ships would anchor off the Grand Canary Island the next day, July 5, 1565. He would send two of his shuttle ships back to Cadiz. Meanwhile he would wait for Alas and his five Bay of Biscay ships. Menendez waited for three days.

Those three days were anything but boring. Menendez was informed by lieutenant Luis Enriquez that his captain, Francisco Sanchez, was planning to take his ship, the *Vitoria*, to the African Barbary Coast. There he planned to sell his 40-man crew to the Muslims. As soon as Menendez became aware of this scheme, he took the only appropriate action. He hanged the renegade captain.

Meanwhile, Menendez developed his plan. He would let the African trade winds push him to the island of Dominica. Then he would hop to nearby Puerto Rico, Hispaniola, and Havana. There he would pick up three ships and 550 men that the king had promised him. With good weather and a little luck, he could arrive off of the mouth of the St. Johns River with 16 ships and almost 2,000 men. Once he landed there, he would put troops on an island at the mouth of the river and use his smaller ships to later make an amphibious river attack on Fort Caroline. That should allow him to block the arrival of Ribault's men by positioning artillery on the island and placing his largest ships in the deeper waters outside of the river entrance . . . ready to meet Ribault when he arrived.

But where was Ribault? Menendez had read the Enveja report. *"The course they observe is to seek the Canary Islands and take the course outside the islands, which they call the Antilles, without touching any cape whatever until they enter the River of May (the St. Johns River)."*

Our forensic navigators, Heckrotte and Nelson, believe that the Enveja information gave Ribault only one option. Turn west about 60 miles BEFORE reaching the Canary Islands.[168] Yes, he would have to first spot Mount Teida in the Canaries. But he would probably want to turn west at about the 29-degree north latitude line for one reason. That latitude terminates north of Cape Canaveral . . . not that far from the St. Johns River. With Pedro Menendez's self confidence in his sailing skills, he had to be thinking, *I will take the steady trade winds off of Africa before taking any other path to La Florida."*

CHAPTER X

Menendez Lands!

enendez departed the Canary Islands on the morning of July 8. He waited three long days for Alas and his five Asturian ships, but they did not arrive. He left with a reduced armada of only eight ships and 1040 men.[169]

Before Menendez and his eight ships departed the Canary Islands, he made the standard muster of his crew. To his surprise, his future son-in-law, Pedro de Valdes, was discovered as a stowaway. When this 25-year-old first approached his future father-in-law, the captain-general said, "NO." The trip was too dangerous. It would put his daughter's fiancé at great risk. Nevertheless, young Valdes disobeyed his future father-in-law's wishes. Menendez had to have shown his disfavor. But he also knew that young Valdes had five to six years of land-based experience fighting the French in Italy. In fact, he was only one of two known senior members of the "Men of Asturias" who had infantry experience.[170] Menendez had to have had a frown on his face. However, it did not surprise anyone that he allowed young Valdes to continue as a member of the Spanish armada.

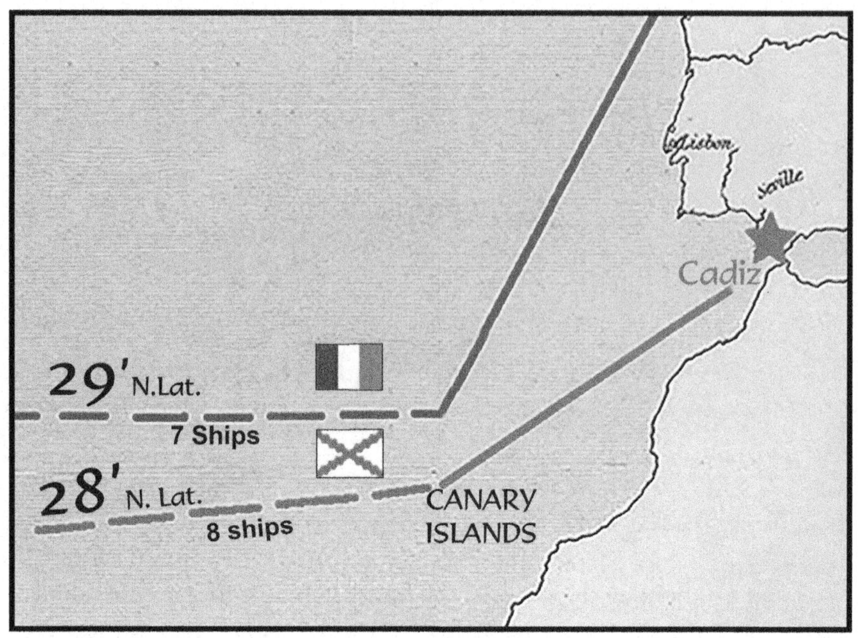

Spain's Race Plan.

Menendez departed the Canary Islands on the morning of July 8th. He now had a reduced armada of eight ships and 1,040 men.[171] The eight remaining Cadiz ships included the flagship *San Pelayo* and admiral Diego Flores Valdez's Almirante; the *San Andres*, the large galeota; *La Vitoria*, the bergantine; *La Esperanza*, the caravel; San *Antonio*, and the shallops *Magdalena*, *San Miguel*, and *La Concepcion*. The revised plan was simple. Once his armada refueled at Dominica, they would take a short hop to Puerto Rico, Hispaniola, and Cuba to collect the three ships and 550 men that the king promised him. Hopefully, Alas would follow him to Havana with his five ships and 324 men. With Alas' arrival at Havana, Menendez expected to arrive at Fort Caroline with 16 ships and 1,914 men . . . 327 seamen and 1,621 soldiers.[172] It would be a massive amphibious attack on the island at the mouth of the St. Johns River.

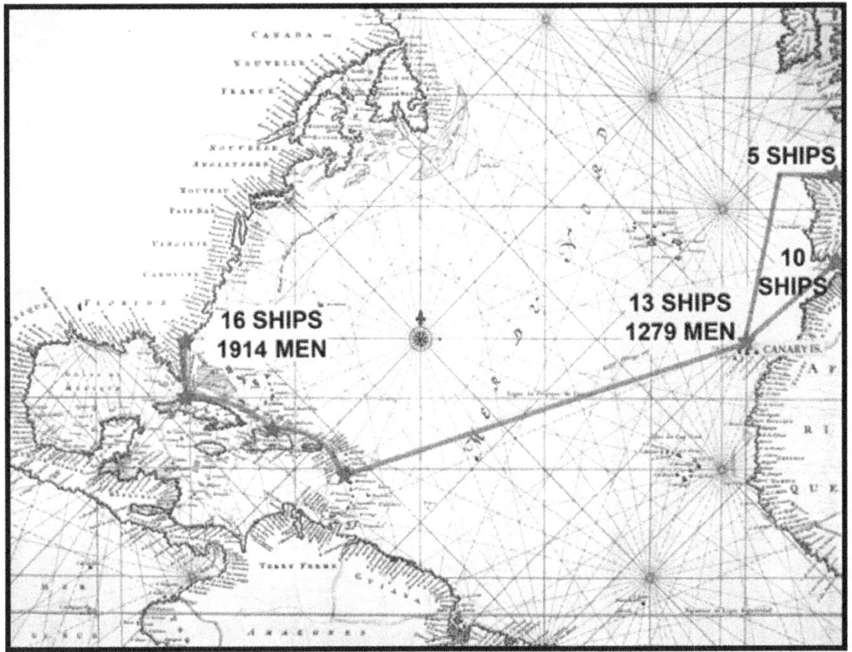

The Race Begins.

Menendez led his eight-ship armada out of the Canary Islands during the afternoon of July 8, 1565. Once he reached the open seas, a tempest filled the sails of the *San Pelayo* and a nearby patache. It quickly pushed them out to sea. But the remaining six ships were left in a dead calm. By dawn on the next day, July 9, Menendez, and his accompanying patache, were 24 nautical miles ahead of the admiral's six ships.[173] Now, instead of crossing the Atlantic together, the armada was split in two.

On July 9, one day after Admiral Diego Flores Valdes' group of six ships departed the Canaries, he received some bad news. One of his ships fired a cannon twice. Then the captain of the endangered ship sent the message, *"I am in trouble."* The ship was developing a hull leak, and more water was entering the ship than the pumps could push out.

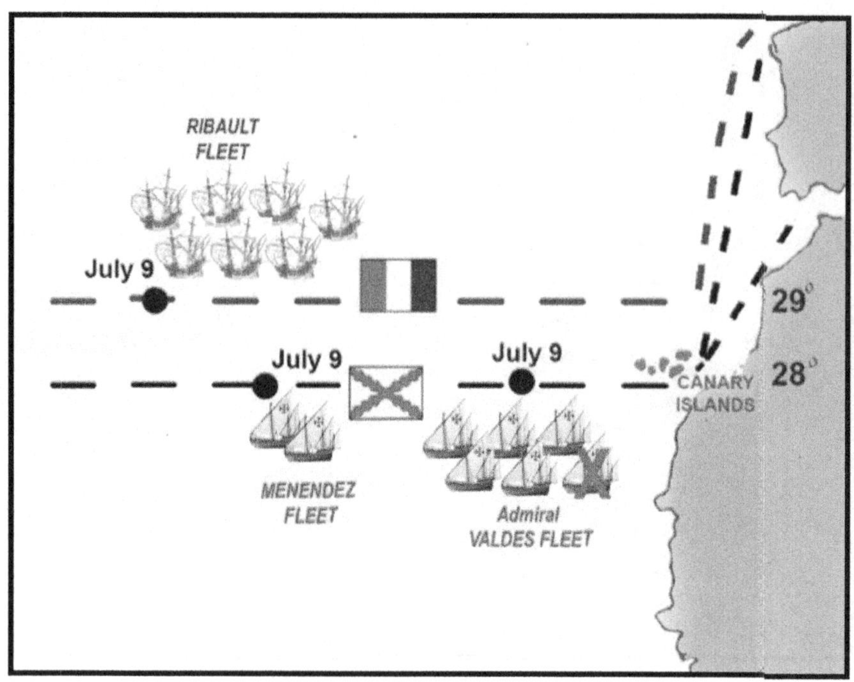

One day after leaving the Canaries

The Admiral immediately sent the ship back to the nearest point of land.[174] Now Menendez would be crossing the Atlantic with seven ships. With his companion patache, he soon found himself 70 miles ahead of Admiral Valdes' lagging group of five ships.[175]

On the morning of July 19, Admiral Valdes and his five ships awakened to spotty rain clouds. But more importantly, Admiral Diego Flores Valdes and his boatswain smelled a "heavy odor." It was the type of smell one notices when one has been in a room that has been closed too long. When they scanned the sky, they saw another weather indicator. The sky was beginning to show a brassy color. Seamen in the mid-16th century knew that if the sky turned a slightly brassy color, there was a storm coming their way from the Sahara Desert. That color appeared only when the clouds picked up sand off the desert and later dropped it when it rained. Now Admiral Valdes was concerned. A bad storm could tear apart an armada of wooden ships.[176]

Throughout the day, the waves were becoming higher and higher and farther apart from each other. The sea was turning to more of a green color surrounded by foam. A breeze soon came up. That was a clear sign that a storm was coming from the East. The admiral and his ship captains knew exactly what they had to do. Immediately they fed the crew a hearty breakfast . . . and ample diluted wine. They knew that this storm could last for days. And the crew needed to eat well before they had to extinguish the fire under the cook stove.

The admiral's five ship captains were more than concerned. With this early indicator, each ship lashed down all deck gear and sea chests. As evening came, additional seamen were put on an intense lookout "watch." It is very doubtful that anyone slept during the evening. However, when morning appeared the next day, July 20, the weather was even more threatening. Ocean navigator Heckrotte believes that this is the likely picture that the crew saw on the morning of July 20th.

"The waves were now running 10 to 15 seconds apart from each other instead of the normal 7 to 8 seconds. And they were getting taller and taller. Cirrus clouds were now appearing. The barometer was rapidly falling. Light rains turned into rain squalls. Wind gusts increased up to 70 nautical mph. The waves became mountainous. They began to crest and turn into a waterfall. Young apprentice seamen now climbed the slick masts to furl (shorten) the sails. Admiral Valdes and his five ship captains were worried. The growing waves were now getting under the bow of the ship before they crested. That caused the bow to rise sharply while the stern fell with a thud. Then the bow rose again, and the stern fell again. The ship was being rocked so violently that the tips of the masts almost touched the ocean. Some of the rope lines that ran from the deck to the sail spars began to snap. Anyone on the ship had to feel that their ship was almost out of control. It jolted wildly up and down and sideways. Almost immediately, the crew got seasick. They were all vomiting. The sea state was very dangerous. Wind appeared to be coming from all directions.[177] Admiral Valdes knew one thing. Such a storm could turn an armada of wooden ships into splinters.

"The older sailors, who, in the past, had belittled every religious service now had a change of heart. They promised God that they would do anything if He would save their lives. The apprentice sailors lashed down everything on the deck before they climbed the slick masts to furl, or shorten, the sails. The larger ships put their caulkers and carpenters to work. They went below decks and began looking for cracks and leaks between the hull planks."

The breeze grew stronger and stronger. Admiral Valdes' group of five ships was hit by a 70 mph anvil.[178]

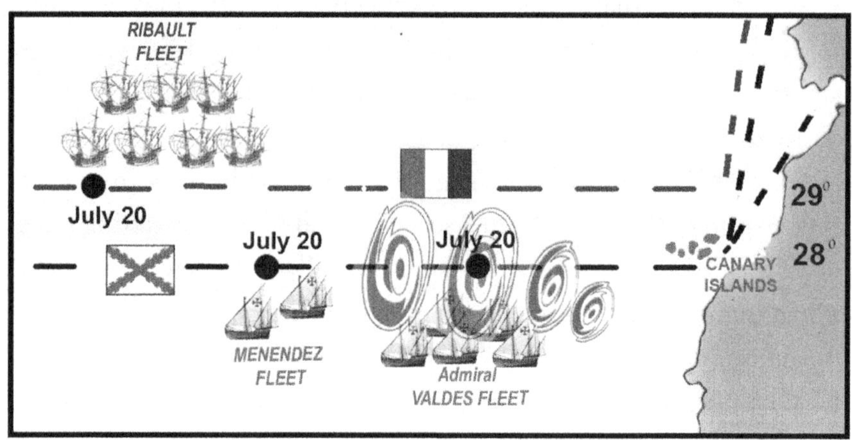

The hurricane hits Spain's armada.

The armada's chaplain, Father Francisco Lopez de Mendoza Grajales, was aboard the Admiral's ship, *San Andres*, when the storm struck on the 20th. He described the situation this way:[179]

"By 10:00 am on the 20th, a violent wind arose. By two in the afternoon it became the most frightful hurricane one could imagine. The sea, which rose to

the very clouds, seemed about to swallow us alive . . . very often the sea washed completely over the deck where we were gathered. One hundred and twenty men had no other places to go, as there was only one space below and that was full of biscuit, wine, and supplies. We were in such great danger that it was necessary to lighten the vessel.

We threw a great many barrels of water into the sea, as well as our cooking apparatus and seven millstones. Most of the rigging and the great ship's cable were pushed overboard.

Still the waves continued to break over us . . . When night came, we were in the same situation. We thought that we must surely perish. I preached to the whole crew to put their trust in God."[180]

The storm that hit the Admiral's five-ship convoy lasted two and one-half days, from 10:00 am on Friday, July 20 to Monday noon on July 23rd.

Forensic Navigator Heckrotte believes that when the storm hit the admiral's five ships on July 20, the Adelantado and his companion patache were 100 miles further west at 23 degrees, 20 minutes north latitude.[181]

When the storm eased up on July 23, however, Admiral Valdes did not see his four other ships. His flagship, the *San Andrea*, was by itself. The other four ships were not in anyone's view.

Thanks to the hurricane attack on the Spanish armada, France's Jean Ribault now had about a 500-mile lead on the Spanish armada.[182] Was that close enough for Jean Ribault to feel the edge of the storm? Navigator Nelson believed that it was. He would have felt the increasing breezes from the southeast.[183]

It is entirely possible that he would have turned to his navigator and offered these thoughts. *"There may be a troubling storm southeast of us. I can feel it now. Menendez may be in the middle of it. If he is, he will be either losing time, losing ships, or both."*

Menendez got all the storm indicators one day after his admiral Valdes first felt them. The same storm that battered Flores' ships was now beginning to strike him. He described this in his August 13, 1565 letter to King Philip II:

" . . . I was hit by a hurricane and it was a miracle that we did not sink . . . We had to throw much of the artillery into the sea . . . The wind was so great that it swept away all of our masts and sails, except the main mast, which was without the main topmast. This lasted for two nights and a day. As the ship (the San Pelayo) was so watertight and so strong and seaworthy, Our Lord was pleased to spare us. When the weather improved, I turned around to make repairs as best I could with some spare topmasts we were carrying and canvas, out of which we made masts and sails."[184]

THE SPANISH ARMADA IS SCATTERED TO THE WINDS.

As soon as Admiral Valdes saw the storm pass on July 23, he experienced a very lonely feeling. There were no other ships around him. The other four had been scattered to the winds. His only thought had to be, "I need to make emergency repairs and try to reach Dominica . . .

and then Puerto Rico. Maybe I will be able to see one or more of my ships there."

On the way to Dominica, the Admiral did find one of his four lost ships. On August 10, Admiral Valdes and one recently found ship entered San Juan, Puerto Rico's harbor. Immediately they spotted the *San Pelayo* and its patache anchored in the harbor. It was one of those rare moments of surprise—joy, tears, and hugs. Menendez had arrived earlier in the day.[185] It was a very happy reunion. But behind the tears and joy, the captain-general had to know the seriousness of the situation. King Philip II had given him the most important mission of his life: Remove the French from his new North American colony. But for the last 30 days, he had been blocked at every turn. His plan was to arrive at Puerto Rico with 13 ships, 1,100 soldiers, and 400 seamen. Now, however, he had only four badly damaged ships and a total crew of about 500 soldiers, 200 seamen, and 100 settlers.[186]

The Adelantado knew that, if he had any chance of beating Admiral Ribault to Fort Caroline, he had to quickly make his four ships seaworthy. And that meant caulking the holes in their hulls, replacing masts, sails, and miles of cables . . . and resting an exhausted crew. That would not be an easy task.

All of this would have to be done in five days or sooner. And there were no spare supplies of masts, sails, and running gear on the island. Menendez also needed some critical information before he could get underway. *Have Alas' five ships from Asturias arrived? Are the governor of Cuba and the government of Santo Domingo ready to turn over to him the two ships and 350 men that they promised the king? And has Pedro de las Roelas, the captain-general of the New Spain armada, returned from Seville? Is he ready to turn over his flagship and 200 men?* Remember, Menendez's original plan was to land at the mouth of the St. Johns River with 16 ships and 1,914 men.

Beached for repair at San Juan.

To get that information, or at least some of it, Pedro Menendez quickly met with the Governor of Puerto Rico, Francisco Bahamonde de Lugo and twenty-five-year-old Juan Ponce de Leon. Young Ponce de Leon was the proud descendant of the explorer who first discovered the "island" of Florida. He was also a well-respected rancher, the king's accountant for Puerto Rico, and the Commander of the island's fortress. The governor and the young rancher, however, knew that they could be supportive only by being candid with one another. More than likely, the governor would have opened the conversation something like this:

"Let me tell you what we know. Admiral Alas and his five-ship armada have not yet arrived from Asturias. Furthermore, Pedro de las Roelas, the captain-general of

the New Spain Treasure Armada, has yet to arrive from Seville. We understand that he was to turn over to you his flagship and men. He may have been caught in the same hurricane that hit you."

If that was not enough bad news to hear in one meeting, there was more. The governor informed Menendez that he was aware that he'd "lost" three ships after the storm hit his armada. However, he now knew what had happened to two of them.

"The Vitoria was lost on the island of Guadalupe, next to Dominica. Most of the 72 men were eaten by the Carib Indians. The San Antonio ended up at Cape Tiburon on the island of Hispaniola. The ship's crew of 139 mariners and soldiers were taken by four French corsairs and either thrown into the sea or carried off."

Pedro Menendez would later hear that his shallop, *La Madalena*, was found badly damaged near Honduras.[187] There was more bad news. The Audiencia of Hispaniola was reluctant to turn over to Menendez the one ship and 300 men that the king had ordered. He believed that the risk was too high. There was also a rumor that Cuba's governor felt the same. That was enough bad news to make any Spanish leader decide to abandon an attack. The Adelantado, however, received one additional piece of discouragement.

About a month earlier, King Philip II had sent three courier ships from Seville to Puerto Rico, Santo Domingo (Hispaniola), and Havana, Cuba. These ships had one mission . . . to remind each major Indies leader of the ships and men that they were ordered to deliver to Menendez and to share with them his battle plan. One of those courier ships was captured by French corsairs. Now France may know exactly how they can ambush your armada, if you stay on-plan."[188] Pedro Menendez de Aviles, however, was more than a gifted military leader. He was an extraordinary leader, and that became evident in how he took his next step.

He did not take much time to mourn his losses. The captain-general showed an inner character that very few men had in the 16th century. Menendez never let a bad situation get him down. In past situations when the odds were against him, he almost always acted based on what he knew he could do . . . not based on the odds at the time. He did it fighting the French pirates off of the Bay of Biscay. He did it off the coast of Normandy, when the French admiral had him cornered.

The situation facing him could not have been more bleak. His king had directed him to remove France from Spain's North American colony. Menendez, however, now knew that he would probably have to face a French resupply force of at least 1,000 men with only five battered ships and maybe 500 soldiers.

The questions he had to answer were difficult ones. *"Do I wait for Alas and his five ships? Do I wait for the promised ship and 200 men from the flagship of the Treasure Fleet . . . or the two ships and 350 men that Hispaniola and Cuba promised to provide? Or do I wait until next year, when all of the promised ships can be collected? Do I try to beat Ribault to Ft. Caroline with the few ships that I have? How do I do that and avoid a possible ambush? The French now know that we are coming. They intercepted our courier ship. Maybe we should immediately avoid these barriers by taking our ships through the Bahama Islands. Maybe we should depart ASAP. As dangerous as it would be, that route could also save a few days."*

Menendez mirrored the rationale behind his final decision when he penned a letter to King Philip II on August 13th. *"If neither the people nor the horses should arrive in time from Santo Domingo, that will not stop me from landing soon in La Florida with any men I may find . . . If the French get to La Florida first, then all the forces I command, even if they all went together, are not going to be sufficient to attack them."*[189]

Menendez gave his king a definite "we-have-no-choice" message. He certainly knew that he could throw his original plan out of the window. He would **not** be arriving at Fort Caroline with 16 ships and 1,914 seamen and soldiers. He would be arriving with only four ships and 700 men. In fact, those ships would be held together by splices, moss, and oakum. And the sails will resemble Raggedy Ann's stitched face.[190]

For the first time, Menendez had to realize that Jean Ribault may reach Fort Caroline before he did. He still believed, however, that he had a reasonable chance of winning the race if he left within a few days. In other words, his option was to leave now with four badly damaged ships and 700 men, or wait a few days with many more ships and men. But if he left now, he might have a chance to win the race.

Taking a Route That No Armada Had Ever Taken

He made the hard choice. Menendez left on August 15 and headed north through the dangerous Bahama Islands. He would not wait.

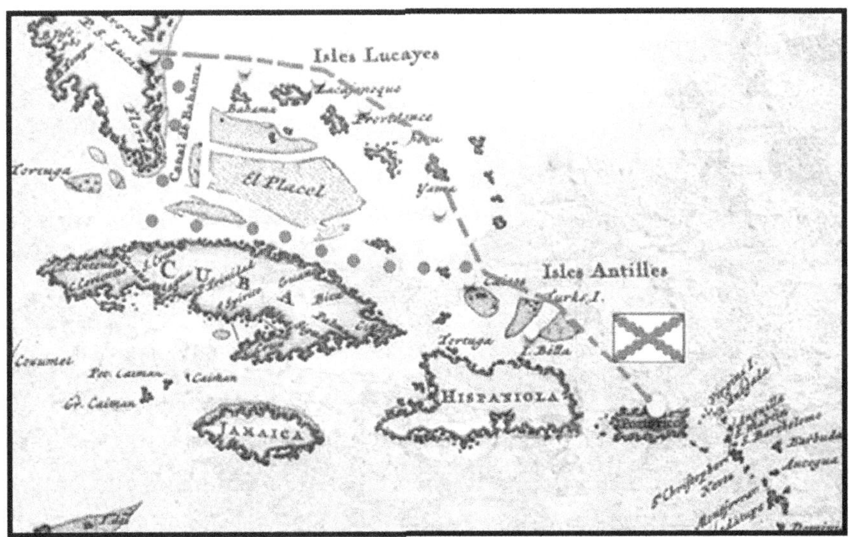

A Change in Course Through Uncharted Waters."

There were no known charts for sailing through the Bahama Islands in 1565. Before Menendez "raised anchor," he informed his crew that he intended to "leave for Havana." He obviously did that to let any French spies located in San Juan know that he was sticking to his "old plan." When he left, he sent a ship's pilot and one of his barks to Santo Domingo and Cuba. He had to make every attempt to collect the 350 men that they were reluctant to give him. Those men could be valuable . . . even if they arrived a few days later.

Menendez had to do one other thing before he departed for Ft. Caroline. He had to organize his 500-man infantry so that there would be one experienced captain for every 50 men. He would then train them to operate as a "tercio," which had been very effective when Spain had fought the French in Italy. A "tercio" has two elements: lightly armored men in the center that carry long (12 to 14 feet) pikes, and rows of men on each side that carry the heavy handheld arquebuses. When the enemy charges, they tend to be stopped by the forward-leaning pikes, while the arquebusiers on each side plasters them with shot.

Now it was time for Pedro Menendez de Aviles to appoint his top infantry commander, or "Master of the Camp." When he looked at his band of brothers from Asturias, he had one candidate . . . his 25-year-old future son-in-law, Pedro Menendez de Valdes. This had to be a difficult decision. The Adelantado had firmly discouraged him from joining the expedition because of the expected risk. Then, he was reluctantly surprised when the young man was discovered in the Canaries as a stowaway.

The 25-year-old had served five years in the Spanish infantry in Italy. Unlike the rest of his "men of Asturias." who only had experience as seasoned mariners, Menendez's son-in-law knew how to lead an infantry. On August 13, the Adelantado asked his future son-in-law to meet him on his flagship, the *San Pelayo*. It was anchored in San Juan's harbor. By the time young Valdes left this meeting, he had recommended Gonzalo de Villaroel as his executive officer, or second-in-command. Together, they would select ten captains to lead each of the 50-man components of his infantry.[191]

Before Pedro Menendez de Aviles departed on August 15, 1565, the governor of Puerto Rico gave him a strong gift of support . . . 43 soldiers, 30 horses, and two large barks. He also showed the Adelantado where he could buy that fifth ship. However, Pedro Menendez still knew that, when he arrived at the mouth of the St. Johns River, he might see nine to ten French ships and 1,000 to 1,200 entrenched Frenchmen. The odds were becoming increasingly poor.

It soon became clear that Pedro Menendez de Aviles would have to attack Fort Caroline by sailing directly to Fort Caroline. He had to avoid an ambush. And he had to save time. Menendez knew that the Spanish courier ship that was carrying his battle plans had been captured by the French. He had to assume that the French believed that he would be taking the Puerto-Rico-to-Havana-to-Fort-Caroline route. And Menendez also knew that they would probably try to ambush him if he took that track. Instead, he would now take an alternate route . . . a track north through the uncharted and dangerous Bahama Islands. Before he got underway on the morning of August 15, 1565, however, he received another piece of bad news. He mustered all of his men to get a head count. Regrettably, 30 men had deserted when he had been anchored at San Juan. More hurtful to the Adelantado was the fact that, among those deserters, were three of the armada's six Catholic clerics.[192]

A Risky Change in Plans

The Adelantado departed San Juan at 3 p.m. on August 15, 1565, with five ships, four of them held together by "bailing wire."[193] He did not depart with the 16 ships and 1,914 men as he had planned. He departed with 500 soldiers and 200 seamen who were less than highly motivated. And they believed that they were headed to Havana. But they were not headed for Havana. As they approached the waters on the north side of Hispaniola at 4 p.m. on August 17, Menendez sent a flag message to his ships and infantry captains: *"Meet me in my cabin once we anchor off of Hispaniola."*

Once they got together, Menendez had an almost-impossible assignment. He literally had to move his tired, depressed, and demoralized officers to a point where they wanted to attack Fort Caroline with fewer resources. But first, he had to give them confidence that they could still win the race. He also had to inform them that they faced an added threat of an ambush and that their best option was to take a direct course north through the dangerous Bahama Islands . . . the uncharted Bahama Islands. Menendez was very aware of what most mariners thought of the Bahama Islands. They were cursed. If you entered them, you would be under the "evil eye." The only way an apprentice seaman would feel safe in the waters of the Bahama Islands were if he was wearing a *figa* . . . a small amulet shaped like a hand with the thumb placed between the index finger and the middle finger.[194]

When his officers met in his cabin on August 17, 1565, Menendez began by saying, *"I believe that our Lord allowed us to lose good men and ships for one reason when we crossed the Atlantic. When we succeed in attacking Fort Caroline and the French, He will be telling us that only He could have made us successful in the face of such a loss."*[195]

Then the Adelantado outlined the options that they were facing. *"We could return to Puerto Rico, wait for our ships, and attack next year. That, however, would give Ribault a year to strengthen his position. Or we could go to Hispaniola and Havana and wait for the ships and men that they promised us. We could also wait for Alas' ships to arrive at Puerto Rico or Havana. However, we would still be taking the Bahama Channel north to Fort Caroline. Again, we would be ripe for an ambush. Or we could turn our bow north and reach Fort Caroline by going straight through the Bahama Islands."* When he made that statement, he had to see some frowns. The Bahama Islands were known as a very dangerous place—no navigational charts, shallow waters, and a record of having created many shipwrecks.

Then Pedro Menendez de Aviles made his recommendation. *"I believe we would be much better served if we immediately set a course for Fort Caroline by going north through the Bahama Islands. It's both a safer and quicker route.*

We will save days. Once we arrive, I want to take the island at the mouth of the St. Johns River and place both our infantry and cannon on it. This will divide their forces. Laudonniere's ships will not be able to leave Fort Caroline or the river. And Ribault will not be able to enter the river and reach Fort Caroline. Once we have secured the island, we can then send one of our ships to Havana and retrieve some of the late arrivals. Furthermore, we have more than enough forces to take their harbor, as long the French fleet has not yet arrived."*[196]

As soon as Menendez proposed his new plan, discussions led to arguments. The leader of his infantry, his future son-in law, Don Pedro de Valdes, spoke up. *"The proposal looks good to me. The more we delay the voyage, the less chance we have of succeeding."* Others, like Captain Juan de San Vicente, argued that it would be better to remain in Hispaniola and wait for the late-arriving ships. Some of the captains, such as Gonzalo Solis de Meras, took San Vicente's comments as a sure sign that he was looking for any reason to desert and go to the silver and gold fields.[197]

As quarreling began, Menendez stepped in. *"Gentlemen, let me suggest how we should settle this question. I will leave this meeting and go topside for the next two hours. I want you to critically discuss the pros and cons of the proposal I gave you. Be as critical as you can. Pray to God for help in arriving*

---

* The "late arrivals" included Alas' Asturias fleet of 5 ships and 324 men. The King also promised Menendez 1 ship and 300 men from Hispaniola, 1 ship and 50 men from Cuba, and the flagship and 200 men from the captain-general of the Treasure Armada. Lyon, *The Enterprise of Florida*, p. 58–69.

at a decision. When I return in two hours, let me know if you can or cannot support this plan. I will follow the direction of your answer."

Menendez's brother-in law, Gonzalo Solis de Meras, described what happened next. *"The Adelantado left them closeted in his cabin and went out on to the ship's deck, where he ordered prayers and litanies to be recited. He asked all the men in the fleet—everyone in his ships—to kneel and beseech Our Lord to enlighten the Adelantado so that, in a decision he wanted to make, he would decide what was best for the service of Our Lord God and the spreading of His Holy Catholic Faith. All of which they did with great devotion. After this was done, the Adelantado withdrew to the stern castle of the galleon with a Book of Hours in his hand, and he prayed for an hour in front of a crucifix and an image of Our Lady. Then he left there, since the two hours' time that he had given his captains would have passed, and went to them in the cabin where he had left them closeted, and asked each and every one of them to tell him openly and clearly what they felt in their hearts and souls, what they thought about his plan, and if he should change it."* When he returned two hours later, he got his answer. *"We are unanimously behind your proposal."*[198]

The leadership that Menendez displayed during this period defined him. Under the burden of continuing setbacks, he held himself together. He did not buckle. Rather than show anger, he showed patience. That allowed him to assess his options and focus on the next step. When the Santo Domingo government defied the king's order, he did not strike back. He offered a solution. *"I will send a bark to you to collect your men. It will be piloted by a friend of mine who knows the waters he will sail."* Menendez, in fact, had skills that only the best senior corporate officers have today. For example, when he got the support of his captains to take a northern course through the dangerous Bahama Islands, he knew that he also had to turn around the minds and hearts of the common soldier and sailor. Thus, as soon as his meeting with his officers ended on August 17, he ordered a celebration for everyone in the armada. Menendez's 1567 biographer, Bartolome Barrientos, recorded the event this way: *"Drums were sounded and fifes played; banners, standards, and fleet pennants were run up over all the ships. As the royal standard was raised, an appropriate salute boomed out. All the arquebuses and cannon fired at once. A double ration was issued to every man that day. Everyone was vastly pleased, and the demonstration of pleasure was universal. The Adelantado's determination was lauded and that of every man pledged.*"[199]

Menendez had done what no one expected. He removed the fear from his armada and reinvigorated his crew at a time when they had just lost many friends and had the odds turned against them. His skills came very close to mirroring those which we know from the mythical stories of Robin Hood. Both put their loyalty to their friends and country above their love of gold. Both held their men together under the worst situations. And both were highly skilled military tacticians who creatively won battle after battle. Is that possible? Could Pedro Menendez de Aviles have been "as Robin Hood as Robin Hood"?

Pedro Menendez de Aviles took only eleven days to travel from the waters off of Hispaniola to the shores of Cape Canaveral. But it was not an easy trip. In today's world, it would have been like flying without radar, sonar, maps, or GPS. Admiral Valdes and his ship, the *San Andres*, led the way. Without charts, they were sailing blind and constantly using sounding lines to find the depth of the shallow water. Suddenly, they would spot a small island. Aggressive waves would hit its banks. That would push the ship in the opposite direction toward what was the banks of another small island. Without any charts or pilots who knew the best navigational track, everyone was on edge. And they had good reasons to feel that way. During the first two evenings at sea, the admiral and his fellow pilots and sea captains pleaded with the Adelantado to turn around and return to Puerto Rico. He refused to do that. But he appeased them by saying, "*From now on I will take the lead with the Pelayo.*" That helped relieve their anxieties. They knew that the *Pelayo* had the deepest hull.

Menendez had to do more, however, than relieve his crews' anxieties. He also had to use his time to prepare his captains for a worst-case scenario. What if they were to arrive at the harbor near Fort Caroline and discover that the French admiral had gotten there first? On the 25 of August, Menendez gave a speech to the men on the *San Andre* (the admiral's ship) as the armada was sailing through the Bahama Islands. During his talk with the crew, he made this comment: *"If we find that Ribault has arrived before us, we will defeat him."*[200]

On the next day, August 26, the armada's anxiety barometer went from high to low to very high again. The sounding lines showed that the depth of the water was dropping, and fast. One ship reported a depth of two and one-half fathoms. Then, as night appeared, the *San Pelayo* struck bottom three times. The bounce from the first two hits pushed the galleon into slightly deeper waters. Seamen began to shout, *"We're at 6 fathoms. We're at 10 fathoms. We're at 12 fathoms."*[201] By this time, every member of the rag-tag armada was fatigued and tired of praying. They were all wondering, "How long will it take to find the coast of Florida?" No one knew the answer. Without the discovery of "longitude," some would say, "I think we are 30 miles away." Others would say, "No, I believe that we are at least 300 miles from shore." Then, at 9 pm on the 27 of August, the crew got a signal, and some of them believed that it came from God. Chaplain Francisco Lopez de Mendoza described the event this way: *"It was about the ninth hour of the night when a comet came out of the sky. It was born almost above us, toward the part of sunrise. It was giving so much light from itself that it seemed like the Sun. It went running to the West, where Florida is. Its splendor lasted for the time it would take to say two Creeds. We took it for a good sign, as the men of the sea so considered it."*[202]

On the very next day, August 28, the five ships entered a calm. There were no winds. The ships did not move. And the ship pilots still did not know where they were or how far the Florida coast might be. The chaplain and the crew were literally tired of praying for wind. Then at 2 p.m., a steady wind developed that immediately took away their tears. Within a few minutes, they sighted the shoreline of La Florida. Immediately, they all knelt and praised God for their safe trip. But they also prayed for victory when they would face the French.[203]

CHAPTER XI

A Rogue Commander

It would only take the Spanish armada six days before they passed the harbor off of St. Augustine on September 3rd. As they were sailing north the very next day, September 4, they spotted four French ships anchored off of the mouth of the St. Johns River. They were Ribault's four largest ships. As he scanned the horizon, the other three French ships could be seen in the distance. They were snuggled inside the shallower mouth of the St. Johns River, just waiting for Menendez's smaller ships.

The Adelantado immediately called a meeting with his ship and infantry captains. One can only imagine the disappointment that Pedro Menendez de Aviles felt. Since April, he had told everyone in Spain that he could succeed in ridding the colony of the French only if he arrived first. He'd held that position until only a week ago.

ADMIRAL RIBAULT'S ARRIVAL AT FT. CAROLINE

Admiral Ribault had been able to make a direct track to Cape Canaveral from the Canaries. Because he sailed 60 miles north of Menendez's cross-Atlantic track, he avoided the heart of the storm that had smashed and divided the Spanish armada. Although the winds were less than the trade winds to the south, Ribault had a route to the peninsula that was about 700 miles shorter. That would give him at least a ten-day advantage if he were lucky enough to escape the frequent "calms." And he was very lucky. With the storm that hit the Spanish armada, France's Jean Ribault clearly had a two-week advantage . . . if he could avoid the frequent "calms."

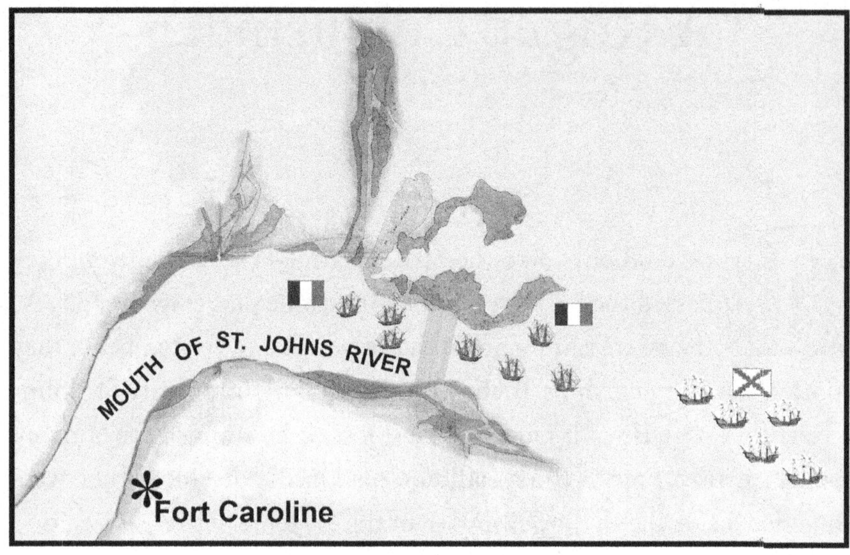

Approaching the St. Johns River.

Why then did Ribault take two weeks (from August 14 to August 28) to arrive at Fort Caroline? The answer is fairly simple. Ribault loved exploration. The historian, Jeannette Thurber Connor, assessed Ribault's actions this way: *"He actually reached the coast of Florida on August 14 . . . but he enjoyed himself going from river to river, a hobby of his, when he should have been settling affairs and unloading cargoes at Fort Caroline and preparing for a Spanish attack."* [204] Instead of racing to Fort Caroline and preparing the French fort for an attack, he slowly meandered into every river between Cape Canaveral and Georgia. He clearly discounted the message that the Admiral of France had given him: *"Pedro Menendez de Aviles and a Spanish armada are also headed to Fort Caroline with many ships and men. If you make contact with him, do unto him as he will do unto you."*

As a result, Jean Ribault and his seven ships did not reach the mouth of the St. Johns River until August 28, 1565. Meanwhile Pedro Menendez was on his heels. He had just spotted Cape Canaveral and was headed north. Ribault had thrown away a two-week lead on Menendez.[205]

By the time that Menendez spotted the four French ships anchored off of the mouth of the St. Johns River, Ribault had only started to unload his ships. Most of his crew and passengers were six to nine miles upriver at Fort Caroline. He had only a skeleton crew on-board his four largest anchored ships.[206]

A Change in Command at Fort Caroline

As Menendez and his five ships approached the anchorage off of the St. Johns River, he was completely unaware of the unrest that was building between Admiral Ribault and Rene Laudonniere, the commander of Fort Caroline. Ribault's problems with Laudonniere had actually begun when Laudonniere dispatched two ships from Ft. Caroline on July 28, 1564, with instructions to return to France and inform the Admiral of France, Gaspard Coligny, of the new garrison's status. Then they were ordered to return with needed supplies. But the report that Laudonniere's men gave to the Admiral of France, Gaspard Coligny, painted a dark picture of their leader. They informed the admiral that Laudonniere sent letters directly to the Lords of the King's Council and acted more like a monarch than the head of a military garrison. Furthermore, they reported that he was unusually cruel to his men. And to top it off, they informed Gaspard Coligny that Laudonniere had brought a woman with him. That had to inflame Gaspard Coligny. He was honored throughout France for his reform of the French army. Because of Coligny, the French army no longer allowed dueling, coarse words, attacks on homeowners, rape, or women in their camps. More than anything, this report sent a message to Gaspard Coligny that Rene Laudonniere did not have the respect of his men.

Thus, when Jean Ribault's fleet of seven ships was off the coast of the St Johns River on August 28, 1565, Ribault did not know if he was about to meet the commander of a French garrison or a rogue deserter. As soon as Laudonniere's sentries spotted Ribault's boats headed toward the river's entrance, he sent a boat to greet them. But instead of responding to that greeting, Ribault was more than guarded and apprehensive. Laudonniere felt Ribault's anxiety. While his men lined the St. Johns River with their arquebuses at the ready, there were no shouts of greeting to Ribault's boats that were moving up the river. The men on Ribault's boats rowed toward Fort Caroline in a tense, all-guns-on-alert manner. They sensed that, at any moment, the air could fill with smoke and musket balls from Ribault's men. Both sides were ready for some unexpected conflict—until the admiral reached Fort Caroline and was recognized. Then Laudonniere ordered his cannon fired to greet the distinguished admiral. Pennants waving, they came onshore and were greeted by firm salutes. Tensions quickly dropped. But Laudonniere had to wonder, *"Why were Ribault's men so apprehensive?"*[207]

After a welcoming meal and many friendly conversations between old friends, the admiral asked Rene Laudonniere to join him outside for a conversation. Within a few minutes, Jean Ribault informed Laudonniere that he would be replacing him as Governor and Viceroy of New France. Then he outlined the concerns that his shipmates shared with the Admiral of France: He had sent letters directly to the Lords of the King's Council. He acted more like a monarch who was running his personal empire. He was cruel and inconsistent in his discipline. And he had a woman with him. Laudonniere made his defense: The woman was only a chambermaid. The men had little experience working in a disciplined manner. But only one thing changed the Admiral of France's orders. [208] Ribault suggested that Laudonniere should remain with him at the settlement instead of returning to France, as Gaspard Coligny had suggested. It was a kind gesture. Ribault was trying to say, *"You remain important to us. Stay here and help us achieve our plans."* Laudonniere, however, responded differently. *"I cannot and should not accept your offer, since you have come here to take the place that I had held, and it would be a rebuke for me not to be in command any longer."*[209]

MENENDEZ ANCHORS AT THE MOUTH OF THE ST. JOHNS RIVER
Menendez certainly knew that, with the delay from the hurricane, there was a good chance that he might not win the race. Up until September 4, he did not want to believe it. Now he knew the answer. As his lookouts spotted the mouth of the St. Johns River in the distance, they clearly saw four large French ships anchored outside the entrance.

They also saw the tall masts of three smaller French ships immediately inside the mouth of the river. **Menendez and Spain had lost the race.** Now he had to reboot and again move the minds of his men. Instead of drowning in failure, he needed to find a way to still win the war. Menendez knew from the past that the only way he could do that was to meet with his Men of Asturius, and let them release their frustrations. But could he do this once again? If he could, he had the possibility, albeit a small one, of losing a race but winning the war. More than ever, he needed that meeting **NOW**. He immediately called a meeting with his ship and infantry captains.[210]

When he opened the meeting with his men, it went something like this: *"We lost the race, but that certainly does not mean that we will lose the war. Now we need to change our strategy. I need your ideas."* Almost immediately, most of the captains recommended that they return to Hispaniola and recover the ships that should be waiting for them. (That would include 1 ship promised by Santo Domingo and 1 ship promised by Cuba; 5 ships delayed from Asturius, and the flagship of the Treasure

Armada.) Then they could return in March with an overwhelming force. Pedro Menendez had a different thought. *"I believe we will face defeat if we take that direction. Skeleton crews are on the ships that we are near. But most of their men are upstream at Fort Caroline. They are onshore. Once they see our damaged fleet, they will have one option . . . attack us in our disadvantaged position . . . but they will not be able to do that until tomorrow morning. I believe that our next move should be to attack them early next morning before they have a chance to be fully manned. We can't attack them tonight because we know that they have incendiary weapons. However, we can get close to them tonight and attack them in the morning. If we can sink or badly damage two or three of them, they will be in no position to attack us the following day. Then we can fall back to the anchorage off of St. Augustine and dispatch a ship to Santo Domingo and retrieve the ships and men that we will need, both to blockade the river's entrance and destroy the French fort."*[211] As soon as the captains heard this recommendation, they approved it. Then, they all fell to their knees and asked God to favor them with victory.

In the words of the Adelantado's biographer, Bartolome Barrientos, this is what happened next: *"Before a fair wind, the Spanish squadron sailed up to within three leagues of the French, at which point the wind died. Thunder and lightning then rent the sky, and a heavy downpour commenced. The rain did not cease until 9 o'clock that night, when the sky cleared, and the wind shifted toward the land. It would be almost midnight when they reached the enemy."*[212]

The Adelantado decided to anchor right up under their bows, so that, by playing out the cables, once the anchors had caught, the sterns of the Spanish ships would lay up against the bows of the enemy. Then at dawn, by pulling in the cable, the Spanish could board them. The Adelantado was convinced that the French galleons could not be protected by the smaller ships that had been waiting inside the mouth of the river. Those ships could not be moved at night, and, by dawn, it would be low tide.

They would have to wait until it was high tide again before they could leave the river. That would not occur until noontime.

Immediately, Pedro Menendez started issuing orders. He told each of his captains where he wanted them positioned against Ribault's anchored ships.[213] Then, at eleven-thirty that night, the French ships "fired some artillery pieces." But the balls passed between the Spanish ships' masts. The Adelantado did not allow the firing of a single cannon against the French ships.

The Spaniards then passed the French flagship, the *Triniti*, without making any overt move. With all flags flying, the Adelantado then brought his five ships to anchor with their bows toward land. Slacking away on the cables, the stern of his flagship, the *San Pelayo*, came to rest between the prows of the French flagship, the *Triniti*, and the Spanish Admirante, the *San Andre*. At this point, the Adelantado ordered the trumpeters to hail the enemy. The skeleton crew on the Huguenot ships replied in kind. When the trumpet flourishes stopped, the Adelantado hailed them most courteously, addressing those aboard the enemy's flagship:[214]

"GENTLEMEN," HE SAID, "WHENCE COMES THIS FLEET?"

"From France," they replied. And he asked again:

"What are you doing here?"

They replied, "We brought infantry, artillery, and supplies for a fort which the king of France has in this country, and for others which he is to build."

Adelantado: **"Are you Catholics or Lutherans, and who is your general?"**

They answered.: "We are all Lutherans of the new religion, and our general is Juan Ribao."

Then they asked Menendez, "Who are you? Who is it that asks these questions? Whose armada do you represent? Why did you come to this country? And who is your general?"

Menendez replied. "He who asks this of you is called Pedro Menendez. This armada belongs to the king of Spain, and I am the general thereof. I come to hang and behead all the Lutherans I may find on this sea and in this land. These are the Instructions from my king, which I will fulfill at dawn when I board Your ships; and if I should find any Catholic, I will give him good treatment."

At this, the Lutherans jeered him and shouted insults. Unable to bear this outrage, the Adelantado ordered the call to arms sounded and the attack launched. But the French turned tail and headed for the open sea. Menendez pursued them. This proved to be one of the few times where Menendez let his emotions change his plan of attack. And it was not the best decision.

Since the *San Pelayo* was between the flagships of Admiral Ribault and his admiral, Menendez and his patache followed two of the four French ships as they turned north. The other three Spanish ships followed the remaining pair as they turned south. Before the chase began, however, Menendez ordered his ships to return to the waters off of the mouth of the St. Johns River by mid-morning of the next day, September 5th.[215]

Menendez and his admiral, Diego Flores Valdes, led the Spanish fleet in a night-long chase of the four French ships. But it was a useless race. Pedro Menendez's small five-ship armada were slowed by damaged masts and missing spars.[216] Because of this, they were unable to catch the faster French ships. By 10:00 a.m. on the next morning, September 5, Menendez returned to the waters off of the mouth of the river. Immediately, the French mobile shore cannon began to fire as the Spanish approached. Inside the St. Johns River, Menendez could see five French ships ready to leap over the sandbar at the mouth once high tide arrived. During the night, Admiral Ribault had moved his infantry and artillery to the island at the mouth of the St. Johns River. When the Adelantado saw this, he was not about to fight on their terms.

The odds were against him. Instead, he ordered his five ships to retreat 32 nautical miles south to the waters off of St. Augustine. He would now put into play the fallback plan that he'd shared with his men on September 4th. *"If we cannot land at the bar of the St. Johns River, we will drop back south to St. Augustine, fortify our position on land, and send our largest ships to Santo Domingo and Havana. Then we will collect the ships and men that should be waiting for us and return en masse in March and destroy them."*[217]

The shallow inlet to St. Augustine

A RETURN TO THE "FALL-BACK" POSITION . . . ST. AUGUSTINE
Menendez and his five ships arrived at an anchorage outside of St. Augustine early in the morning of September 6th. They were about a mile and a half from shore. Soon after they anchored, they began to

unload 200 soldiers. On the next day, September 7, Menendez sent his three smallest vessels and the remaining 300 soldiers into the protection of St. Augustine's shallow harbor.

The three smaller ships could clear the bar at the entrance of the St. Augustine channel (it would only be 1.5 fathoms, or nine feet, at low tide). It was too shallow for any large ship to clear. Because of that shallow harbor entrance, St. Augustine was never targeted by either Spain or France as an initial settlement. But it was soon to become a military garrison . . . by accident.[218]

SEPTEMBER 7 AT ST. AUGUSTINE: RIBAULT PREPARES FOR A COUNTERATTACK.

While Menendez was unloading on his first full day at anchorage off of St. Augustine, Jean Ribault got vital news from Captain La Grange. He had just returned from scouting the seas off of St. Augustine. The message was simple. Menendez had anchored his two largest ships offshore and sent his three smaller ships into the much-shallower St. Augustine harbor.

Ribault immediately called a meeting of his captains. That included Rene Laudonniere and Ribault's captain of the infantry, La Grange. The admiral made a simple announcement: *"Prepare to attack Menendez's armada at St. Augustine. We now know that their two larger ships are at an anchorage outside of St. Augustine and their three smaller ships are within the harbor."* His message was clear. "If we don't destroy them while they are unloading, they will have the ability to attack us again. So, let's destroy them now, while they are vulnerable."

Laudonniere vigorously objected on two points. *"You don't want to leave now because we have frequent storms in September that can immediately turn success into failure. Furthermore, if you leave now, you leave Fort Caroline literally defenseless. We should use the time to strengthen the fort."* The back-and-forth argument between Ribault and Laudonniere grew to the point where the admiral had to remind Laudonniere of the message that the Admiral of France, Gaspard Coligny, had given him: *"If you make contact with the Spanish armada, attack them just as vigorously as they will attack you."*[219]

It was not surprising that the recently disgraced Laudonniere objected to the plan. But it was surprising that Ribault's own captain of the infantry, La Grange, sided with Laudonniere. Captain La Grange had been a thorn in the admiral's side before he'd departed Dieppe. Nothing changed once the armada landed at Fort Caroline.[220]

The admiral, however, was determined. He not only wanted to leave immediately, he insisted on taking thirty-eight of Laudonniere's Fort Caroline men and his personal ensign. However, he had one obstacle to overcome . . . Captain La Grange. He refused to join the fight until September 10th. That two-day delay became very important to the outcome of their plan of attack on the Spanish armada off of St. Augustine.[221]

On September 8, the *San Pelayo* and the *San Sebastian* were anchored 1.5 miles east of the St. Augustine harbor. The three smaller ships were inside the shallow St. Augustine harbor. Since early morning, the ships' crews had rapidly unloaded artillery and food supplies onto the shuttle boats that would head for shore. By noon, the Adelantado and his captains climbed into a boat and headed for the harbor. With his crew and settlers and invited Native Americans, the Adelantado attended Mass. When Mass was over, he formally took possession of St. Augustine for Spain. It was a solemn, yet regal, ceremony. After the ceremony, Menendez celebrated the event by sharing a meal with his captains and a number of friendly Indians. The natives had to feel the tension within the Spanish camp. Their newfound friends were facing the type of setback that disappoints the soul. Their enemy, the French, had beaten them to the St. Johns River. They clearly had the upper hand. The French now controlled the St. Johns River and the resupplied fort. Their infantry held the island that blocked anyone from entering the river.

However, the Indians had something to offer Pedro Menendez de Aviles. During the meal, a few of the Indian chiefs dropped an intriguing idea when they made this remark: *"It is possible to go to Fort Caroline by going inland . . . without going to sea. It might take you two days, but you can reach Fort Caroline and bypass the French-held island at the mouth of the St. Johns River."*[222] Time was short, however, to let that suggestion penetrate any deep thought. Menendez had to call a meeting with his captains and accelerate the unloading because he strongly believed that Ribault would attack them by September 12th. That was only four days away. In Menendez's mind, he had to do everything to unload the *San Pelayo* and *San Sebastion* by September 11th. Simply put, they had to unload two large ships in three days instead of the usual fifteen.

Chapter XII

Menendez's Premonition

The fear that Ribault might attack before September 12 was constantly on Menendez's mind. At midnight on September 9, while he was in bed, he had a premonition. *"Ribault will attack the very next day."* With just that thought, he arose and ordered the *San Pelayo* and *San Sebastian* to raise anchor and depart for Hispaniola. It was a smart move.[223]

Back at Fort Caroline, Admiral Ribault was in a tight spot. His own Captain of the Infantry had again challenged his authority by refusing to attack the Spanish armada on September 8th. Jean Ribault had to wait at the mouth of the St. Johns River for two days until La Grange changed his mind. It was insubordination at its highest level. On September 10, he finally agreed to follow the Admiral's orders.

The mood of the attacking four French ships could best be described as "vigorous and aggressive." It was reported that, upon the departure of the fleet, the French officers held a getting-underway party on one of their four departing ships. At that party, the men reported that Ribault and his captains drank two whole pipes of wine to the health of the Spaniards. *"I drink to the head of Pedro Menendez and those with him,"* one cried, *"Cursed Spaniards! We will hang them from the yardarms of their own ships as well as from ours, so that they will not come again to smell out this country of ours!"* cried another. [224]

Ribault and his four ships departed for Menendez's anchorage off of St. Augustine early on September 10th. Being 32 sea miles away, it was at least a six-hour trip. Meanwhile, the disgraced Rene Laudonniere lay in bed in a very depressed mood. Admiral Ribault had taken 38 of his best men for a foolish attack on Menendez. Of the men who remained who were able to defend the fort, four were young boys, and one was a cook. The others included a 65-year-old carpenter, a beermaker, an old crossbow maker, two shoemakers, four or five men with their wives, a spinet player, two servants of French nobles, and 85 or 86 laborers. Maybe he had 16 or 17 who could bear arms. But many of those were either sick or injured. Laudonniere believed that the fort was very vulnerable to an attack.[225] But, of course, Menendez was in no position to attack Fort Caroline. At least not now!

Nevertheless, Laudonniere soon put what energy he had into strengthening the defenses of Fort Caroline. He put the fort's guard on special alert. He organized two shifts of guard "watches." That allowed one shift to gain valuable rest. And he ordered two soldiers to make continuing rounds with lighted candles.[226]

At midnight on September 10, Menendez waved to the skeleton crew that raised the anchors of the *San Pelayo* and *San Sebastian.* As their sails unfurled, they were underway to Hispaniola and Havana before Ribault had a chance to attack them. As they departed, the one shallop and two trailing shuttle boats that unloaded the last provisions started to return to the shallow entrance of the St. Augustine harbor. By dawn they had traveled far enough to hear deckhands call out, *"We're at two fathoms and approaching the inlet."* They also noticed one other thing. When they scanned the horizon, four French ships were closing in on them.

Those French ships had been looking for the two large Spanish ships, the *San Pelayo* and *San Sebastian*, that had just departed. But seeing that they were missing, they turned their prows toward the port-bound Spanish shallop. Menendez was on one of two trailing boats. As his men expected, he was helping to unload the last of the two departing ships.

Ribault's Ships Closing In

Altogether, there were 150 Spaniards that were straining to sail across the shallow harbor inlet that was just yards away. But they soon entered a calm. The sails were dead flat. One of the four French ships was within shouting distance from their stern . . . and closing. Low tide was approaching. The depth of the inlet would be only nine feet in minutes. That gave the shallop no clearance. Its hull reached nine feet down. However, the four French ships had deeper hulls. The Spanish were in a heavy sweat. They did not know if they would clear the inlet before the French attacked and boarded their ship and boats. Everyone prayed and prayed and prayed. All of a sudden, a miracle happened. A stiff breeze came up. It was just enough to push the shallop and its two trailing boats across the inlet's bar. To the Spaniards, it was nothing less than a miracle. Outside of the harbor entrance, the frustrated French waited for the tide to rise so that they could enter the harbor. But after a two-hour wait, the winds of a real northeastern tempest appeared. It was now too dangerous for the French to remain near the shore. Ribault's four ships took off to find the *San Pelayo* and *San Sebastian*, but they were at least fifteen miles south at that time.[227]

Menendez and his men had again survived a near tragedy. After they attended Mass to thank the Lord, the Adelantado could not help but notice one thing. The storm that had pushed the French out to sea was increasing in its intensity. *This storm may be a nor-easter. If that is the case, it will continue for days. That means that Ribault's ships may not be able to return to their fort. The winds are blowing in the opposite direction that they need to return to the fort,* Menendez thought to himself.

A Surprise Attack Like No Other

Soon after they landed, the Adelantado requested a Mass to thank the Lord for their safe delivery. Three days later, on September 13, the storm that had pushed Menendez's small ship across the inlet bar turned into a genuine "nor-easter." At that point, Menendez asked his captains to join him for a special military council. At that meeting, on the evening of September 14, 1565, the Adelantado introduced an idea that he believed had the potential to win the war for Spain.

After Menendez thanked his men for their hard work and determination, he said in so many words, *"We have an opportunity that we should not let pass. When Ribault attacked us at the inlet to St. Augustine, he attacked us with his four largest ships. That means when he attacked us near the inlet on September 10, he had to have taken the best men from Fort Caroline. Fort Caroline must be weakly defended. The storm that is upon is a 'nor-easter.' It will last for days. Because it is coming out of the north, there will be no way that Ribault's armada can return to Fort Caroline by sailing north. They will either have to drift south or be crushed against the shoreline.*

"Now is our opportunity. We need to attack Fort Caroline now by reaching them through an inland route . . . across streams, rivers, and thickets. And we must do it while it is raining. We will take 500 soldiers—two parts arquebusiers and one-part pikemen—and rations for a week in our packs but no porters. We will carry our weapons on our backs and attack Fort Caroline from inland. No one will expect us to do that. But we know how to get there. Our French prisoner, Jean Francois, worked at that fort for one year. He will guide us along with two local Indian brothers who were at the fort only six days ago. They tell me that the fort is only fifteen miles from here. With my compass alone, I can take us to within two leagues of the fort."[228] His men were not quiet. They had many questions. Should they tackle this risky venture or not? They finally agreed to support the plan. Menendez then informed his men that he wanted to leave in two days . . . the morning of September 16th.[229] The group nodded their heads in agreement. Before they departed, the Adelantado informed them of the command structure he wanted to use. His campmaster, or head of the infantry, Pedro de Valdes, would organize the surprise attack. Valdes' executive officer would be Captain Gonzalo de Villarroel. Menendez's brother, Bartolome, would remain at the St. Augustine Fort and supervise the remaining soldiers. His admiral of the fleet, Diego Flores de Valdes, would also remain to guard the three remaining ships and artillery. Then Pedro Menendez de Aviles underscored one more point: *"I will lead the surprise attack."*

Attitudes, however, can change overnight. By the next morning, Pedro Menendez was informed that some of his captains were critical of his plan. Several of those who supported the plan yesterday were against it today. And the side conversations were making many concerned about the dangers ahead. One of the captains who led this opposing view was Juan de San Vicente. He was one of the men who'd argued against taking a northern route through the Bahama Islands at the August 17th council meeting aboard the *San Pelayo*. When Menendez heard of this side-talk opposition, he immediately convened a meeting of his captains. It was a relatively short meeting. His message was hard and to the point. It went something like this: *"By now you have shared your concerns with others who are not on this trip. That violates every rule of military secrecy. We can never succeed if we have public discussion of a secret plan. Your violation should be reprimanded. But I am not going to do that if you agree to use better judgment from now on. Success is seldom attained in war when there is no secrecy. If our men become disheartened, we have only to look at their captain. If he is disheartened, and not leading, his men will be disheartened and scared. And we will know who that captain is. If I see a captain who is not leading his company, I will take his company away from him. I want to depart at dawn on September 17th."* There were no more arguments.[230]

Gonzalo Solis de Meras, the brother-in-law of Pedro Menendez, was one of the captains on the surprise attack. He described the march in graphic detail. *"At dawn Menendez's captains sounded reveille with trumpets, fifes, and drums. And the bells chimed. The men went to Mass first.[231] Afterwards they departed to good-luck wishes and set out marching in formation. Every man carried a knapsack with six pounds of biscuit on his back and a canteen that held two and one-half liters of wine.[232] The Adelantado took twenty soldiers from Asturias and Vizcaya with their axes to lead the way. They cut down the brush and trees in their path. They also left axe marks along the trail to help them remember the path when they returned to St. Augustine. Joining the 500 men were two Indian brothers who had been at the French fort only six days earlier. The Spaniards called them 'angels of God.' They believed[233] that Fort Caroline was only fifteen miles north, northwest of St. Augustine. If that turns out to be true, it should take them about two days to reach the fort."*[234]

The march quickly became an almost-unbearable trip. During the trek, the rain from the "nor-easter" came in a continuous downpour. Two thirds of the men had to carry their heavy arquebuses and backpacks while often wading in knee or waist-deep water. Along the way they had to cross three rivers, all swollen from the torrential rain. However, not every soldier knew how to swim. They solved that problem by attaching a series of their long pikes, holding them together with tree vines. Then those who knew how to swim guided the non-swimmers across the rivers with their twelve-foot-long linked pikes. Of course, some were fearful of the idea. But their fear vanished when Pedro Menendez crossed the river first using those lashed-together pikes.[235] At night there were no

Painting by Birney Lettick, *for* National Geographic

places to stay dry and warm. The storm continued to blow and pour down on them. That rain also drenched the fuses of their arquebuses. Their main weapon was now useless. Their clothes became soaked and heavy with water. Their biscuits became wet and moldy. The gunpowder was too wet to use.

At this point, the men were tired, wet, hungry, and exhausted. And that generated a feeling of already being defeated. Some of the men began to complain. *"The only smart thing for us to do is to return to Fort Augustine."* Others talked loudly enough so that the Adelantado could hear their slanderous comments of him. One of them was ensign Fernan Perez. Not surprisingly, he was the ensign of Captain Juan Vicente. He came close enough to the Adelantado so that he could hear these words: *"Look how we are being misguided by this fainthearted Asturian, who is as ignorant of land warfare as an ass! If it had been up to me, the same day he left St. Augustine on this journey, he would have gotten what is now coming to him!"*[236]

Pedro Menendez just ignored those comments. Finally, sensing that his captains needed a stiff shot of adrenalin, he called an early-morning meeting on the third day. As soon as they arrived, he set the stage. *"Gentlemen, we are now without ammunition or food, and the men are tired, lost, and disheartened. Let's discuss what is best for us to do."* Gonzalo Solis de Meras, who was in the march, recorded what happened next. *"Some of the men replied that they did not see why they would agree to do anything other than to retreat to St. Augustine."* The Adelantado expected that reply. Then, he made this comment. *"Gentlemen, are you confident that we are very close to Fort Caroline?"* They replied, *"We are."* Then Menendez said to them, *"It seems to me that we need to go and trust our luck as we agreed. When we sound our trumpets and raise our flags, we will **not** need our arquebuses.*[237] * *That in itself will cause the French to get out of bed. If we retreat, the French will see us as cowards. And we are not cowards."* That was enough of a reminder for the captains to agree, after some discussion, that they should follow their plan.[238]

The Spaniards pushed on in knee- to waist-deep water. There was no trail to follow. At night it was difficult to find dry higher ground to start a fire. On the evening of the third day, September 20, Menendez reached the neighborhood of the fort. He encamped in a pine grove less than a mile away. It was too close to light a fire. It would be noticed by the French. At dawn on the next day, September 21, 1565, the Adelantado gathered his captains around him. They knelt down and prayed for victory. Then he set out on a narrow path that led to the fort. His French prisoner led the way. His hands were bound behind him. But it was so dark that Menendez had to stop and wait for daybreak. Then, in historian Woodbury Lowery's words, this is what happened next:

---

* While the arquebus was the weapon of choice in Europe, it quickly became less important in southeastern North America. The arquebus could be fired only with a fuse. Menendez quickly discovered that those fuses would be immediately extinguished in any rain. All of a sudden, the older crossbows became the weapon of choice.

"When morning came, Menendez set out in the direction of the fort. On reaching a slight elevation, the French prisoner, Jean Francois, announced that Fort Caroline lay just beyond, down on the river's edge. Then the camp Master, Pedro Menendez Valdez, and the Asturian, Ochoa, went forward to reconnoiter. They were hailed by a man they took to be a sentinel. "Who goes there? he cried, *"Frenchmen," they answered."* As they closed in on him, Ochoa struck and killed him with his sword, but not before he began shouting. That triggered Menendez to immediately shout out *"Santiago! God help us! Victory!"*[239]* At that signal, the entire Spanish force rushed down the path. They immediately killed two French sentinels who were in their way. Then they entered the gates of the fort. The attacking Spaniards were running in a joyful manner. Everyone was trying to outrun the others. Almost immediately a French trumpeter climbed the rampart and, seeing the Spanish rush in, sounded the alarm. Meanwhile a rush of men opened the main gate. Almost immediately two young Spanish ensigns raced to the inside center of the fort and raised the Spanish flag on the two French flagpoles.[†]

The French, who were arising from a sound sleep, were taken entirely by surprise in the blowing rain. Some were only half-dressed. Some were naked. The French were quickly cut down except for the women and children. Menendez repeatedly yelled, *"No French children or women should be harmed."* Then he headed for the breach in the fort's wall. After repulsing its defenders, he came upon Laudonniere, who

---

† "Santiago! God help us! Victory!" was one of Spain's most popular battle yells in the 16th century. The yell started from the ninth century. At the time, Castile was fighting the invading Muslims from Africa. The battle yell apparently came when Asturias's King, Ramiro I, informed his troops that he was visited the night before by the Apostle St. James. The apostle apparently said to the King, *"I will come to your aid by the morrow, and the hand of God will overcome the countless multitude of Saracens. You will see me on a white horse bearing a great banner."* As the legend goes, St. James did appear. The "Spanish" troops yelled, *"May God and St. James help us!"* The battle was won. Since then Spanish troops have often yelled that battle cry as they entered an important battle.

was running to their assistance. With his hands tied behind his back, Menendez's French prisoner pointed him out. Seeing that it was a useless fight, Laudonniere ran through a breach in the western wall and took to the woods. He escaped.

Attack on Fort Caroline

Within an hour, the fight in and around the fort was over. The French were either dead, wounded, or running into the woods. But the river at the edge of the fort was another issue. As soon as the Adelantado had gained control, he noticed three French ships moored in the river . . . within cannon shot of the fort. They were the three smaller ships from Ribault's seven-ship armada. Using a trumpeter, he communicated with Jacques Ribault, who was the son of Admiral Jean Ribault and captain of the *Pearle*, one of the three moored ships. Menendez made young Ribault a fair, and quite frankly, a very humane offer. *"Take any of the three ships that are moored; take the women and children and leave for France."* He would give them the necessary supplies for the voyage. They would need only to leave behind their artillery and ammunition. If they chose not to do this, he would sink the three ships. Young Ribault responded that if the Adelantado wanted war, he would do the same. That answer was enough for Pedro Menendez to fire a bronze cannon shot at the nearest ship and put her to the bottom of the river. That, of course, triggered the French to cut the cables on the other two ships, the *Pearle* and *Levriere,* and sail back toward the mouth of the river.[240]

Almost immediately, Menendez and his men sought any shelter they could find to get out of the rain and rest. They were more than exhausted. At 4 pm, his captains came to him so that they could discuss their incredible win. When they met, everyone's eyes were brimming with tears of thankfulness. The Adelantado addressed them. *"Gentlemen and brothers, God works these miracles once and again for His cause. Let us be able to serve and praise Him for the great mercy He has shown us. It is now time to commend ourselves to Him more than ever and get our things ready to defend this fort against the French fleet when it returns and to secure the men, artillery, weapons, ammunition, and supplies we have left at St. Augustine."*[241]

Then the Adelantado informed his band of brothers that he would rename the garrison "Fort Mateo," because it had been conquered on September 21, 1565, which was St. Matthew's Day on the Catholic calendar. Furthermore, he informed them that Gonzalo de Villarroel, the sergeant major who reported to his future son-in-law, Pedro Menendez de Valdes, would be promoted to Warden of the Fort and Governor of the District around it. He had demonstrated his skills in the most visible way when he participated in the attack on the French fort.

On the next day, September 22, Pedro Menendez de Aviles reviewed the detailed results of his victory. Not a single Spaniard had been lost. Only one had been wounded. Of the 240 French in the fort, 132 had been killed. About six drummers and trumpeters were held prisoner as well as 50 women and children. But he was surprised by one number. When he took muster of his men, the count was slightly less than 400. What happened to the other 100? Did they return to St. Augustine because they were too sick and tired to continue? Or were they just cowards?

That evening, September 22, Pedro Menendez de Aviles again met with his captains and informed them that he would depart in two days for St. Augustine. He would leave with 35 men who were healthy enough to make the trip. However, he would leave 300 of his 400 men at the fort to defend it from any attack by Ribault. He shared with his captains that his plan was to order two of his three ships moored at St. Augustine to return to the mouth of the St. Johns River. Their mission would be to capture the remaining French ships that were at the inlet. Then, he would search for the four ships under Ribault's command that attacked his shallop and two boats on September 10th. Everyone knew that, if he could capture or destroy Ribault's four ships, the war would be over.

Menendez had to be in exceptional shape. At forty-six years old, he was up at dawn and searching through every building for the men who were fit enough to leave for St. Augustine. Just the thought of having to repeat that trip had to frighten the 400 men before they went to sleep. But the Adelantado found 35 semi-willing bodies. He departed the next day, September 23, with the rain continuing to fall. It would be a harrowing return trip. They could not find the ax marks they left from the first march, and the ground was nothing less than one flooded mess. It did not even help to send one of their men up a tall tree to spot the next distant piece of ground. The sky was so darkened by clouds that even the scouts could not see what was ahead of them. Finally, after three days, Menendez and his 35 men spotted St. Augustine in the distance.

But what Menendez and his men did not know was that the men and settlers who'd remained at St. Augustine did not expect them to return. The general feeling in the compound was that Menendez and his men must have died. That impression was believable because one hundred men returned before they reached Fort Caroline. They told everyone how difficult and dangerous the trek became. *"They were running out of food. With the rain they had no use of their arquebuses (their muskets). They had to wade through water up to their waist. They were wet, hungry, and exhausted."* And a few were cowards.[242]

That story was amplified by men such as Captain Juan San Vicente. When Menendez's men departed on September 17 from St. Augustine, San Vicente claimed to have a pain in his leg and a stomachache. It was a strong enough reason for him to stay behind. That, of course, triggered a response from those who were ordered to defend the garrison. They chided him for being a coward. San Vicente reportedly replied by saying, *"I swear to God that I am waiting for the news that all our soldiers are dead, so that those of us who have remained here can embark on these three ships and go to the Indies, for it is not reasonable that we should all die like beasts."*[243]

When Menendez knew that he was within three miles of St. Augustine, he sent a young soldier racing ahead to let the garrison know that he would be arriving soon. The expedition's chaplain, Francisco Lopez de Mendoza, recorded the arrival this way:

> *"The news being known, I went with all speed to my house and took out a new gown, the best I had, and a surplice. I took a cross in my hands and went out to meet him a short distance before he should arrive at this port. He, like a good knight and Christian, and all those who came with him, knelt before I arrived, giving many thanks to Our Lord for the many mercies received. In this manner, I and my companions came in the lead, singing in procession, so that he was received with great rejoicing by us and we by him."*[244]

As soon as the Adelantado rested and got his breath, he ordered two of his three remaining ships to be ready to depart on the morning of September 28th. Their mission? To capture the two French ships at the mouth of the St. Johns River. However, before the ships departed, Menendez received word that those two ships had already sailed. Approximately 56 Frenchmen had escaped the attack on Fort Caroline. Jean Ribault's son, Jacques, quickly departed for France with 26 of them on the *Pearle*. Captain Maillard left with 30 on the *Levriere*. With that news, the Adelantado changed his orders. He would now send only one of his three remaining ships with artillery and ammunition to strengthen the defense of their new fort, Fort Mateo (previously Ft. Caroline). Now there were only two remaining ships at St. Augustine.[245]

Two days after Pedro Menendez had returned to St. Augustine, he received some eye-opening news. On September 28, some Indians arrived and informed the Adelantado by hand-signs that *"many Christians were stranded 12 miles south of St. Augustine on the coast."* This had to be a shocking piece of information for the Adelantado to hear. If these men were from one of Ribault's four largest ships, it clearly meant one thing. The "nor-easter" that drenched his men when he marched to Fort Caroline may have pushed Ribault's ships onto the shore. Menendez had to have had a fleeting thought: *"If that is true, we have won the war. We control Fort Caroline. And Ribault's remaining armada of four ships has to be too damaged to continue the fight."*

More than likely, Menendez would have had one other thought. *"If there are more than 50 or 100 French survivors, do we have enough food to keep them and ourselves alive? And with only two small ships remaining at St. Augustine, how could we accommodate a large group of French prisoners without running the risk of being overtaken by them?"* His answer to himself would have to have been . . . *"NO! We have neither the food nor the number of ships that we would need."*

Menendez would not have much time to ponder those questions. What we do know is that he immediately departed with 40 soldiers to find those shipwrecked survivors. When he arrived near midnight, he saw soldiers on the other side of an inlet. The historian Woodbury Lowery later reported that there were about 140 surviving Frenchmen from two ships that first landed on the shore south of St. Augustine. As that first group of Frenchmen began to walk north, they became stranded at the south side of an inlet that separated them from St. Augustine's southern shoreline. When Menendez arrived on the northern shore of that inlet, he saw two French flags on the other side. Under a white flag of truce, a French officer informed Menendez that all four French galleons and several smaller ships had been shipwrecked south of St. Augustine.[246] Menendez asked, *"Are you Catholic or Lutheran?"* The French officer replied that they were all Lutherans. Within a few hours the French told Menendez what they desired . . . a ship to return to France and a promise of safe passage for all their men. Some of the men who were nobles would also be willing to pay a ransom for their freedom. The Adelantado said that he would do that if they were Catholics and if he had the ships to spare. But he replied that he did not have ships to spare. In effect, the French pleaded for help, and the Adelantado did not agree to anything. His only offer was to have the shipwrecked men join them. Then he would decide what would be the right thing to do.

When the Frenchmen crossed over the inlet to the Spanish side, they were fed quickly. Then they were marched beyond the sand dunes and executed.[247] Menendez immediately returned to the garrison on St. Augustine. On the very next day, September 30, the same Indians who'd reported the first group of stranded Frenchmen returned. They informed Menendez that there were many more Frenchmen who had arrived at the same point where they found the first group. Menendez immediately thought that this group could be the men from Ribault's flagship. And that could include Jean Ribault himself.[248]

The Adelantado immediately departed with 150 soldiers. At midnight he set up camp at the same place as before. When dawn arrived, they could see many Frenchmen on the other side of the inlet. The shipwrecked French soon spotted the Spanish and sounded a call to arms. They unfurled their royal standard and two campaign flags. Then they assembled into a formation, ready to fight. But Menendez did just the opposite. He ordered his men to sit and eat, and not show any sign of unrest. Soon the French did the same. They got out of formation and raised a white flag signaling, *"Let's talk."* Both sides then agreed to meet. Pedro Menendez received the French admiral with the utmost courtesy. He offered him food, drink, and straight talk. The discussion went the same as two days before. Pedro Menendez de Aviles would not guarantee Jean Ribault anything. He would just have to trust the mercy of the Spanish conquistador. Ribault returned to his encampment to get the opinion of his captains. When he returned to Menendez, Ribault informed him that only 150 of the 350 men would agree to place themselves at his mercy.

As soon as the French cautiously landed on the Spanish-controlled shore, their hands were immediately bound behind them. Then they were marched inland, beyond the sight of the others, and put to the knife. However, as one Frenchman's hands were about to be bound behind his back, he informed the Adelantado that he had information that should spare his life. Menendez responded by saying, *"Tell me what you know, and I will decide if your life should be spared."* The Frenchman was apparently the pilot of Ribault's flagship, the *Triniti*. His story was simple: *"I know France's real plans for this country. Next April the Admiral of France, Gaspard Coligny, plans to send a great fleet here with the intention of capturing the returning Spanish Treasure Fleet, which, by necessity, has to pass here from New Spain (Mexico) and Terra Firma (South America). They will be aided by the English, who will also arrive with their ships. With the expectation of a victory over you, Juan Ribault will be ordered to go to the Martires (today's Key West) with his 800 men and build a fort there. The plan is to stop any Spanish ship that either enters the Bahama Channel or comes through it from the south. And then in the Spring of 1567, Ribault will be ordered to attack Havana with the fleet that arrived earlier from France. But that would be a different type of attack. They will use slave revolts to defeat the Spanish at Havana. After they captured Havana, they would use the same tactic in Hispaniola, Puerto Rico, and Terra Firma (South America). That is France's plan."*[249]

When the Adelantado heard this story from the Frenchman, he had to have thought, *"Could this be true?"* But Menendez believed it. He spared the man his life. WHY? Because the Spanish found the written plan that repeated this story soon after they captured Fort Caroline. Historian Gene Lyon relayed this story of what they found in one of the buildings once they captured Fort Caroline. *"In an apartment that belonged to Jean Ribault, they found a small strongbox in which he had all his papers, provisions, and titles, including papers that said what he must do next. There were six decrees, signed by the admiral of France, Gaspard Coligny. In the instructions was a section which stated that, after having reinforced the forts in Florida and fortified others which might seem necessary to him, that which would serve God would be to go to the coast of the Indies and give liberty to the slaves there . . ."*[250]

What was amazing was that the French pilot's report was exactly what Pedro Menendez had expected. When he was asked by Philip II in February of 1565, *"What strategy do you believe France will take?"* Menendez answered with a shockingly bold prediction. He believed that France's most likely strategy would be to establish military garrisons along the southeast coast and then attack and capture the Spanish Main by creating slave revolts. **What Ribault's pilot shared was, "THAT was France's exact plan."**

Was Menendez Unusually Cruel?

Pedro Menendez de Aviles lost the race with France to be the first to reach Fort Caroline. But he won the war. Later, the enemies of Spain would start a campaign to label Menendez and Spain as cruel in their execution of the shipwrecked enemy. The question persists, of course, "Was Menendez cruel?" The facts answer the question:

- 558 Frenchmen from four shipwrecks were spotted south of St. Augustine on Sept. 28 and 29 of 1565.

- Menendez had only 200 men at the nearby garrison of St. Augustine. He left 300 men at Fort Caroline once he'd captured the fort.

- There were only two small 125–150-ton ships at St. Augustine. He had just dispatched one of his remaining three ships to guard the entrance of the St. Johns River near Fort Caroline. Earlier he had dispatched his two largest galleons to the Indies so that they would not be attacked by Ribault.

- There was only a bare-minimum amount of food available. The supply building at Fort Caroline had just burned to the ground.

- If Menendez had offered the 558 men their freedom, he either would have had to put them behind a guarded stockade or ship them to Havana. With only 200 men at St. Augustine, he could not have safely guarded them. He had only two small ships at St. Augustine to take prisoners to Havana, and he did not have enough food to keep them for any period of time.

Pedro Menendez made the decision to execute 334 of the Frenchmen simply because he had no other alternative. What is clear is that he did not do this with any intent to be cruel. He literally had no choice at the time. Was Menendez one of those cruel Spaniards? No! Absolutely not! When Menendez attacked Fort Caroline, he ran throughout the fort shouting, *"Under penalty of death, do not kill any women or children."*

After he destroyed the fort, he offered 30 Frenchmen the option to sail back to France. After he executed the men south of St. Augustine, he assembled a company of men to track down the 200 men who decided to escape. They retreated south and built a fort near Cape Canaveral. When Menendez located those Frenchmen, he offered them their safety if they would surrender. One hundred and twenty accepted his offer.

No, Pedro Menendez was not a blood-soaked Spaniard who would kill any Huguenot he met. All the evidence shows that he was not a man of hatred or cruelty. He simply did what he had to do to protect his men.

There was one other reason that may have influenced Pedro Menendez's decision to execute the Frenchmen who were shipwrecked. Menendez saw the French through two lenses. There was the French Catholic government, ruled by King Charles IX, his mother, Catherine, and the French Catholic party. Then there were the minority Huguenots, led by Gaspard Coligny. During the last five years, when Spain was at peace with France, the ships of the French Huguenots continued to raid Spain's ships and ports in the Indies. Thus, when Pedro Menendez executed his French prisoners, he was reported to have said, "*I end your life not as Frenchmen, but as French Huguenots.*"

Many documents have been published discussing whether Pedro Menendez de Aviles was unusually cruel to his captured enemy. In 1905, Woodbury Lowery published what is probably the most balanced answer to that question. He summarized the conquistador this way:

"His faith was that of a soldier, imbued with all that hatred of heresy peculiar to his age and race. He showed as little compunction in executing heretics upon what was taught to be the will of the Church as relentlessness in performing the commands of his sovereign. He was neither impelled by rage nor violence, nor did he act under the impulse of a blind fanaticism. He deliberately and conscientiously performed what he believed to be his duty towards his King and his faith."[251]

Within a two-day period in late September 1565, Pedro Menendez de Aviles had won an almost-unwinnable war. From the beginning, he knew that he had to arrive at the mouth of the St. Johns River before the French armada. From his experience, that was the only way he could win. In his mind, if Ribault arrived before he did, the French would have an enormous advantage. However, because of the cross-Atlantic hurricane and the fact that France's Jean Ribault chose a shorter route, Pedro Menendez de Aviles and Spain lost the race. Yet, at every barrier, he got his men off the floor. Then he re-motivated them and got their buy-in on another option. His surprising success was not just a result of creatively developing a string of alternative strategies. He had a core of men, his "Men of Asturias," who would follow him in virtually any situation. They were almost a carbon copy of the mythical Robin Hood's "Men of Sherwood Forest." They followed him at every impasse. They were willing to forfeit their lives for Menendez. As a result, he arrived at the mouth of the St. Johns River with only one-third of the ships and men that he'd planned on having. Instead of arriving with 16 ships and 1,914 men, he arrived with five badly damaged ships and 800 passengers. But only 700 were fighting men. The others were settlers. He arrived knowing that he had lost the "race" that he said he had to win. But most importantly, with the odds overwhelmingly against him, he won the war.

Philip II was the first to hear of the total destruction of the French armada. On October 15, Pedro Menendez sent King Philip II a letter that described the victory. The king, most likely, received that letter in early December 1565. Philip responded:

> *"We have been most gratified to learn of the success you have scored in your undertaking . . . As concerns the justice you meted out to the Lutheran corsairs who attempted to occupy and fortify Florida in order to sow the seeds of their wicked sect . . . we believe you were fully justified and acted with entire prudence."*

Philip II waited until January before he informed Catherine de Medici of the extent of her losses in Spain's new colony. At that point, Catherine knew that they lost Fort Caroline. But she had not yet been informed of the destruction of the admiral's fleet and the loss of many of his men. On January 15, 1566, the Spanish ambassador, Frances de Alava, met with France's queen mother. The meeting reflected the character of Catherine de Medici. She put on a performance that mirrored her gigantic hypocrisy. She was, of course, not willing to inform the ambassador that she agreed to the plan to resupply their "unofficial" French garrison. She was also not going to disclose that she backed Coligny's plan to push Spain out of the Americas. And she was not about to acknowledge that the Pope had given Spain the rights to North America as early as 1493. Instead, the Queen Mother stated in a most innocent manner that she believed that the Frenchmen who had gone to the Isle des Bretonnes had already left that country.

When the Spanish ambassador to France heard that reply, he became infuriated and loudly replied, *"I know of no Isle des Bretonnes. You can call Peru the Tierra Firme des Bretonnes, but I know that when the order was given to your captain, he said that he was to proceed to New France by way of Florida. The name of Florida was expressly used."*[252]

Catherine de Medici and her son, King Charles IX, did not press the argument very long. They were unusually quiet about their defeat . . . at least until Spain's enemies in England, France, Germany, and Italy began to create a public relations campaign about Spain's "cruel" behavior.

Contrary to this pretense of being above the fray, the facts tell a completely different story. This was the 16th century. Differences were often settled by duels and by blindly attacking the enemy. In France, the Huguenots burned many Catholic churches and killed their priests. In England Queen Mary Stuart earned the reputation of "Bloody Mary" when she killed thousands of innocent Protestants. England's Protestant queen, Elizabeth I, allowed the pirate, Francis Drake, to freely bomb and destroy the Spanish towns of Santo Domingo, Cartagena, and St. Augustine. And Pope Paul IV decided to initiate a war with Spain just to drive the Spanish out of the Italian Peninsula. This was the norm for the 16th century.

Was Menendez too prejudiced against the Protestants? Maybe. But in the 16th century, almost everyone was too prejudiced. Most of Europe displaced their Jewish population. They hated all Muslims. There was still some slavery. The common peasant could not rise to become a noble.

Soon after the execution of the French, food became very limited. In mid-November, Pedro Menendez departed for Havana to get food, supplies, and some of the 794 men and 9 ships that should be waiting for him. He was especially worried about his Asturian friend, Admiral Esteban Alas, and his five ships. Did they make it to Havana?[253] Menendez knew, of course, that he did not need all of those ships and men. He had already defeated the French. What he needed was his friend, Esteban Alas, his 5 ships, and food and supplies.

When Pedro Menendez departed for Havana, he did not know that some of his men at St. Augustine were planning to mutiny. His "Men of Asturias" had a strong allegiance to him, but not necessarily the seamen and soldiers that they recruited. They became, in fact, no different than many of the men that constantly left Seville for Havana. What was important to them was not serving the king or God. It was finding a way to Havana so that they could hop on the next ship to either Mexico or Peru. They all had gold fever. When Menendez returned from Havana, he had to use every skill he had to hold his men together at St. Augustine and San Mateo (Spain's new name for Fort Caroline) . . . at least long enough for Spain's reinforcement armada of 1,500 men to arrive.[254]

CHAPTER XIII

Where Our America Began!

In early April of 1566, Menendez set sail for the Punta Santa Elena. This was more than a trip to locate the next military garrison. The Punta had been Spain's first targeted settlement. In fact, the Punta Santa Elena had a double value for Spain. It could protect the returning Treasure Fleet, and it could serve as the hub for further expansion into North America.

On April 15, 1566, Pedro Menendez de Aviles saw the mouth of the Punta Santa Elena.* This had to have been an emotional moment. He knew that Jean Ribault, the French admiral whom he had just executed, had established a short-term military outpost there in 1562. But none of the three Spanish explorers before him had found the Punta. And no country had yet placed a real settlement on the shores of the Punta. This was the prize of Europe . . . a location so valuable that Philip II sent a letter to the viceroy of New Spain in December of 1559, ordering him to settle the Punta (point of) Santa Elena before any other location in North America. It was so important that the Admiral of France, Gaspard Coligny, selected it as a possible location from which to ambush the returning Spanish Treasure Armada. With help from two Oristo Indians, Menendez passed the Punta Santa Elena (Hilton Head Island), entered the River of Santa Elena (Spain's name for Port Royal Sound) on April 16, 1566.[255] His ship and two brigantines then sailed up the harbor for another three miles until they reached the eastern tip of a large island at the end of the harbor. After meeting with the Oristo Indians who lived here, Menendez christened his new home "Santa Elena." Today we call that large island "Parris Island, South Carolina." Using his brigantine boats, Pedro Menendez de Aviles and Esteban de las Alas, with about 100 men, rowed to shore. Within half an hour, the Adelantado's two Indians took them to a nearby village. The native Americans were more than welcoming. They helped Menendez's men build Fort San Felipe.

Entering the Punta. Approaching Parris Island.
Sketched in 1564–1565 by Jacques Le Moyne. Engraved by Theodor De Bry

It did not take long for Pedro Menendez to give Santa Elena the attention that King Philip II ordered. By the end of 1567, Captain Juan Pardo was making good progress in building the inland road between Santa Elena and the silver mines in northern Mexico. He reached the Tennessee River in 1567. By 1569, Santa Elena had a formal colonial government. It had a normal mix of men, women, and children. It had a fort, a church, and many homes. There were many artisans and shopkeepers. And unlike the French, the Spanish settlement had farms. In other words, it was a self-sustaining European village. It was a true European settlement. By October of 1569, Santa Elena had a population of 327 people.[256] At that point, it became the first European settlement in North America.

By 1571, Santa Elena had become even more important. Pedro Menendez made Santa Elena his home and the capital of Spain's North American colony. Before Pedro Menendez departed for Spain in 1574, he had seen Santa Elena face the same challenges that the English would later face at Jamestown and Plymouth. There was a continuing shortage of food, periodic mutinies, and an Indian population that swung from being friends to enemies.

Pedro Menendez de Aviles accomplished what no other conquistador had achieved. He established the first European settlement in North America . . . Santa Elena. To do that, however, he literally had to do the impossible to push France out of the continent. As a result, he sealed Spain's claim on North America for the next 42 years. But it was how he lost the trans-Atlantic race, but won the 1565 battle with France, that will long be remembered. To date, our schools have taught us that the first Europeans settled at either Plymouth, Massachusetts, or Jamestown, Virginia. Neither is true. The first Europeans made the Punta Santa Elena their first settlement target. And Spain made Santa Elena the first true North American settlement in 1569. Put another way, *"It was where our America began."*

~ *The End* ~

*

* Spain's Philip II was the first to define what a "settlement" should be. He made that definition in his March 20, 1565, contract with Pedro Menendez de Aviles. In short, a settlement had to be a self-sufficient Continental-style town. It had to be self-sufficient, with all the basics of Spanish life . . . a plaza, church, fort, merchants, both men and women, and farms. Under that definition, France clearly failed. Both Charlesfort and Fort Caroline were manned by a dominance of men. Fort Caroline may have had one to four women out of a total of 300. Without women the French attempts to settle Charlesfort and Fort Caroline were at a big disadvantage. They lacked the families that gave the men the will to survive. Nor did France have farms. They had to rely on being resupplied by ship. France could not supply farmers. Virtually all 16th-century farmers were diehard Catholics. They had no interest in working for the Huguenots. William Blackburn, *Admiral Coligny and the Rise of the Huguenots* (Philadelphia, 1869), 84

Santa Elena's population of 327 may seem small for a town or settlement, but it wasn't in the 16th century. Havana, for example, had a population that is believed to be less than 300. See Alefandro De La Fuente, *Havana and the Atlantic in the Sixteenth Century*, p.82–87.

Epilogue

WAS IT SPAIN'S PLAN TO MAKE ST. AUGUSTINE ITS FIRST "TOWN?"[257] When Pedro Menendez entered the race to North America, his only objective was to land at the mouth of the St. Johns River and push the French out of Fort Caroline. However, when Menendez approached the mouth of the river, he quickly saw that Admiral Ribault had won the race. France's armada had blocked him from entering the St. Johns River and attacking its inland fort. Thus, as a fallback move, he sailed 32 miles south to the harbor next to St. Augustine. Then on September 8, 1565, Pedro Menendez de Aviles went ashore with his men and settlers. Among the sounds of trumpets and waving flags, he fell to his knees before a large cross and took possession of St. Augustine as a "town." In short, Spain never intended to make St. Augustine its first "town." They simply landed there by accident.

But Spain recognized two types of "towns." From a legal point of view, they considered a "town" a location that had a town council, or a "cabido." A "cabido" would usually be made up of town residents or settlers. But St. Augustine had no settlers who had been prior residents. So Menendez asked some of his military officers to be listed as members of the "town" council. That legal move gave Pedro Menendez a big advantage. He could now claim that he had met part of his contractual obligations to the king of "creating two or three towns within three years."

But what King Philip II wanted was two or three settlements, and he clearly outlined his definition of a settlement in his March, 1565 contract with Menendez. A settlement had to be a community that had the possibility of being a self-sustaining town. It had to have both men and women. It had to have a fort, church, businesses, and homes. And it had to have farms. The King went one step farther. He informed everyone that he wanted that first settlement located at the Punta Santa Elena. Nowhere else.

In early April of 1566, Pedro Menendez de Aviles was sailing north searching for the Punta Santa Elena. With the help of two local Oristo Indians, he spotted the Punta on April 9, 1566. It is now known as Hilton Head Island and the large harbor behind it . . . Port Royal Sound. By 1566, both France and Spain considered it the finest harbor in North America. After sailing into the Sound for three miles, Menendez spotted a large island in the center of the harbor. On the seaward side he could see a rising sand-hill. He would make that spot Santa Elena. By 1569, it would meet all of the king's requirements to be North America's first true settlement. By 1571, it would be the first capital of Spain's claim on North America.

WHY WASN'T ST. AUGUSTINE THE FIRST SETTLEMENT IN NORTH AMERICA?*

When Pedro Menendez de Aviles landed there in 1565, he only made it a military garrison. In fact, St. Augustine became a military garrison by accident. When Menendez saw that Ribault had beaten him to the mouth of the St. Johns River, he took his storm-battered armada south to an anchorage off of St. Augustine. The Punta Santa Elena was always

---

* E-mail letter from Dr. Paul Hoffman to Dr. Ferguson, Dr. Rowland, and Stu Rodman, May 28, 2015.

Spain's first targeted settlement site. To be the first North American settlement, it would have been settled before 1569, the date that Santa Elena became a true settlement. But it was not. On March 6, 1580, the king's Royal Accountant, Lazaro Sanchez, sent this summary of his recent trip to St. Augustine to King Philip II.

> *"There are no settlers here, only men of the garrison, whom your majesty pays. If there were (settlers), the land is ready for settlement. For although it is a Coast, there is a great abundance of mulberry trees for silk. The land also raises sugar cane very well . . . Everything that is planted grows excellently. Until this Is done, your Majesty will have much expense and little income."*
>
> Signed, Lazaro Sanchez de Mercado, Royal Accountant[258]

WHEN DID ST. AUGUSTINE BECOME A TRUE SETTLEMENT? Sometime after 1580. It may have become a settlement by 1600. The Punta Santa Elena was not just the primary settlement target for Spain. It became North America's first settlement target.

In short, Spain's Santa Elena was settled in 1569. St. Augustine was settled after 1580. Jamestown was the first English settlement in 1607. Plymouth was settled in 1620. Here is an accurate summary of the key dates:

⚑ **1521: Ponce de Leon**
Spain's first failed attempt to colonize North America.
Landed near Ft. Myers. Repulsed by Indians and mortally wounded.

⚑ **1526: Lucas Vasquez de Ayllon**
Spain's second failed attempt. Ayllon landed on the coast of South Carolina with 600 settlers. His ship captains named today's Hilton Head Island 'Cabo (or head of) Santa Elena. And they named the harbor behind it, Rio De Santa Elena, or River of Santa Elena. Soon

Europe referred to these two names as The PUNTA (or point of) SANTA ELENA.

Ayllon chose a location south of Savannah as his short-lived settlement of San Miguel de Gualdape. It lasted only four months.

1528: Panfilo de Navarez
Third failed Spanish attempt to settle, near Tampa Bay area.

1539–1543: Hernando de Soto
Fourth failed Spanish attempt to establish a settlement. After three years, he had not established a settlement.

1559–1561: Tristan de Luna and Angel Villafane
Fifth failed Spanish attempt. Tristan de Luna attempted to establish a settlement at Pensacola rather than follow the king's order to make the first settlement at Santa Elena. The Pensacola attempt failed. His successor Villafane tried to locate Santa Elena but came no closer than landing in the area.

1562: France's Jean Ribault did find the Punta and established a short-term military garrison on the western end of the harbor. Today we call that large island "Parris Island." Gaspard Coligny's goal was to see if Charlesfort could be used as a point to ambush the returning Spanish Treasure Armada. The French garrison failed after one year. France was in a civil war and could not resupply its North American outpost. Spain later landed at Parris Island in 1566 and named the site Santa Elena.

1569: Spain's Santa Elena. (located on today's Parris Island, S.C.) Spain successfully made the Punta (point of) Santa Elena the first European settlement target in North America. Menendez established a military garrison on Parris Island in 1566. Santa Elena became Europe's first North American settlement in 1569 with 327 settlers: men and women, a fort, church, homes, merchants, and many farms. The town became the first European colonial capital in North America in 1571. It was abandoned in 1587. It survived for 21 years.

⚱ **1587: England's "lost colony."** John White and 116 English colonists made a FAILED attempt to settle on Roanoke Island. After three years, a resupply ship could not find the settlement.

⚱ **1600: (estimate) St. Augustine.**
All evidence shows that it was not a true settlement before 1581. The best estimate is that it became a settlement after 1600. Until then it was a military garrison, but not a settlement that had a strong civilian population. It can claim to be the oldest continuing Spanish city in North America.

⚱ **1607: Jamestown, Virginia**
First successful English settlement in North America.

⚱ **1620: Plymouth**
Second successful English settlement in North America.

WHY WAS EUROPE SO INTERESTED IN THE PUNTA SANTA ELENA? Spain and France saw the Punta Santa Elena as having the best harbor on the southeast coast of North America. It was located on the return path of the Treasure Armada. Thus, they saw it as an essential point that they had to possess before their enemy, France. Soon after a Spanish slaver discovered the Punta area in 1526, both Spain and France defined the Punta on its maps as today's Port Royal Sound, and the large island at its entrance, Hilton Head Island. King Philip II's own orders clarified the importance of the Punta. On December 18, 1559, he penned these words:

"I therefore command, notwithstanding whatever orders you may have to the contrary from our viceroy, to make first a town at the Punta Santa Elena."[259]

Spain also saw the harbor as being its "Grand Central Station" for exploring everything North and West. France saw it as a location where

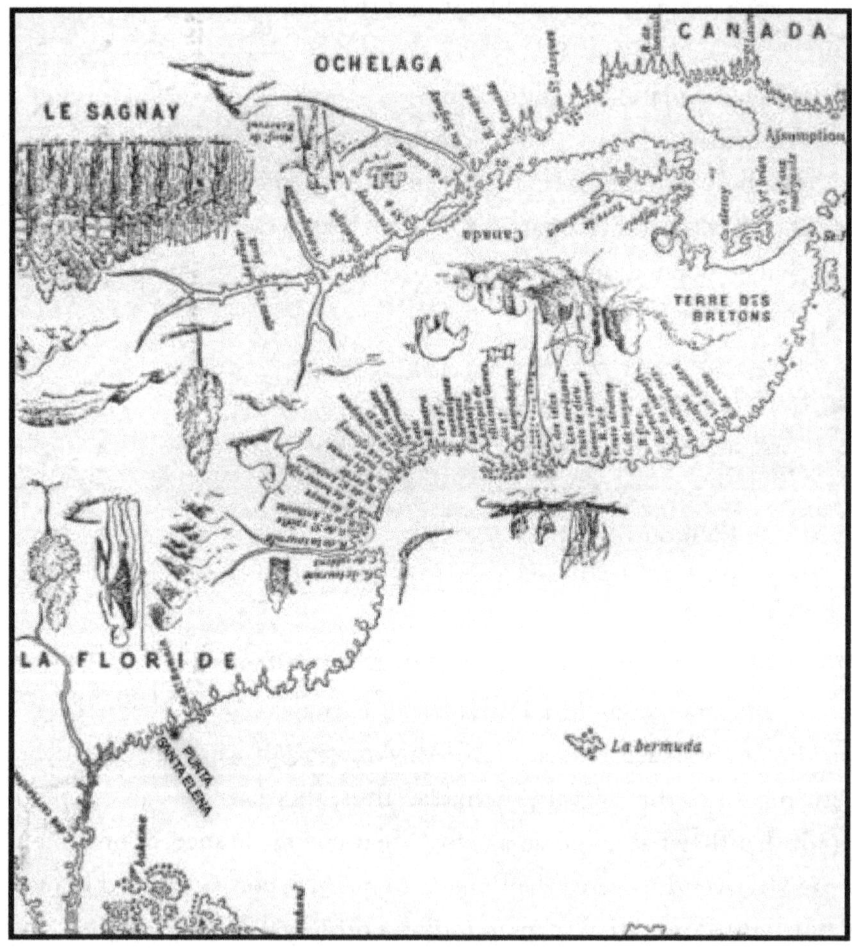

France's "Dauphine" Map of 1543

its ships could anchor before attacking Spain's returning Treasure Fleet from the nearby Indies.

In other words, it was strategically important to both countries. The best proof of that are two maps.

France underscored the importance of the Punta Santa Elena in 1543. It published the "Dauphine" map. Among all the rivers, it placed only one strategically important location on the map that was located below today's Canadian border . . . The Punta Santa Elena.

Le Moyne's map of 1564 was further proof that France saw the Punta Santa Elena as the most important strategic location in North America's southeast. In fine print on this map were the words, 'Punta Santa Elena" and "Charlesfort.

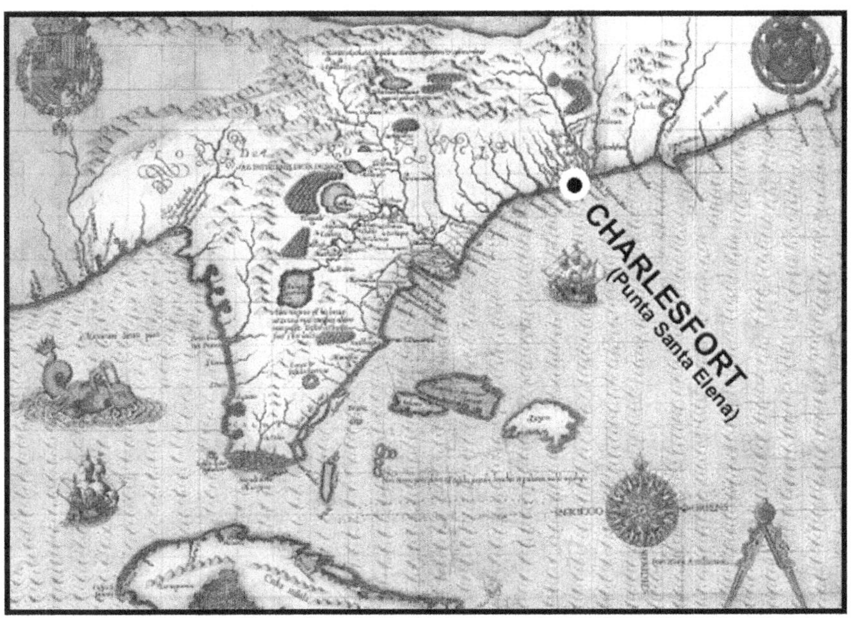

1564 map of the known Spanish colony by Jacques Le Moyne

WHAT BECAME OF SANTA ELENA?

Pedro Menendez de Aviles and 100 men built the first military block-house on Santa Elena in 1566. Later in 1566, Menendez ordered Captain Pardo to begin building an inland road to the mines in Northern Mexico. Pardo extended that road in 1567 and got as far as eastern Tennessee. By October of 1569, Santa Elena had become North America's first genuine settlement . . . 327 settlers, men and women and children, merchants, a Spanish plaza, a church, many farms, and a fort.[260]

By 1571, Menendez and his family made Santa Elena their home. It then became the capital of La Florida (Spain's term for "North America"). Santa Elena went through all the experiences that the English later experienced at both Jamestown and Plymouth . . . a shortage of food, rebellions, and constant strife with the Indians. Spain was much more respectful, however, of the native Americans in the 1560s than either Cortes or Francisco Pizzaro were in the 1520s and 1530s.

In 1587, England's pirate Francis Drake openly attacked Spain's Caribbean ports of Santo Domingo (capital of Hispaniola) and Cartagena (Colombia's Caribbean seaport). Knowing that their next targets would be St. Augustine and Santa Elena, Spain quickly decided to abandon Santa Elena and consolidate its strength at St. Augustine. It was closer to her ports in the Caribbean. Drake destroyed St. Augustine but missed finding the harbor inlet to Santa Elena. Had Pedro Menendez been in command at the time, it is highly unlikely that he would have abandoned the settlement. In fact, some believe that, if Pedro Menendez de Aviles had lived another ten years, we would all be speaking Spanish today.

WHY HASN'T THIS HISTORY SURFACED BEFORE?

The answer is simple. The "winners" write the history books. As Spain was entering the 1600s, it was trying to develop its North American colony while waging war with France and its pirates. It had too many irons in the fire and was struggling just to pay the interest on its debts. It did not have the resources to stop England from landing at Jamestown in 1607. Nor did it have the resources to defend its claim on the Plymouth area in 1620. Spain gradually had to withdraw from its southeast territory in 1763. Then it traded the little ground it possessed in eastern Florida for Cuba.

WHY WERE WE TAUGHT THAT IT WAS THE ENGLISH WHO FIRST SETTLED OUR COUNTRY?

No one has better summarized that myth than the noted historian Dr. Paul E. Hoffman. In a 2017 interview, he made this statement:

"What we have been taught for 450 years is almost completely wrong. It did not happen that way. What the English developed was a 'myth of origin.' That myth was started by the English when they first settled Plymouth in 1621. They believed that they were the first to have settled North America. Then they improved on that myth when they remembered that they had settled Jamestown, Virginia in 1607.

These two stories together became our country's 'myth of origin.' But it was not the English who first settled what is now the United States. It was SPAIN. They first settled at Santa Elena on Port Royal Sound. By 1569, they had approximately 329 settlers. It was a complete Spanish town on our shores. And it became the first European colonial capitol in North America."[261]†

WHAT MESSAGE DID FRANCE SPIN AFTER IT HEARD OF ITS LOSS IN LA FLORIDA?

France used its loss to Philip II to spread a malicious public relations campaign that came to be known as the "black legend." It was largely a series of lies that were difficult for Spain to answer. *"Spain was a cruel and warlike country. Menendez unnecessarily executed several hundred French soldiers. They*

---

† St. Augustine did become Spain's major North American city after 1630. Along with Plymouth, Jamestown, and Santa Elena, it is a "must-see" for anyone that wants to experience the early history of our country.

tortured their citizens via religious fanaticism." There was some truth in a couple of those statements. Cortes and Pizarro certainly conquered Mexico and Peru in the 1520s and 1530s with blatant cruelty. But that changed by the time of Menendez. On the European continent, France was almost always the aggressor against Spain. From 1540 to 1565, it was France that was attacking Spanish shipping and Caribbean ports . . . not the other way around.

The scholar Philip Wayne Powell crisply captured Spain's public relations dilemma when he said, *"Much of the Hispanophobia expressed by Spain's enemies took form as lies, slanders, and exaggerations growing out of wartime emotions or the passions of cultural-social-religious hatreds. There had to be more than enough truth to bait the books. And so it was; falsehood flies on falcons' wings, but Truth pursues in wooden shoes."*[262]

CAN THE PUBLIC VISIT THE SANTA ELENA SITE TODAY?

Since 1891 the Marine Corps has occupied and controlled the 7,800 acre South Carolina island called Parris Island. It has been one of two locations in the country that trains the young men and women who want to become Marines. To almost everyone's surprise, there is a complete 16th-century Spanish town buried under a few inches of soil on a remote corner of Parris Island. When you visit the site, you quickly understand why the early Spaniards called the area the Punta Santa Elena . . . or the "point" and harbor of Santa Elena.

When you reach the site, you will not believe that it is one of the most important pieces of ground in our country. Yet, it is presented in an embarrassing way. One walks along a dirt path until he or she comes to a small waist-high placard that designates a point of interest. However, there is little to see except grass, plastic bottles, and bottle caps next to your feet. The rising sea level has created a situation where the walking path is often flooded with debris from a high tide. As the graphic shows on page 199, the sea has already eroded 125 to 150 feet of the site's shoreline and partially covered two of its 16th centuries forts. You will also not see any archaeologists on the site. There are none.

It's a picture of neglect. But it is not neglect from the Parris Island Recruiting Depot. Nor is it neglect from the civilian manager who manages the site. Dr. Steven Wise is a talented Civil War historian who has managed and protected a site that is at least as important as Jamestown, Plymouth Rock, or the Gettysburg National Park. Yet, the size and adequacy of his budget is a function of the Commandant's priorities.

During the last eight years, several of the region's top historians have tried to communicate the importance of the Santa Elena site to the Marine Corps. No luck. Santa Elena is not a state historical site. It's a national historical landmark. In a way, it's a situation that is somewhat understandable. Since the 1970s, the Marine Corps has been aware that the Santa Elena site was of some historical importance. But they clearly did not receive the continuous reports that we passed to them. **"Santa Elena is not just of some importance. It was Europe's first colonial capital in North America. It was a settlement before the English landed on Plymouth Rock and Jamestown. It may be where our America began."** However, the only reply we received from the Marine Corps was, "We have one mission . . . to recruit and train young potential Marines. Anything else is a diversion."

Now the news is out. America will certainly demand that their children see the site, watch the archaeologists uncover and confirm its history, and hear how our country was settled by the Spanish, English, and French. And they will expect to hear the background story as effectively as they heard it at Jamestown, Plymouth, Mass., and St. Augustine.

Last October I began to ask myself a few questions. "Maybe I am part of the problem? Maybe I need to do a better job in communicating with the Marine Corps. I reminded myself of the steps that I took when I was president of a sizeable company. If I had a significant problem within a certain state, I would sometimes call the governor of that state and ask for help. I almost always received a returned call within a day. And the governor's office always responded with some assistance.

I placed a call to the Commandant of the Marine Corps in early October of 2021. I was quickly routed to the Brigadier General in charge of communications. I explained my concerns and made one suggestion. "Let's set up a conference call where I, and a couple of others, can share our concerns with the Commandant. Together we should be able to frame out a plan that is worth further study." It is now almost February of 2022, and I have not yet received a reply.

Our nation needs to respectfully send the Commandant one message. "Either give the Santa Elena historical site the attention that it deserves or turn it over to someone who can."

WHAT HAPPENED TO PEDRO MENENDEZ DE AVILES?

As soon as Menendez won the war of Fort Caroline, he focused on building a settlement at Santa Elena and fortifying his military garrisons at St. Augustine and Fort Mateo (the former Fort Caroline). By 1571, he moved his family into a home on Santa Elena that had the finest furnishings of the day. Santa Elena was now the capital of Spain's North American colony. Menendez, however, was constantly being pulled away from home. In October of 1567, for example, he was given the additional responsibility of being the Governor of Cuba.

In 1574, King Philip II again pulled him from his job as governor of La Florida (or North America) to help him eliminate pirates in the English Channel near Flanders. In September of 1574, he became bedridden with a severe stomach illness. He died in Spain on September 17, 1574, probably of typhus. A few days before he died, he wrote this letter to his nephew. *I hope to leave Spain by Spring . . . And with that I shall be free to go at once to our North American colony of La Florida, not to leave it for the rest of my life, for that is the sum of my longings and happiness.*[263]

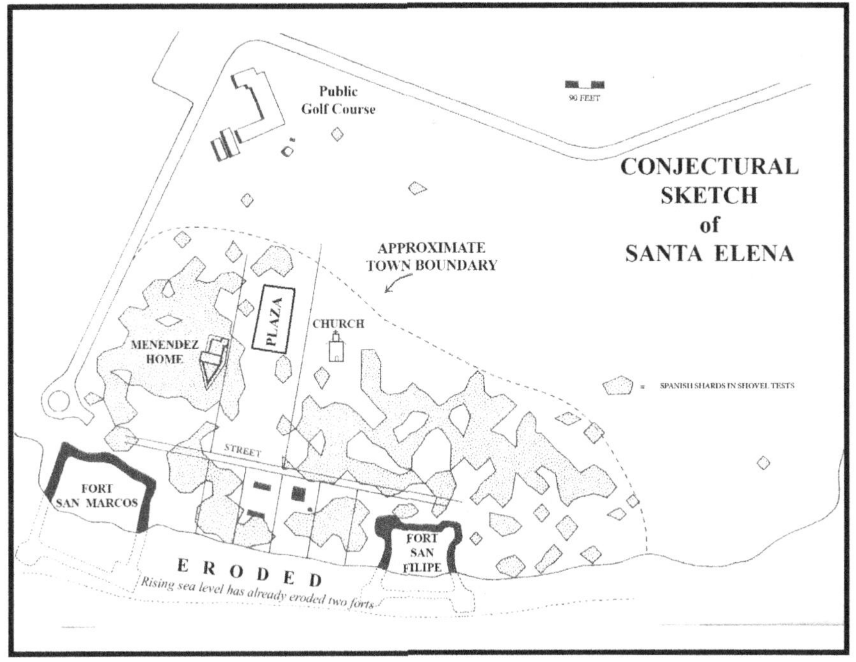

The South Carolina Institute of Archaeology and Anthropology

What Happened to Gaspard Coligny?

His strategy to start a war with Spain in an attempt to weaken the Catholic hold on France did not work. Philip II saw through it and immediately placed his anger on Gaspard Coligny and his Huguenot pirates. Catherine protected Gaspard Coligny . . . at least for a while. Instead of being weakened by Spain, Coligny actually became a stronger power within France. By 1571, he was placed on the King's Council. At the same time, Catherine de Medici found herself in a situation where her son, King Charles IX, was listening more to the Admiral of France than herself. That was a threat to her power base that she could not tolerate. On Friday, August 22, 1572, one of her assassins wounded Gaspard Coligny. With that disappointment, she communicated a second round of lies. *"Coligny and his Huguenots were planning to overthrow the king.*" That quickly triggered riots throughout France that caused the massacre of 50,000 Huguenots. The Admiral of France, Gaspard Coligny, was finally assassinated two days later, on August 24, 1572.[264]

OF THE 15 SHIPS (5 FROM SPAIN AND 10 FROM FRANCE) THAT PARTICIPATED IN THE 1565 BATTLE FOR FORT CAROLINE, HOW MANY RETURNED TO EUROPE?

Only two French ships returned . . . the *Pearle,* captained by Jean Ribault's son, Jacques, and the *Leverier,* captained by Maillard. None of Spain's five ships safely returned. (The average life of a wooden ship in 1565 was 3–4 years.) When Pedro Menendez dispatched his prize flagship, the *San Pelayo,* from St. Augustine on September 10, 1565, the ship was overtaken by English prisoners and run aground off of the coast of Denmark.

WHAT HAPPENED TO FRANCISCO GARCIA OSORIO, THE GOVERNOR OF CUBA, WHO REFUSED TO GIVE MENENDEZ THE SHIP, THE MEN, AND THE SUPPLIES WHICH PHILIP II HAD ORDERED HIM TO TURN OVER TO MENENDEZ?

Pedro Menendez de Aviles informed the Crown that the governor refused to give him the promised aid. Governor Osorio was removed from his position in November of 1567. Pedro Menendez was given the added responsibility of being named Governor of Cuba.

WAS THE 1565 FRENCH-SPANISH RACE TO CONTROL NORTH AMERICA PART OF EUROPE'S PROTESTANT REFORMATION?

Yes! It was very much a part of the 16th-century Protestant Reformation. The Protestant Reformation is recognized as that pivotal period in our world history when Europe challenged the Catholic Church and its many abuses. It is also recognized as the time when the challengers established the Reformed or Protestant Churches. Thus, the French-Spanish race to North America was more than a fight between two countries to claim North America. It was actually a part of the Protestant Reformation. Gaspard Coligny and his minority French Huguenots raced to La Florida to create a war with the all-Catholic Spain. They believed that if they created that war, France would have to take a more anti-Catholic position. And that would allow the French Protestant minority to have more religious rights. This 1565 struggle, therefore, was clearly a part of Europe's Protestant Reformation. For those who believe that America should keep *"In God We Trust"* on our coins and buildings, they now have another arrow in their quiver. "God" and "Christ" were the central themes in Europe's attempt to colonize North America.

DID SPAIN AND EUROPE LOSE MALTA TO THE MUSLIMS?

King Philip II was fortunate. The June, 1565, Muslim attack on Malta lasted until October. At the last moment, Spain's Viceroy of Sicily arrived with 8,000 men. That was enough to send the tired troops of Suleiman the Magnificent back to Constantinople. The Catholic Order of St. John was saved as well as the western Mediterranean. The Muslims lost 20,000 of their 31,000 troops.

People of Importance in This Story

☗ The Duke of Alba.
Fernando Alvarez de Toledo was considered Spain's toughest army general. As the Viceroy of the Kingdom of Naples, he successfully led the Spanish forces in the Italian peninsula against France's Duke of Guise in 1557.

☗ Pedro Menendez de Aviles
The Spanish Conquistador who loved his country, his God, and his "Men of Asturias." He broke all barriers to become the Adelantado and captain-general who pushed the French out of Spanish North America. He became the first European colonial governor in a colony that Spain claimed to include the entire 48 states. As a leader, he was possibly more Robin Hood than Robin Hood.

☗ Esteban de las Alas
Admiral of Pedro Menendez's Cadiz fleet. A longtime friend and ship captain of many of the Adelantado's voyages. Later, the vice-governor of the Spanish colony. One of Menendez's "Men of Asturias."

⚑ Admiral Alvaro Bazan

Ordered to command a coast-guard style fleet of ships to defend Spain's northern Bay of Biscay from French pirate attacks. Pedro Menendez joined his fleet in 1543 as a young sea captain.

⚑ Nicolas le Challeux

A French carpenter who escaped from Fort Caroline when it was under attack. Worked under the command of Rene Laudonniere in 1564 and 1565.

⚑ Charles IX

Young prince, son of Catherine de Medici and Henry II who assumed the Crown upon the death of his brother Francis II in December of 1560. Because he was only 10 years old at the time, his mother, Catherine de Medici, assumed control of the country as his regent. Charles IX was very close to Gaspard Coligny. That close relationship led to the assassination of Coligny.

⚑ Louis, the Prince of Conde.

One of the Bourbon princes who had a minority claim as a king of France if the Valois family could not produce a male offspring. Joined Gaspard Coligny in 1559–1560 as co-leaders of the new Huguenot movement.

⚑ Gaspard Coligny

France's Admiral of France, a high-level administerial position in which Coligny led the appointment of all French privateers (legal pirates.) The nemesis of Menendez. Coligny became the leader of France's Huguenot movement. He organized France's race against Spain and Pedro Menendez.

⚱ Louise Coligny.

Mother of Gaspard, Odet, and Andelot Coligny.

⚱ Odet Coligny

Appointed as a Catholic cardinal at age 16. Older brother of Gaspard and Andelot Coligny.

⚱ Andelot Coligny

Younger brother and best friend of Gaspard Coligny. A highly successful army officer who rose to command France's infantry.

⚱ Charles V

Spain's first king, in 1516. Grandson of an offspring from the marriage of Juana of Castile (daughter of Queen Isabelle and Ferdinand II) to Philip I, the son of the ruler of the Habsburgs, Maximillian I. Charles became the monarch of both the Habsburg Empire and the Spanish kingdom in 1519, as well as the titular Emperor of the Holy Roman Empire.

⚱ Francisco Duarte

One of the three nobles who managed Spain's CASA. He handled all business transactions. He represented the CASA in assembling the ships and supplies that Menendez needed for his 1565 cross-Atlantic attack on Fort Caroline.

⚱ Dr. Gabriel Enveja

A high-ranking Spanish spy working in France. With only rumors, he visited Jean Ribault's armada that was about to depart from Dieppe to reinforce their Fort Caroline garrison. His report put the race to North America in high gear.

- Francis I (King Francis Valois)
  King of France from 1515 to 1547. Remembered as the prime enemy of Charles V, King of Spain and the Habsburgs. Had a reputation of hating Spain, loving women, and breaking treaties.

- Francis II
  Weak offspring of Henry II and Catherine de Medici. At the death of his father, he assumed the title of King of France in name only. The Guises ran the country.

- Father Francisco Lopez de Mendoza Grajales
  The colorful chaplain of Menendez's armada that raced to Fort Caroline in 1565. He captured the key events of the "race" in a detailed report. One of Menendez's "Men of Asturias."

- Francois Guise, The Duke of Guise
  A boyhood playmate of Gaspard Coligny and King Henry II. He grew to become a very effective army commander. He would do anything that would push the Huguenots out of France and advance his own reputation. Became a lifelong enemy of the Colignys.

- Charles Guise, The Cardinal of Lorraine
  Cardinal brother of Francois. Worked with his brother, the Duke of Guise, to seize command of the government under Francois II. He joined in every scheme that would push the Huguenots out while improving the power base of his family.

- Captain La Grange
  Appointed head of the infantry when Ribault raced to Fort Caroline in 1565. He was a disciplinary problem for Ribault before he departed and once he landed at Fort Caroline.

Henry II
Considered only a cut above his father Francis I. He was driven to win control of Spain's duchy of Milan and the Kingdom of Naples. Married to Catherine de Medici. Father of Francis II and Charles IX.

Maximillian I
Grandfather of Charles V. Through a planned marriage with Isabel's and Ferdinand's daughter to his son, Philip I, Castile became part of the Habsburg empire. Then upon the death of Charles V, Spain separated from the Habsburgs and became its own country, controlling Spain, the Netherlands, Milan, Naples, and the Americas.

Catherine de Medici
Married to Henry II. Had little power until her son, Francis II, died. She then seized control of France as the regent of her 10-year-old underaged son, Charles IX. Gained a reputation of being deceitful to anyone who would challenge her current policies. Backed Coligny's planned attacks on Spanish America. Eventually killed Gaspard Coligny when he was seen as too powerful and too close to her son, Charles IX.

Pedro Menendez de Aviles
A Spanish Conquistador who rose from the lower ranks of society to become the first leader of a European colony in North America. He led much like the mythical Robin Hood. He loved his country, his God, and his "Men of Asturias." He rose to the top by often breaking the rules of a highly structured government. He became a real-life Robin Hood in the 16th century. He arguably became one of our first "founding fathers."

⚜ Bartolome Menendez

Brother and best friend of Pedro Menendez. Father Francisco Lopez de Mendoza, the Chaplain of the 1565 Spanish armada that raced to North America, said this about Bartolome: *"When Bartolome was left in charge of the St. Augustine fort while Pedro attacked Fort Caroline, so great was his diligence that I never saw him undress or lie down in the bed. In the nights when we had alarms, he was the first man who came out fully dressed and with the zeal to serve his God and King. Even when it was necessary to go up to the topsails of a ship to assist others, he was the first to get there."*

⚜ Gonzalo Solis de Meras

Menendez's brother-in-law. Wrote the most detailed diary of the 1565 expedition. Outside of being the armada's scribe, he was also made an infantry captain. One of Menendez's "Men of Asturias."

⚜ Anne (An-nay) Montmorency

Gaspard Coligny's uncle. Considered one of the wealthiest nobles in France. Made Constable for life by Francis I. Next to the king, he was the most powerful man in France for a number of years. Mentor of Gaspard and his brothers.

⚜ Francisco Garcia Osorio, the Governor of Cuba

He refused to provide the men, supplies, and a ship that King Philip II had ordered him to provide Pedro Menendez. He was removed from office in November 1567, and replaced by Pedro Menendez de Aviles, who was also Governor of the North American colony.

⚜ Pope Paul IV

The anti-Spanish elderly Pope who promoted a war with France against Philip II of Spain in 1556.

- Emanuel Philibert, The Duke of Savoy, Regent of the Netherlands
  He lost his Italian duchy until he conquered the French northern border town of St. Quinten in 1557 for Spain.

- Philip II
  Son of Charles V. King of Spain at the death of his father. Monarch of the most powerful empire in Europe by the mid-16th century. Saw himself as Europe's protector of Catholicism. Constant enemy of France. Backed Pedro Menendez's plan to push France out of North America. A king who was tied up in paperwork and micromanaging others. He had little understanding of financial planning.

- Guillaume Rufin
  The lone French teenage soldier who decided to stay in the Charlesfort area rather than try to return to France in a homemade boat in 1563. He was captured by Spain in 1564 and became a valuable interpreter for Pedro Menendez. When captured, he informed Spain of France's real intentions at Charlesfort.

- Pedro de las Roelas
  The captain-general of the New Spain (Mexico) Treasure Armada in 1565. Ordered by King Philip II to turn over his flagship and 200 men to Menendez before he attacked Fort Caroline.

- Jean Ribault
  Considered France's greatest admiral in the 1560s. Led a small squadron of ships to enter the PUNTA in 1562 and establish a military garrison on today's Parris Island. He called the garrison "Charlesfort." But it only lasted one year. Later, in 1565, Gaspard Coligny ordered Ribault to race Spain, and Pedro Menendez de Aviles, to North America to resupply and defend France's second

planned military garrison . . . Fort Caroline. This race would ultimately decide whether it was Spain or France who would first claim control of North America.

⚱ Jacques Ribault

Son of Jean Ribault. Captained the Pearle. Escaped to France after the attack on Fort Caroline.

⚱ Diego Flores Valdes

Worked 15 years as either a captain or admiral under Pedro Menendez. Made admiral of the armada during the 1565 race with France. He was one of Menendez's "Men of Asturias."

⚱ Elizabeth de Valois

Second child of France's Henry II and Catherine de Medici. As part of the 1559 peace of Cateau-Cambresis, the defeated French were forced to offer Elizabeth as the new wife to King Philip II of Spain. She then became known as Isabel in Spain. Ironically, as Philip II was waging war against Spain and Catherine de Medici, her daughter was the queen of Spain.

⚱ Captain Juan de Vicente

One of the few Men of Asturias who did not come from northern Spain. He was hired because he had infantry experience in Italy. He proved to be disloyal and a constant headache for Menendez.

⚱ Spain's ambassadors to France:
1559-January, 1564: Thomas Perrenot de Chalntonnay
January 1564–1586: Don Frances de Alava

Major Sources

⚜ Gonzalo Solis de Meras, The Conquest of Florida
Seen as one of the most important documents. Gonzalo Solis de Meras was Menendez's brother-in-law. He was given the title of an infantry captain during the 1565 expedition. He wrote a day-by-day detailed record of the race and the following battle. The original document found itself in the Archives of the Indies. The current Adelantado, the Conde De Revillagigedo, Alvaro Armada Barcaixtequi, has a copy of the Solis de Meras document.

⚜ In 2017, David Arbesu wrote a translated reprint that included the lost pages that were not in the Adelantado's copy of the Solis de Meras "Memorial." This should be considered the most complete document of Solis de Meras' The Conquest of Florida.

⚜ Father Francisco Lopez de Mendoza Grajales wrote the earliest journal of the 1565 expedition. He was the chaplain of the Spanish armada. Considered the second-most important account of the Menendez 1565 race.

⚜ Rene Laudonniere, "Three Voyages." This is a translation by Charles E. Bennett of the book that Rene Laudonniere wrote after he escaped from Pedro Menendez's attack on the French fort, Fort Caroline. Laudonniere was second-in-command under Ribault when he tried to settle Charlesfort at the Punta Santa Elena in 1562. Then while Ribault was imprisoned in England, the Admiral of France, Gaspard Coligny, asked Laudonniere to command the next planned settlement on Spanish American soil . . . Fort Caroline. He escaped to France after Menendez chased him out of La Florida in 1565.

🔱 Nicholas Le Challeux was a French carpenter. He escaped to France after Fort Caroline was captured by Pedro Menendez de Aviles. Once he landed on French soil, he wrote a book in 1566 that described the French-Spanish battle between Pedro Menendez and Jean Ribault. His book was titled *Discours de L'historie de la Floride*.

🔱 Henry Lancelot Voisin wrote a book called *Les Trois Mondes* in 1582, which described the French expedition of 1565. A summary of it is in Charles E. Bennett's *Laudonniere and Fort Caroline*.

🔱 Jacque Le Moyne and Theodore De Bry made it possible for us to see what this new American colony looked like in 1565. Le Moyne was in the French group that attempted to settle Fort Caroline in 1564. His sketches of the wildlife and Indians on the Florida peninsula gave Europe its first look at our America. The engraver Theodore de Bry purchased these original engravings and made them available to the world. Historian John de Bry is a direct descendant of this engraver. Source: John White and Jacques Le Moyne, *The New World*. Edited by Stefan Lorant.

🔱 Pedro Menendez de Aviles
The Edward W. Lawson Collection includes 101 translated letters written by Menendez or to him. It also includes documents relative to

his career. These files are held by the University of Florida's Smathers Libraries in their Special and Area Studies Collection.

⚓ *New American World*, ed. by David V. Quinn, Volume II, includes translated copies of most documents related to the 1565 race between Spain and France. Volume II includes a translated copy of Admiral Jean Ribault's *The True Discoverie of Terra Florida*. The documents in *New American World* cover the period from 1526 to June 1574.

Appendices

Appendix I

Frequently Used Terms

Adelantado: A Spanish colonial official who was directly appointed by the king to develop a frontier area or colony. In most cases, the Adelantado was required to finance the entire expedition by himself. In return, the Adelantado, or Conquistador, would receive grants of authority, titles, certain revenues, and exemptions from taxes. Pedro Menendez de Aviles was made an Adelantado in March of 1565. That title made him a true Spanish noble and, arguably, one of America's founding fathers.

Admiral of France: A high ministerial or administrative position under the king in the 16th century. The Admiral of France had three major responsibilities: During war, he gathered the needed merchant ships and converted them into warships. He licensed ship merchants and fishermen to become privateers who would attack Spanish shipping. And he protected the northern ports and coastline of France. The Admiral of France had no direct authority over field admirals. However, he held a powerful political position. Gaspard Coligny was appointed Admiral of France in 1552 and became the one who organized pirate attacks on ships commanded by Spain's Pedro Menendez de Aviles.

Alcabala: A Castilian excise tax that was paid to the Crown and levied in every city upon goods as they passed to a ship. This tax literally killed most major Spanish industries that sold goods throughout Europe.

Almirante: In the Spanish fleet system, the second-in-command of an organized fleet was called the "Almirante" or Admiral. He sailed in a ship designated as the almirante. When at sea, the almirante guarded the rear of the formation. Pedro Menendez's second-in-command, his almirante, was his longtime friend and ship captain, Diego Flores Valdes. During the "race," his ship, the *San Andres*, was referred to as the Almiranta, while Menendez's ship was referred to as the Capitana.

Arquebus: Spain's infantry weapon of choice when Menendez attacked the French in 1565. The arquebus was the forerunner of the modern rifle. The soldier who carried and fired the arquebus was referred to as the arquebusier. The arquebus weighed around 18 pounds and required the strongest soldiers to carry them. To fire the weapon, the soldier had to pull a trigger which moved a lit fuse toward a flash pan of powder that was located on the gun. Then there would be a substantial recoil. In Europe, the arquebus quickly replaced the windlass-drawn steel crossbow. It was both more rugged and simpler than the crossbow. Menendez, however, had great trouble with it when he led his men on the surprise attack of Ft. Caroline. The continuing rains extinguished the fuses on the guns.

Armada: An organized fleet, squadron, or flotilla of ships.

Armada Real: The royal-guard fleet placed under the command of Pedro Menendez de Aviles. Its mission was to provide escort for the Treasure Fleets at critical times.

Asiento: Any agreement or contract.

Averia: An export tax on all ships leaving Spain for the Indies. Its purpose was to fund the Spanish armada that would protect the ships going to the Indies and return with silver and gold bullion.

Barco: Usually used for small craft in harbor, or to transfer passengers or cargo.

Battle Yell: "Santiago! God help us! Victory!" This was Spain's most enduring battle yell during the heat of 16th-century battles. The yell came from a story reported within Spain during the 9th century. Spain was fighting the invasion of Muslims from northern Africa. The yell apparently began when Asturias' King Ramiro I reported that he had been visited by the Apostle St. James prior to a battle that he would face with the Muslims. The apostle is reported to have said to the King, "I will come to your aid and on the morrow by the hand of God you will overcome the countless multitude of Saracens . . . you will see me on a white horse . . . bearing a great white banner." As the legend goes, the Apostle James appeared on horseback, and the Spanish troops shouted, "May God and St. James help us!" After this reported story, Spanish troops would often enter battle with a yell that requested help from God, the Virgin Mary, or diverse Catholic Saints like St. James.

Bergantine: A small, two-masted sailing craft provided with lateen sails.

Cabildo. Spain's name for a New World town council. Menendez's 1565 contract required him to establish two or three towns. To confirm that an area was a legal "town," a conquistador had to record that the area had a town council, or cabildo. Therefore, when Menendez retreated to St Augustine on September 6, 1565, he landed and recorded the town as a cabildo. Of course, that was only a paperwork entry. The names that were recorded as members of the "town council" were only the senior military officers. There were no civilian town "leaders" to list. Menendez did the same when he landed on today's Parris Island in 1566. He recorded Santa Elena as a legal town or cabildo. Thus, between 1565 and 1569, Pedro Menendez had fulfilled his contract obligation as having established two towns or cabildos. During that period, the true government was wherever Pedro Menendez de Aviles and his lieutenant, Alas, were sleeping. And they were constantly moving around during this period. The first real town was established only when there was a settlement that had a mix of men and women, merchants, and farmers. Santa Elena met those requirements in 1569, when it recorded 327 settlers.

Capitana: The flagship of the fleet general, upon which all convoys formed and whose signals and commands were to be obeyed by all vessels in the fleet. The galleon *San Pelayo* was the capitana of Pedro Menendez de Aviles.

Caravel: A mid-sized ship, sometimes with both sails and oars. Menendez departed the Canary Islands with two caravels, the *Sant Antonio* and the *Concepcion II*.

CASA: The Casa de Contratacion, or House of Trade. The CASA soon became the government regulatory agency that controlled almost every phase of life in the New World. It was founded in 1503, but was later put under the authority of the policy-making Council of the Indies. The CASA trained ship navigators, secured and updated all charts, authorized the departure of Treasure Armadas, collected the ships for the armadas, and inspected all shipments from smuggling. It was so powerful that it had its own police force and judicial system. Pedro Menendez got caught in the CASA's fury when Philip II directly appointed him as a captain-general in 1554. That action removed the CASA from their longtime right of appointing the powerful captain-generals, or fleet admirals, of the Treasure Armadas. The CASA showed their anger toward Menendez instead of the king, who had ordered the change.

Castellano: Spain's standard gold coin in the early 1500s.

Cedula: A written royal order, having the force of law.

Chalupa: A small, decked craft, usually furnished with two masts and rowed with six to eight oars per side; usually less than 100 tons. Menendez departed the Canary Islands for the Indies in 1565 with four chalupas . . . the *Magdalena*, *San Miguel*, *Sant Andres*, and the *Concepcion*.

Chatillon-Sur-Loing: This was the sleepy little town one hundred miles southeast of Paris. It was the home of Gaspard Coligny and his family. During his active career, Gaspard was head of the household. His older brother, Odet, was made a cardinal at age 16. His younger brother, Andelot, became Gaspard's best friend. Gaspard's mother, Louise de Montmorency Coligny, focused on educating her three sons. She was also the sister of the highest noble in the land, Anne (pronounced An-nay) Montmorency.

The Chatillons: This was a term describing the politically powerful Coligny family headed by Gaspard.

Conquistador: The Spanish Crown-appointed official vested with the rights to conquer and govern a new territory. Pedro Menendez de Aviles was considered an Adelantado, Conquistador, captain-general of the Armada, and Governor of Europe's first North American colony, La Florida.

Constable: The Constable commanded the military, which in the 16th century was largely the army. He was responsible for financing the army, managing it, and administering military justice. Reporting to him were the captain-generals of the *Infantry* and *Cavalry*. By being in command of France's Army, the Constable was seen as being in the most powerful position under the king. Some saw the position as equivalent to a Prime Minister in authority and power.

Cochinal: A dye that came from an insect. It was Mexico's (New Spain's) second most important export after silver in the 16th century.

Consulta: The formal opinion of a royal council upon a particular matter, delivered to the King for his information.

Corsair: A commerce raider or other intruder in the Spanish Indies, not licensed by the Spanish Crown. During the first half of the 16th century, Spain referred to Corsairs as "French pirates" or "privateers."

Ducat: The unit of greatest value coined in both gold and silver. To understand its value, a ship captain would often be paid 100 ducats a year. A seaman would be paid 1–3 ducats a month. Ten pounds of sugar would cost 1 ducat, and a pair of boots would cost 1 ducat.

Factor: One of three principal officers that governed the CASA or House of Trade. The factor was responsible for provisioning all ships; leasing needed ships; arming them from the government's armory; and paying for everything necessary to get an armada underway and keeping it operational in the Indies. No ship could get underway without the factor's approval that it met all ship regulations. The factor was the businessman of the CASA.

Fathom: When referring to the depth of water, one fathom equals six feet.

Fragata: A sailing vessel with one or two masts and also provided with six to twelve oars for propulsion. Used by Spain to enter shallow rivers and harbors. Used by Spain in 1564, to see if France was still in control of Charlesfort.

Galeota : A medium-sized galley. Equipped with oars and sails. Menendez departed from the Canaries with one galeota in his armada, the *Vitoria*, an 80-ton ship.

Galleon: A large oceangoing ship, with two or more masts, square-rigged sails, plus a lateen sail on the mizzen mast. Galleons were rated up to 900 tons in the mid-16th century. Menendez's *San Pelayo* was rated at 906 tons.

Grand Master: One of the highest positions in the French government, largely because the position placed the Grand Master very close to the king. The Grand Master was responsible for managing the French Court and the king's household. That included the king's palace, kitchen, guards, and lands. Combined with the responsibility of managing who is and is not invited to become a member of the court, this was one of the most powerful political positions in the nation. While Anne de Montmorency was Constable of France from 1538 to 1558, he was also the Grand Master. He was the most powerful noble in France during that period.

Hidalgo: A higher class peasant. A hidalgo was seen as having some honor because a previous family member had courageously served his country. Hidalgos rarely became "real" nobles. They did not have the leadership that was believed to only came from true nobility. Menendez was an exception. He was born a hidalgo, but broke the glass ceiling when he was promoted to the rank of captain-general and Adelantado.

Huguenots: This was the term that most French Catholics used after 1561 to describe members of the Reform Church. Before 1561, French Protestants were usually labeled "Lutherans."

Maestre: An official aboard a Spanish ship whose duty it was to assume charge over all cargo and passengers aboard ship.

Maestre de Campo: The military officer in charge of a 16th-century Spanish *tercio*. Pedro Menendez appointed his 25-year-old future son-in-law,

Pedro Menendez de Valdes, as his Maestre de Campo. Valdes, in turn, appointed Gonzalo de Villaroel as his second-in-command.

Matrimonial Imperialism: A term that describes the strategy that a 16th-century European monarch would use to strengthen their country by pledging the marriage of a son (prince) or daughter (princess) to the son or daughter of the monarch of another country. That future marriage would then, hopefully, make the two countries either one consolidated country, or at least strong allies. This was a term that was made popular by the historian Jeffrey Parker.

Memorial: A brief report or memorandum.

New Spain: This was both a reference to Mexico and the armada that went to Mexico to deliver goods and collect bullion. The New Spain armada usually departed in late spring to early summer of each year.

Patache: A small ship of about 65–85 tons used as a reconnaissance or courier vessel by Spanish fleets. It usually had two masts and, at times, a main lateen sail. It may have had oars. Typically manned by 50 mariners.

Pendant: A sort of long narrow banner, displayed from the masthead of a ship of war, and usually terminating in two ends or points.

Pilot: The ship's pilot was the ship's navigator. Considered very valuable, it was often a very unpopular position. Without knowledge of longitude, pilots were often off their projections by hundreds of miles.

Pinnace: A small vessel navigated with oars and sails and, generally, having two masts, which are rigged like those of a schooner.

Pipe of Wine: A "pipe of wine" was a standard measurement of a cask of liquid in 1565. It was considered to be equal to 4 barrels, 2 hogsheads, or half a ton. It was considered to contain 136 gallons of wine.

Pirate: Those who plundered vessels on the high seas and raided ports and harbors. Pirates operated without a license or sanction from a particular nation. They were lawless and stateless predators.

Privateers: They carried out acts of piracy with special charters or licenses from their respective monarchs. France treated them as "their Navy." Gaspard Coligny, who was the Admiral of France, was the one who charted all French privateers after 1552. Pedro Menendez made his reputation by being unusually successful in capturing French privateers. They generally did not operate in times of peace. However, the French privateers seldom made that distinction. The privateers were often regular fishermen and operators of merchant ships when not raiding Spanish ships and ports. During the 1560s a large percentage of the privateers were French Huguenots.

Poder: A power of attorney

Punta Santa Elena and Santa Elena: Before Menendez's 1565 victory over the French, the Punta Santa Elena described the oceanfront island (Hilton Head Island) and the adjoining harbor behind it (today's Port Royal Sound). The promontory point of Hilton Head Island was easily spotted by ships as they exited the Bahama Channel and traveled north along the southeast coast. The Punta was strategically very important. It was located on the vulnerable return route of the Treasure Armada. It was an ideal spot for any Spanish enemy to locate there so it could ambush the returning Treasure Armada. After Menendez's 1565 victory, Spain located its first colonial settlement, Santa Elena, on the western end of the harbor. Today we call that island Parris Island. It was first occupied by the French (Charlesfort) in 1562, and later occupied by the Spanish in 1566. Spain's Santa Elena became the first North American settlement in 1569 and the first European colonial capital in 1571.

Roberge: A mid-sized French ship. These vessels were long and narrow. Each had three masts and were rigged with both square and lateen sails. Each also had a single bank of oars for fast acceleration near the shore.

Sargento Mayor: The executive officer, or second-in-command, of a Spanish infantry *tercio*. This position was usually held by a hidalgo, a man of honor. Menendez's second-in-command of the infantry was Gonzalo de Villaroel. He reported to the Adelantado's future son-in-law, Pedro Menendez de Valdes, who was the armada's Maestre de Campo, or head of the infantry.

Scrivener: The secretary or recorder on a ship. He would write wills, document supplies, record notes from a meeting, and verify what writing was on a box or barrel.

Scuppers: Certain channels cut through the waterways and sides of a ship, at proper distances. Lined with plated lead in order to carry the water off of the deck into the sea.

Ship's biscuit: The standard food element on a ship. It consisted of unleavened bread that was twice-baked. That preserved it from deterioration for a long time. To eat the biscuit, one had to soak it in either wine or water for several minutes. Soaking in wine was a mariner's first choice.

Sounding line: When a ship entered shallow water, a "leadsman" was often ordered to throw out a sounding line. This was a small line of rope with a lead weight at the end. Pieces of leather were tied onto the line at every second or third fathom. When the leadsman pulled the line upward, he would see where the water had hit specific leather pieces. That would tell him the depth of the water.

Tender: A small vessel. Also commonly referred to as a "patache." Usually used to pick up passengers destined for a nearby ship or used to carry information and intelligence from shore to ship or shore to shore.

Tercio: The essential 16th-century military formation that Spain used to defeat the French in the Italian wars. Menendez formed a *tercio* when he attacked the French fort of Fort Caroline in 1465. The formation required pikemen to be organized in the middle of the formation, with arquebusiers flanked on each side of the pikemen. As infantry or cavalry charged the middle, they were slowed down or stopped by the pikemen. Then the arquebusiers fired into the charging enemy.

Tierra de Firme: During the 16th century, it was the Spanish fleet that usually departed in July or August of each year to deliver goods and collect bullion from the South American mines in Peru and Colombia. Organizationally, it also referred to the Spanish lands in South America that were below Panama.

Watch: The space of time wherein one division of a ship's crew remains on deck to perform the necessary services, while the rest are relieved from duty. Usually the Watch periods change every four hours.

Zabra: A small ship of 40–70 tons about 47 feet long. In addition to having two masts, it also had oars that could give it a fast acceleration when it pursued an enemy.

Appendix II

The Importance of the Treasure Armada

Soon after Spain's Cortes discovered that there was vast silver and gold in Mexico, France deployed its privateers to get part of Spain's treasure. These French privateers were in reality France's navy. They became successful by waiting offshore of those Caribbean ports from which treasure ships would depart. Spain responded. By 1522, Spain selectively escorted certain treasure ships in their return to Seville. The French attacks increased as Spain discovered vast silver deposits in Peru and Colombia in the 1530s and mined more silver and gold. The French attacks triggered Spain to strengthen its treasure fleet.

Neither Charles V nor his son Philip II were strong in financial management. By the time Philip became King of Spain in 1556, Spain owed its bankers more than 25 million pesos. That debt came from two actions. They fought France with Europe's only full-time infantry from 1500 to 1559. They also handicapped their industries with a destructive distribution tax . . . the alcabala. That tax virtually eliminated most of their major industries. They were no longer competitive with other European countries. Thus, when Spain went to war with France, Spain had to purchase much of its artillery from Italy; its sailing running gear from Russia and Germany; and its marine hardware from its enemy, France. Because of this, Spain had a negative trade balance. That, in turn, required them to dedicate two-thirds of their entire budget to paying their debts.

Thus, the return of each treasure armada became increasingly important. As the amount of bullion increased year to year, Spain was using most of its bullion just to pay demanding bankers. It was the one fund to which Spain had quick access. Spain was able to bank from 20% to 33% of all mined bullion. That, however, made up no more than 20% of their annual income. This gave Spain quick access to cash that was under their complete control. What this meant was that Spain's financial system became closely intertwined with the size and timing of the treasure fleets' arrivals from the Indies.[265]

DESIGNING THE TREASURE FLEET

Spain, therefore, had to design and improve its Treasure Armada based on the trade winds and ocean currents; the hurricane season; the unbearable temperatures in Panama in the summer; and the changing tactics of the French privateers.

By 1565, Spain's Council of the Indies had instituted a Treasure Fleet route that included two departures each year. The New Spain (Mexico) armada would leave Seville or Cadiz in May or June for a ten-day sail to the Canary Islands. That would be their cross-Atlantic starting point. At the Canaries, they would catch the trade winds that constantly blew from the Sahara Desert to the Indies.

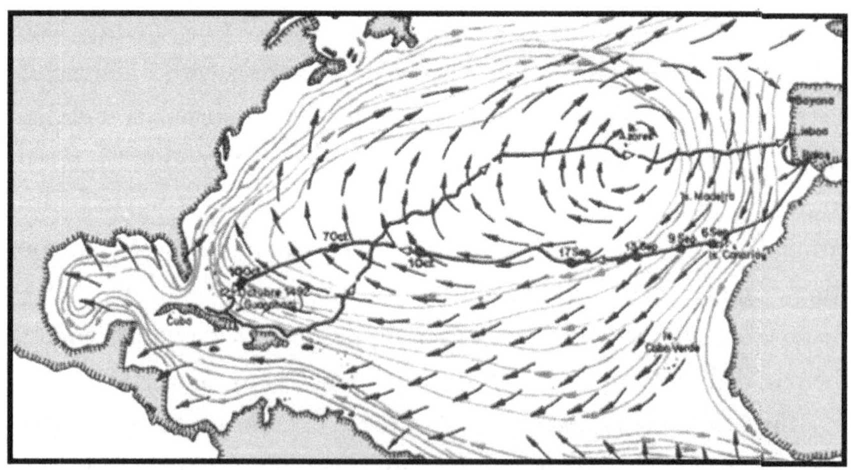

A Treasure Route That Followed the Trade Winds

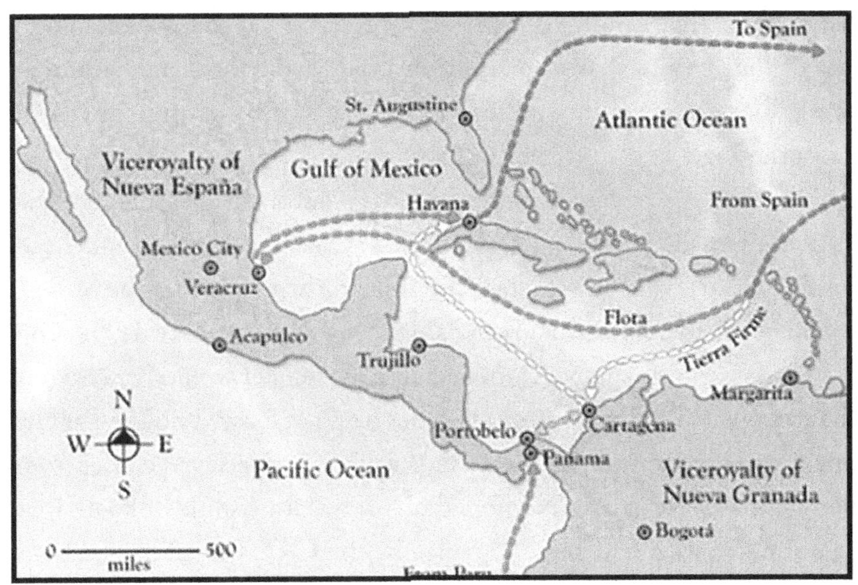

Route of the Treasure Armada

After reaching the Canary Islands, a ship captain would refuel with wood for the cooking stove and water for the crew. Then he would head due West for four to six weeks. That would almost always let him arrive at the Antilles Island of Dominica in the Indies. Dominica was a perfect place to stop for two or three days for wood, water, and rest. From there, the New Spain (or Mexican) ships would pass Puerto Rico, Hispaniola, and Cuba until they reached the Gulf Coast town of Veracruz, New Spain (Mexico). They would usually arrive in either late August or early September. Within days, the Viceroy would send wagonloads of silver from Mexico City to Veracruz to meet the arriving treasure armada.

By 1565, the Tierra Firme (South American) armada was scheduled to retrieve the bullion from Peru, Colombia, and Panama. It was the most important armada. Twenty to forty merchant ships would typically be escorted by the six to eight heavily gunned galleons. It was those armed escort ships that would carry the silver and gold bullion. Spain scheduled this armada to leave the Canaries in late August or early

September. That would allow them to reach Cartagena (Colombia) in late October. With that schedule, they would avoid the deadly heat that would hit Panama in the summer. However, they always ran the risk of encountering a late-summer hurricane.

The travel path would be similar to the New Spain Treasure Armada until they reached the island of Dominica. Once there, they would head south for Cartagena (Colombia) and unload the goods that the settlers would need. Then they would send a smaller ship to Nombre de Dios, on the Gulf coast of Panama. Immediately a messenger would be sent over the narrow neck of the country to Panama City, located on the Pacific. Spain would then transfer the silver that they had received earlier from Peru and send it back to Nombre de Dios by either mule or boat. That would take just a few days.[266] Typically, the CASA would order both armadas to winter over in either Cartagena (Colombia) or Veracruz (Mexico). In January or February, they would depart for Havana. That harbor was the best equipped to make any repairs before they departed for Seville. By early spring, each armada would head north to grab the Bahama Channel and the Gulf Stream. It was this stretch of the southeast coast where the Spanish Treasure Armada was in the most danger. The Bahama Channel was relatively narrow, with unknown shoals. All the ships had to pass by the harbor of Santa Elena. Once they passed Santa Elena, it would not be long before they would capture the westerly trade winds that would send them to the Azores. Then they would be just a couple of weeks away from landing near Seville.[267]

Appendix III

Menendez's At-Sea Instructions

When Pedro Menendez de Aviles began his cross-Atlantic race with France, he gave his ship captains specific instructions to follow. He first used these rules when he was ordered to be the captain-general of the 1562 Treasure Armada.

Date: January 1562

To: Captains, Masters, and Pilots (Navigators)

In the name of God: Amen. I, Pedro Menendez de Aviles, Captain-General for His Majesty in the Trade with the Indies and of the Fleet and Armada that at present I take in my charge; say to you, the captain, Master and Pilot of the nao you have in your charge; what you shall keep to in the present voyage is the following:

When the Capitana wishes to make sail, she will fly a flag on the quarter of the poop and will fire one piece (cannon). Then you shall be ready and prepared to make sail when she does.

You shall follow the Capitana, without passing before or remaining behind her, and you shall navigate in this manner for all of the voyage.

You shall pass close to the Capitana twice each day, once in the morning, the other time in the afternoon, and then you shall take the password and, in giving it to you, you will salute with the whistle as is customary. If the day is calm, or the wind rough so that you cannot take the word, you shall have the following names for each night:

Sunday:	*The Holy Trinity*
Monday:	*Saint John*
Tuesday:	*Saint James*
Wednesday:	*Saint Peter*
Thursday:	*Saint Lawrence*
Friday:	*Saint Christopher*
Saturday:	*Our Lady of Victory*

You shall keep these names, written on a piece of parchment or paper in this order, in the binnacle, so that if anyone asks for the word at night, he who is steering will know how to give it.

At the time you pass close to the Capitana to take the word and have taken it, you shall sheer off and give room to the naos that are following, so that one does not collide with the other.

Whenever you shall have need for help, if it is day, you shall fly a flag on the main topmast and fire two shots. If the necessity should be very great, you will fire four, one after another, and fly another flag on the foretopmast, so that it will be understood that the necessity is great. If it should be at night, you shall hoist a lantern on the main topmast and fire two pieces. If the necessity is very great, you shall hoist another lantern on the foretopmast and fire four shots.

When the Capitana is navigating, and it is suitable to change the course she was following at nightfall, she will show two lanterns, and on each side of the signal lantern on the poop, and fire a shot. Then each one will put another lighted lantern on its poop and fire a shot, so it will be better seen and understood between them, although it may be cloudy, and each one will keep its lantern lighted until the Capitana removes hers and only the signal lantern remains.

When the Capitana wishes to take in sail at night, being in a beam sea, she will have her signal lantern lighted and a lantern on her main topmast. Then each nao shall hoist a lantern on its main topmast. When the Capitana wishes to put sail on again, she will take down her lantern and fire one piece (cannon shot). Then all the naos shall do the same.

When the Capitana fires a shot and flies a flag on the poop mizzenmast, she wishes to hold a consultation with the pilots of the armada. Then they shall all come on board.

The nao who discovers enemies that are not in the convoy shall put a flag on the mainmast and wave it, fire one piece and bear to the leeward upon the Capitana to give her advice. If there are more than four enemy ships, she will fire four pieces.

You shall have the greatest care and vigilance to guard the fire, not consenting that there be any in the galley unless there is a very cautious man there. At night it must be killed, and you shall not consent to there being fire in any part of the nao, except it be in the binnacle and another lighted lantern close to the helmsman which must not be taken from there and carried to any other part without permission from the Captain, Master or Pilot; and because of the losses that usually happen, very great account must be taken of this.

You shall give very good treatment to the passengers who may go in your nao; and you must give the mariners in it their complete ration, as is customary, so they do not get sick; and you shall cure them according to reason.

You shall not consent in any manner that there be outcries, blasphemy, arguments or oaths. If there should be, they being people in your charge, you will arrest them and give me advice of it, so that they may be castigated in conformity to justice. If they be passengers, give them their lodging as a jail and advise me of it.

If by any chance, while navigating, any nao should get separated from the Capitana; if it should be before arriving at the Canary Islands, it will not go on until the fleet arrives there and it has joined with it. If it should be beyond the Canary Islands, it shall not pass beyond Dominica, because I will lay my course for there. If it should be beyond Dominica, and it is one of the naos going to New Spain, it shall not pass beyond Santo Domingo (capital of Hispaniola). If it should be a nao for Tierra-Firme, it shall not pass beyond

Santa Marta, and if such a nao should be at Nombre de Dios (trading port on the eastern shore of the Panama isthmus) and by unexpected chance it cannot make Santa Marta (a secondary Gulf of Mexico port in Colombia), it shall go to Cartagena (Gulf of Mexico port in Colombia) and not leave there until the fleet arrives. This I command that you keep and comply with this under the penalty of permanent loss of your office in the Trade of the Indies, and of all possessions, and of your said naos and freight; all to be applied to his Majesty's Chamber. And the mariners and all other people of the sea in the said nao to be exiled to the galleys for six years.

All of which, and all the rest contained in this Instruction, you shall keep and comply with under the said penalties, and more, for whatever thing contained in these paragraphs you shall not comply with. And for every time you shall break one of them, you will be condemned to pay a fine of fifty thousand maravedis for his Majesty's Chamber, and thus you shall keep and comply with him, and in everything, contained in this said Instruction.

You shall carry the artillery, arquebuses and other munitions ready for instant use, and in places where they may be made use of every time it is necessary.

Signed, Pedro Menendez de Aviles[268]

<h1 style="text-align:center">APPENDIX IV</h1>

THE MEN OF ASTURIAS

In 2017 the author visited the home of one of the highest regarded 16th-century historians . . . Dr. Eugene Lyon. The author had one of those questions that should never be asked of an historian. But it was always in the back of his mind, and he had to have an answer. His question had nothing to do with the historical accuracy of the Pedro Menendez de Aviles story. When the author arrived at Dr. Lyon's home, he finally asked his deep-seated question. *"When we look at the life of Pedro Menendez, is it possible that we are looking at a man who comes very close to being very similar to that of the mythical Robin Hood?"* Dr. Lyon showed a small smile. Then he said, "Make your case, Daryl." Then the author made this case.

"The Robin Hood classic reminds me of our day-to-day frustrations with power, politics and bureaucracy. Robin represented the ideal noble and the best of mankind. He saw the injustice in how Prince John and the Sheriff of Nottingham treated the common man. To even the playing field, he stepped out of his normal role as an affluent noble.

"Then he used every skill he had to help the peasants. Moreover, he had a little lighthearted fun mixed in with a little swagger. One of his strengths quickly appeared. He guided his "Men of Sherwood Forest" with a small core of closely held confidants . . . Little John, Will Scarlet, Friar Tuck, and 'Much,' the miller's son. With a few differences this story is almost a carbon copy of the Robin Hood epic. There is only one significant difference. The Pedro Menendez de Aviles story is not fiction." Dr. Lyon leaned back in his chair. You could almost hear him challenging every comment

in his mind. Then after a minute, or so, he leaned forward and said, "YOU ARE ABSOLUTELY CORRECT. PEDRO MENENDEZ WAS ALMOST MORE ROBIN HOOD THAN ROBIN HOOD."

MENENDEZ'S MEN OF ASTURIAS

Who can forget Robin Hood's Friar Tuck, Little John, Will Scarlet, and "Much," the miller's son? Pedro Menendez de Aviles had the same core of close confidants and lieutenants. They followed him wherever he sailed from 1550 to the great 1565 race to North America.

HIS CORE "MEN OF ASTURIAS" INCLUDED:

⚑ Bartolome Menendez

His brother and closest friend. He had been at his side as either a ship captain or admiral since 1550. When the CASA arrested him and his brother in 1563, Bartolome spent 25 months in prison. He was an exceptional leader.

⚑ Diego Flores de Valdes

A distant relative. A very close friend and confidant. He was second-in-command of the 1565 race to North America. He donated much of his estate to help finance the expedition.

⚑ Esteban de las Alas

He worked under Menendez as a ship captain for twelve years before the 1565 race. He was admiral of the Asturias, or northern armada during the expedition. When Santa Elena was made the capital of Spain's North America in 1571, Esteban de las Alas was his second-in-command.

☖ Father Mendoza Grajales

He became Menendez's trusted chaplain and confidant during the 1565 race to America. He was a colorful priest who always supported his captain-general. Menendez shared many of his inner thoughts with Father Mendoza. And Father Mendoza recorded those experiences during the entire race to North America.

☖ Pedro Menendez Marquez

He was Menendez's close friend, nephew, and ship captain for twenty years. Like Alas, Valdes, and his brother, Bartolome, Pedro Menendez Marquez was part of that inner circle of close confidants. They were also considered some of the best mariners in Spain.

THE UNIQUENESS OF HIS MEN OF ASTURIAS

This small group of core followers was unique in several ways. First, they were all from northern Spain. They were from Asturias, the Spanish province that bred men of the sea who were unusually strong fighters. Second, they developed their leadership skills as mariners, not as land-based military officers. In short, Menendez's men did not have the military experience that the CASA either traditionally expected or required. They did not have a land-based military background. At that time in the 16th century, Spain saw their "Navy" as part of the Army, not a separate maritime fighting force. Menendez put leadership experience and loyalty over everything else. And he found those men largely from Asturias. That can be seen in who he chose as his second tier of leaders. Among them were:

☖ Pedro Menendez Marquis, Asturian

☖ Captain Diego de Amaya, Asturian

- Captain Diego de Alvarado, Asturian

- Alonso Menendez Marquis, Asturian

- Thomas Alonso de las Alas, Asturian

- Diego de Hevia, Asturian

- Gonzalo Solis de Meras, Asturian

Appendix V

The Memorial (Report) of February, 1565

Introductory note from the late Dr. Eugene Lyon:

Early in 1565, Pedro Menendez, now freed from the strictures of his imprisonment by the House of Trade (CASA) officials, was consulted by Philip II about the best policy for Florida, where enemies of the Crown might at any time set foot, endanger the Spanish Crown's North American rights, and put in peril the treasure galleons returning to Spain through the Bahama passage. Although rumors of possible enemy settlements were rife in Spain and the Indies, ironically, both parties were at that moment ignorant that Frenchmen had already built a fort and planted a settlement on the River May (St. Johns River), in the northeast corner of the Florida peninsula. It was not until after Menendez's Florida contract was signed on March 20, that belated word came from the Governor at Havana about the French settlement in Florida.

This letter illustrates some of the underlying dynamics of Menendez's relationship with Philip, but it also demonstrates that the future Adelantado intended to settle in the Santa Elena area, as the primary focus long before the disclosure of the French presence at Charlesfort in 1562. Two themes which continue to concern Menendez are featured here: his fear that slave rebellions and Native American enmity to the Spaniards will be encouraged by French or English corsairs; and his preoccupation with the Northwest Passage and its branch that may reach from Newfoundland to Mexico. Here Menendez also expresses his peculiar belief, to be repeated in later letters from Florida, that "Lutheran" French or Englishmen share the same basic beliefs with the Native Americans. At the end of the letter, Menendez follows another familiar pattern: he asks the king to finance the Florida expedition of settlement, which he would lead. Instead, the king agreed to an Adelantado's contract in which Menendez would bear the cost. When the news of the French incursion reached Spain, the Crown added its own support to the venture. He then laid out his plan for Florida: its fortification, population, agricultural development, and the evangelization of the Indians by Jesuit missionaries. If Menendez had followed his initial plan, it might have led to settlement of the Carolinas, the North Atlantic states or New England by Spaniards.

Signed, Dr. Eugene Lyon[269]

The Memorial to King Philip II:

Pedro Menendez says that in which Your Majesty orders him, that he declare what he knows and understands about the coast and land of Florida, and of the corsairs who it is said have gone to settle it and make prizes of ships which come from the Indies, and the damage they might do, and the remedy which could be applied in case they had gone and settled in some part, in order that they not be allowed to take control of that coast and land, and in order that they might easily be expelled from there, and in order that Your Majesty might order to establish and preach the Gospel in it, and that the damages which might be made in the fleets and ships which come from the Indies might be avoided. He states the following:

He says that, being in Seville last May, he knew and understood for certain from persons who came from the Canary Islands who had been on the island of Tenerife, in the port of Panachico with a Portuguese named El Mimoso. He is a pilot in the Indies trade, who has his wife and his house in France, and goes as a corsair robbing the vessels of Your Majesty, taking four warships. And he is said to have gone to settle on the coast of Florida, and that two large companion ships were awaiting while he took refreshment and sought intelligence in that port. And in a zabra he saw them there, without disembarking five or six hours, where some employees came to talk to him, who said they were his relatives, and they went to their ships, and he made sail on his voyage of return from the Indies.

Item: He says that he learned in Seville and in this court about Englishmen who went in a war fleet to go to the coast of Florida to settle in it, and to await the ships of the Indies. And a month ago, he learned that five very heavy and very well armed English galleons had passed the Galician coast at the end of December, and had been driven with a storm into the bay of Gerrol, where they were for a day and a half without putting a man on land, but fishermen went aboard to talk with them.

And thus he says that if the above mentioned is true and the said French or English or any other nation is disposed to wish to go and make some settlement in the other Florida, it would do great harm to these kingdoms, because on the other coast of Florida, near the Bahama Channel, in some port or ports, they could make their establishment and fortify themselves in such a way that they could have galleys and other fast warships to take the fleets and other private ships which come from the Indies and leave (the Channel) there, and all of them would run a great risk of being taken.

Item: That if Frenchmen or Englishmen have gone to Florida last summer, as he is certain that they did, and made some settlement or fort in some port, or have wintered there, and given notice of how they would remain there, if they be reinforced this summer before we come upon them and expel them from the land, it will afterwards be impossible to do, due to the friendship which they will have made with the natives, because the same natives will aid them in such a manner that only with the greatest difficulty even though great costs are incurred and expenditures made, could they be expelled. In addition to which, even though they be expelled, the same Indians would remain as our enemies, and would not come readily to our friendship, and this would be of great harm. And also, if they are reinforced with armadas this summer, the fleets awaited from the Indies would be in danger.

Item: It would be greatly inconvenient that the above-mentioned or anyone else might settle in Florida, because in the islands of Santo Domingo, Puerto

Rico and Cuba, which are near to there, there are a great number of blacks and mulattoes, people of evil intent, who outnumber the Christians in each of these islands thirty to one, and it is a land in which this generation is greatly multiplying. And, in possession of the French and English, all these slaves will be set free. And because of this, in order to enjoy this liberty, the blacks will aid them against their own lords and masters, in order that they rebel and take over the land. With the blacks helping them, it would be a very easy thing to do; to illustrate this one may cite the example of Jacques Sore, the Frenchman who in the year of 1553, with only one 100-ton ship with eighty men, while giving liberty to the blacks, took and robbed the island of Margarita, Cabo de la Vela, Burburate, and Santa Marta, burned Cartagena, and burned and robbed Santiago de Cuba and Havana, even though there were two hundred Spaniards there in Havana. And they took the fortress and twelve pieces of bronze artillery that were within and carried them off.

And I hold this matter of the blacks to be a great inconvenience; it seems to me that, just knowing that Frenchmen or Englishmen may settle Florida, and having them so near, this alone might be cause for them to rebel, even though they might not have help from the French or English, because there are many polyglot persons among the slaves who desire liberty. And I am certain that the design of those who might go to settle Florida is to seize control of those islands and impede the Indies navigation, which they will be able to do very easily, having settled or settling the other Florida.

Item: He says that in the year of 1554, he brought a man from New Spain who said that a French ship had entered an arm of the sea in Newfoundland, which branched off down into Florida and it entered four hundred leagues into it a little more or less. And when that arm of the sea came to an end, the people landed and a quarter of a league farther on they found another arm of the sea. And in order to know where it ended, they made four small brigantines and went three hundred leagues on it, until they found themselves in 48 degrees, due north of Mexico five hundred leagues. There they found great settlements and much sustenance, near to the mines of Zacatecas and

San Martin, so that boats could go there from Newfoundland. And there is reason to believe that this arm of the sea discharges in the South Sea on the course for China and Molucca. And this ship, having made this discovery and returning to France, was sunk, as I have already now given an account to Your Majesty. And a Portuguese ship which came from Newfoundland joined up with it, and when it sank, certain persons escaped to the Portuguese ship, and this man among them.,

And thus, if the said French or English come to settle Florida understanding this secret, it would be the greatest inconvenience, as much for the mines and territories of New Spain as for the navigation and trade of China and Molucca, if that arm of the sea goes to the South Sea, as is certain. And this can be done with great ease for being a master of Newfoundland, and a settlement and fort can be made in that strait where the two arms of the sea join, which would be of the greatest increase for them and great harm for Your Majesty.

Item: He says that due to the said inconveniences, and many others which may follow, it seems to him that it befits the service of God our lord and of Your Majesty, and the general good of his kingdoms and all the Indies that, with brevity, Your Majesty proceed to master that land. And because it is such a great land. And it is situated at such a good juncture, that if some other nations go to settle it, taking, as they will take, friendship with the Indians of the land, it will afterwards be most difficult to take and master it. This is especially true if French or English settle it, Lutheran people, and since they and the Indians are of one law, as I have said, they will very easily have friendship, one with another. And through that land being so close to France and England, and the French controlling Newfoundland, since more than two thousand of their ships alone go there each year, and for that reason they will easily be able to trade in that land and sustain it. Especially since they say that it is very large, and well fitted for sugar mills, which they lack, and for which they are accustomed to be provided from these kingdoms. And they might have much livestock in that land, for wool and wool cloth, of which they have great need.

That which it seems that Your Majesty ought to provide, that which involves the service of God Our Lord and of Your Majesty, and the salvation of so many souls, and the growth of your kingdoms and territories and of your Royal treasury, and to avoid the said inconveniences, is the following:

He says that, there not being French, English or any other nation to hinder in the land and coast of Florida, it would be fitting that five hundred persons go—sailors, soldiers, farmers, all working people, and that among them there might go almost one hundred craftsmen; bricklayers, sawyers, carpenters, smiths, stone masons, all with their tools and equipment for their trade. And thus these, as the rest with their offensive and defensive arms, arquebuses and crossbows. And that there go in the said number of the five hundred men, twelve friars, four Jesuits and 12 boys to help in the teaching of the Gospel, in order that the chief Indians might give their children to read and learn the doctrine. And that three surgeons, six barbers should go. These must go in fast shallops and zabras, with oars, and supplies for a year in one or two galleons.

And they must go directly to Cape Santa Elena, and with the fast ships run and discover all the bays, rivers, sounds and shallows which there are in the route to Newfoundland. And to provide settlers, in the largest number possible, for two or three towns in the places which seem best to the person who goes there, and after seeking out the best ports, having first explored inland for four or five leagues, to see that it might have a good disposition of land for farming and livestock raising. And each town would have its fort, their best which could be at the time to defend against the Indians if they should come upon them, or against other nations; and in each one of these forts there would be artillery and munitions.

All of which would cost 80,000 ducats for a year, rather more than less, with food, salaries paid, and with ships, artillery, munitions and tools and everything necessary for the voyage; I will give a memorandum of each item. And the ships will remain very sufficient to put a number of livestock into the land. And this is impossible if not from these kingdoms, because in the Indies one can neither find ships for this purpose nor people or craftsmen of the proper quality and much more money would be spent, and you would in no way have the necessary effect. Worse, the delay would be of the greatest harm, even if you gathered together the people available in all the ports of the Indies to make the said expedition, because it would not be possible to find there people similar to this and the necessary craftsmen need for the said expedition.

And when some might be found, it would be a very great cost, since each craftsman earns much money in those parts and the same is true for farmers and sailors. And from Havana one can do less than in another part since there are no resources or people there. And from the place where one must settle if you wish to go to Havana, you must go such a long way around through not being able to go back south through the Bahama Channel, when one can come to Spain as quickly as going to Havana and with less risk. And it will be of most importance that Your Majesty do this at your cost, because it would be done with more brevity, secrecy and diligence, which is most important. And when Your Majesty might no longer be served in this, and it must cease, a person can be found to take this in charge with the conditions which Your Majesty shall contract with him, then it is better that it cease to be done, even though, as I say, the first part would be done at Your Majesty's cost, since brevity is so important.

Item: He says that in case that there be Frenchmen in the land, and that might have an armada at sea awaiting the fleets, and ships of the Indies, it will at least be necessary to increase the effort beyond that which is said, by four heavy galleons with a thousand sailors and soldiers. These will cost, for the six months, 50,000 ducats, a little more or less.[270]

Signed: Pedro Menendez de Aviles

Appendix VI

Highlights of Pedro Menendez's Contract of March 20, 1565

When Menendez signed his contract with Philip II on March 15, 1565, he accepted a mission of settlement and pacification. Under this contract, Menendez would pay for the entire expedition. The Crown gave him the authority of a royal prince. He was almost a government of his own, reporting only to the king. His mission was simple. Pacify the Indians, settle two or three towns, and search for new territory. Menendez was given broad powers. If successful, he would also be given broad rewards.

Ten days after Menendez and the king signed this contract, everything changed. With knowledge that France was resupplying a second fort on Spain's new colony, Philip II literally said, "Put this original contract on hold. Before we do anything, we have to push France out of our colony." The text in this contract, however, was very important. It literally outlined the strategic plan that Pedro Menendez and King Philip II would use to settle North America's first European colony.

Summary of the Contract:[271]

- ♗ The contract was structured between "duties" and "rewards."

- ♗ Menendez would bring 10 ships fully equipped, including his large galleon, the *San Pelayo*. He would also bring 500 men.

⚑ He would bring 100 farmers and 100 sailors and a mix of artisans . . . carpenters, blacksmiths, etc. At least 200 of the 500 new settlers would have to be married men and their wives.

⚑ He would locate the best place for settlements. (We already know that the Punta Santa Elena was both his and the king's preference).

⚑ He was to make two to three settlements in the first three years.[272]

⚑ The colony of La Florida was defined as extending from the Florida Keys to Newfoundland and as far west as they had identified. (That would be a few miles west of the Mississippi River. No one knew what was west and north of Newfoundland. Most thought it was probably China and Moscovy (Russia).

⚑ Every attempt was to be made to bring the native Indians into the Christian faith . . . and to loyal obedience to the King of Spain.

⚑ Pedro Menendez would pay for the entire expedition.

THE BENEFITS INCLUDED:

⚑ He was to enjoy the title of Adelantado into perpetuity. (Today, a distant heir of Pedro Menendez, Count Alvaro Armada Barcaixtequi, has the official title of Adelantado)

⚑ He would receive the title of governor and captain-general for two lives . . . his own or that of his son or son-in-law.

⚑ He would be captain-general of the ships in the expedition.

- He could also pursue private business on the side . . . such as shipping or farming.

- He would have the power to distribute land.

- He was granted 75 square miles of the land of his choice, that is, 48,000 acres.

- He could bring into his colony 500 slaves duty-free.

- He was promised two fisheries.

- He was granted licenses for 10 private ships for the first year to support his private income.

Menendez's contract told a story well beyond the duties and benefits that related to the Conquistador. In his contract, King Philip II clearly noted that Spain had been unsuccessful for the last 50 years in establishing a real settlement in North America. **Thus, if Menendez were successful, Spain would be the first country in Europe to develop a settlement in North America.**

To date, our history books have confused us. They constantly refer to England as having the first American settlement . . . either at Plymouth or Jamestown. But our historians have never defined "settlement." **What constitutes a settlement?** King Philip II defined that important word in Menendez's contract. First, he implied that **a settlement had to be a targeted destination (have some reason to be settled). He noted that it should have a fort, church, merchant buildings, government buildings, farms, and homes. Its inhabitants should include men and women, men of the church, merchants, soldiers, and artisans.** And unlike the strategy of France's Gaspard Coligny, a settlement had to have farmers.

They had to have a local self-sustaining supply of food. He also implied that a settlement should have a life beyond a few years. In other words, a foreign settlement should mirror an active trading village in Europe.[273]

Appendix VII

Menendez's Ordinances

Soon after Pedro Menendez established Santa Elena, the men of the garrison began to show a complete lack of discipline. Menendez was very much like the Admiral of France, Gaspard Coligny. He knew that he had to quickly instill a strict discipline. Otherwise, his chances for success would be challenged. With that in mind, he quickly introduced these "Ordinances."

Ordinances

Whatever person, of whatever condition he might be, who is present and serves in these provinces, who gives reproof or considers it . . . shall be eight days with his head in the stocks and eight more with his feet (in the stocks). He shall not be given a wine ration for the said fifteen days, or he may have the punishment doubled . . . to six months dismounted with a (tie, hobble) on his foot; and, in all this time, he may not bear arms.

He who might give his support to such as one who is in the stocks, two days and loss of ration of the two days. He who speaks evil against the saints shall have his wine ration taken away for that day, and all these rations shall be given to charity for the poor in the hospital, and the other half to the denouncer.

That every Sunday and feast day . . . all shall hear Mass, and he who does not shall lose his ration for that day; if he should already have received it, he shall not get it the following day, and it shall be applied to the poor and to the denouncer as stated above. Those days the curate shall pronounce the Christian doctrine.

Every day, morning and evening, the Christian catechism must he said, and within a year each soldier must be obligated to know it, and the curate who resides there shall examine them, and he who does not know it must pay three months' salary, which shall be taken for the said hospital and the sick and to saying Mass for the souls generally of the Catholic dead who have died and who may die in these provinces later, if provided for them, friends as well as enemies.

Any soldier who might laugh on such an occasion shall be punished with all rigor—and the determination of this shall be by the Governor and Captains who were in such a place where this happened, so that all agree in the determination.

That he who puts his hand to a sword or dagger or any other offensive arm to harm another serves here, six months on the King's works, or dismounted without pay, and they shall not give him wine.

Whatever person who shall thrash with a stick or give hard slaps to anyone, he is sent to perpetual service in the galleys and, in the meantime until there is a means to send him, he shall serve with irons on the works of the King.

Whatever person who gives the lie to another who is shown to be offended and lied about, he shall then be given three lashes with the whip.

Any squad leader may arrest any soldier whom he catches in the act, and give occasion by laughing, bringing him as a prisoner to the public jail in order that he may be punished no matter which company he might belong to. He who does not do this shall incur the same penalty.

In all the forts of these provinces, soldiers shall lodge in groups of ten and thus shall they draw their rations and in no other way. They shall agree upon and set up their comrade groups, and one shall draw rations for all ten; it shall not be given to the squad leaders. As time goes on, if one of these ten shall become evil and rebellious, he shall be punished and another comrade be ordered to take his place so that they shall all live peacefully and quietly and with good discipline in all, and it shall be divided at the place where the said ten soldiers must be dismissed, in order that they shall all be together by their order because all should work on equal terms.

In all the forts, the cabildo (the official town council) must meet twice each week, land at other necessary times to deal with the matters of government and the municipal republic. In this must enter the Governor, captains and treasury officials of His Majesty, the Alcalde, attorney and cleric who might be in that fort, and the supply master. These offices of Alcalde, attorney, a bailiff, and the jailer must be named by the cabildo, in order that they might be qualified persons. Each year there shall be a new election of this.

No Governor shall punish or settle a lawsuit unless it be done by vote in cabildo (the town council), nor shall a captain. He may not punish nor free any soldier in the event of a mutiny, unless it be with the accord and resolution of the cabildo.

In civil cases, the cleric shall have a vote.

After the Governor, the first votes shall be those of the captains and then the treasury officials of His Majesty and then of the Vicar and then the Alcalde, the attorney, and the supply master.

In all criminal matters, any appeals to go before the superiors of the provinces shall be granted by the cabildo, in order that justice be executed so that the penalties of these ordinances might be executed here notwithstanding such appeals in the same way, all sentences for mutiny shall be executed; whatever sentence is given, the parties shall not appeal, and all sentences for mutiny shall be executed, and sentences of ten thousand maravedis and below.

In those matters which apply to things of war, the Governor and captains must enter into council and no one else, except the cabildo's notary, if they need him and call for him.

No soldier may go from one fort to another without the permission of his superior under penalty of death.[274]

Appendix VIII

Ships and Men

This book raises a number of obvious questions. How many ships did Spain and France lose during this important 1565 "race"? How many French were killed in battle, executed, or set free? The author soon discovered that there was no summary of this data. However, in writing this book, he developed one. His major source was Gonzalo Solis de Meras' MEMORIAL. Dr. Eugene Lyon also provided a valuable analysis of the Spanish ships that were promised in his *The Enterprise of Florida*. The Count of Revillagigedo's copy of "Ships Lost in the Florida Conquest" was invaluable.[275]

Spain's Plan

Spain's plan was to beat France's resupply armada to Fort Caroline. Their tactical plan was to seize an island at the mouth of the St. Johns River and block Admiral Ribault from reaching Fort Caroline, which was several miles upriver. Then Menendez would make an amphibious attack on the fort with his smaller ships. The size of Menendez's attack appears to be planned from a rumor he heard in Vizcaya around April 16. *"The French were planning to attack with 16 ships and 2,000 men."*

	Ships	Men
Leave Spain: (May 15-July 1, 1565)		
From Cadiz, commanded by Menendez	10	1,100
From Northern Spain, commanded by	5	324
Admiral Esteban de las Alas.		
Total:	15	1,424
Depart the Canary Islands		
Cadiz component (2 shuttle ships to return)	8	1,040
Northern Spain component.	5	324
Total:	13	1,364
Depart Hispaniola	+1	+ 300
Total:	14	1,664
Depart Cuba		
Governor delivers 1 ship and 50 men	+1	+ 50
Capt.-Gen. of Treasure Fleet delivers ship		
and 200 men	+1	+200
Total:*	16	1,914

*The ship and head count varies between that recorded by de Meras, the CASA, and the late historian, Dr. Eugene Lyon. For example, Dr. Lyon noted that the CASA believed that Menendez's armada departed Cadiz with 995 persons. Menendez said he left with 1,504 souls. Using the inventory of ships, the author believes he left with 1,100 people. The total Spanish force arriving at the mouth of the St. Johns River should be fairly close. Dr. Lyon records the king's promise of an additional 550 men and 3 ships being promised to Menendez once he reaches the Indies . . . 1 ship and 50 men from Cuba; 1 ship and 300 men from Hispaniola; and 1 ship and 200 men from the captain-general of the Treasure Armada. See Gonzola Solis de Meras, Pedro Menendez de Aviles: *Memorial*, trans. Jeannette Thurber Connor (Florida State Historical Society, 1923), 72. Also note Dr. Eugene Lyon, *The Enterprise of Florida*, (Gainsville, U. of Florida Press, 1974), 98.

WHAT HAPPENED?
Departure from Spain

	Ships	Men
Cadiz component (led by Menendez)	10	1,100
Alas northern Spain armada	5	324
(Delayed by bad weather)		

Departure from the Canary Islands (July 8, 1565)
    Only Cadiz component departs. Two shuttle
        ships return to Cadiz.   8   1,040

One day after Canary departure: July 9, 1565
    Lose one patache due to hull leak
        (Assume 15 mariners escort ship's return)   7   1,025

Departure from Puerto Rico: August 13
    Lose 235 men and 3 ships from hurricane   4   790
        Lose 30 men due to desertion.
    Buy one ship and receive 43 men from Gov.
        of Puerto Rico   5   833
    Government of Hispaniola did not turn over
        promised one ship and 300 men.
    Governor of Cuba did not turn over one ship
        and 50 men.
    Treasure Armada flagship and 200 men were
        delayed due to weather.
            Total on August 13.   5   833

FRANCE'S PLANNED ARMADA OF 1565

France's plan was to do much more than just resupply their Fort Caroline garrison. Gaspard Coligny's orders were for Admiral Jean Ribault to first replace the commander of Fort Caroline, Rene Laudonniere. Ribault would then become the Viceroy of New France. In the following spring, he would lead a joint French-English attack on the Spanish Treasure Fleet that would pass the mouth of the St. Johns River. Then he was to establish a secondary ambush fort at today's Key West. Following that move, France was to take the one action that should guarantee Coligny a war with Spain in the Americas . . . descend to Havana and the other key Spanish ports in the Caribbean, and conquer them using slave revolts.

THE FRENCH PLAN

	Ships	*Men*
Ribault leaves Dieppe, France on February 18, 1565	7	800–900

Avoids contact with Spanish enroute. Best approach would be to turn west before he reaches the Canary Islands. Once he reaches the mouth of the St. Johns River, he expects to find either two or three French ships and at least 200 men under Laudonniere's command.

9–10	1000–1,100		9–10	1000–1,100

WHAT HAPPENED

Following orders from the Queen Mother, Admiral Ribault avoided the normal route that the Spanish, and most Europeans, took to reach the Indies. That required Ribault to take a more direct route to the Florida peninsula. Our forensic navigators believe that route would have required Ribault to turn west 60 miles before he reached the Canary Islands. Although a slower route, it was about 800 miles shorter. And it was not in the direct path of summer hurricanes that develop off the shores of western Africa.

Ribault and his seven-ship armada landed at the mouth of the St. Johns River on August 28, 1565.[276] Menendez and his five ships arrived on September 4 . . . seven days later.[277] When he reached Fort Caroline, he found approximately 240 men. He also discovered that Laudonniere had at least three ships inside the mouth of the St. Johns River. Of the five Spanish ships that arrived on September 4, only four of the eight Cadiz ships that departed the Canaries survived the mid-Atlantic storm. The fifth ship was a recently purchased ship from Puerto Rico, and it was leaking badly. Menendez arrived at the mouth of the St. Johns River only to see that Ribault had won the race to Ft. Caroline.

French Losses at the Battle of Fort Caroline

Losses at Fort Caroline:
142 Killed in battle
60 Escaped
50 women and children saved
110 French offered safe conduct with surrender

Executions at site near first three wrecked French ships:
208 Made it safely to shore from wrecks.
8 Given safe-conduct.
200 Executed.

Second group of French shipwrecked survivors:
350 No. of French in Ribault's flagship that made shore.
150 Were willing to surrender to Menendez.
16 Given safe-conduct.
134 Executed.
200 Escaped and went south.

Menendez meets many of 200 escaped French near Cape Canaveral.
    150 Meet with Menendez.
    21 Refuse to surrender.
    129 Surrender and given safe-conduct.

Summary of French killed, executed, or given safe-conduct
    Number killed at Fort Caroline: 142
    Number executed at shipwreck sites: 334
    Number offered safe-conduct: 263
    Number who accepted safe conduct: 203

SHIPS THAT SURVIVED THE EXPEDITION

Spain:

Of the 16 ships that eventually joined the Menendez Expedition, only one survived. That ship was a shallop, one of the five ships from northern Spain that later arrived at Havana. When Menendez's prized ship, the *Capitana San Pelayo*, departed its anchorage off of St. Augustine on September 10, 1565, it was soon overtaken by English prisoners. They took the ship to Denmark, where it was run aground.

France:

Of the ten ships that were under Admiral Ribault's control at Fort Caroline (seven from Dieppe and three from Ft. Caroline), only two returned to France . . . the *Pearle* and the *Levriere*. The *Pearle* was commanded by Admiral Ribault's son, Jacques Ribault. Vivien Maillard captained the *Levriere*.

Endnotes

1. Gonzalo Solis de Meras, *Memorial,* trans. Jeannette Thurber Connor, (Deland, Fl., Florida State Historical Society, 1923) 41. Albert Manucy, *Menendez* (Sarasota, Pineapple Press, 1992), 9–13.

2. Albert Manucy, *Menendez: Captain of the Ocean* (Sarasota, Pineapple Press, 1983) 11,13.

3. Marcelin Defourneaux, *Daily Life in Spain in the Golden Age,* (Stanford, Stanford University Press, 1979), 35.

4. *Time and Space: Living in Sixteenth-century Europe,* accessed in November, 2019 from Blackwell Publishing, www.blackwellpublishing.com/BPL.

5. William Beik, *A Social and Cultural History of Early Modern France* (Cambridge, Cambridge University Press, 2009), 20.

6. Eugene Lyon, *The Enterprise of Florida* (Gainesville, University of Florida Press, 1974) 9.

7. Woodbury Lowery, *The Spanish Settlements Within the Present Limits of the United States* (New York, Knickerbocker Press, 1905), 121.

8. Pablo E. Perez-Mallaina, *Spain's Men of the Sea,* trans. Carla Rahn Phillips (Baltimore, The Johns Hopkins U. Press, 1998), 36.

9. Lowery, *The Spanish Settlements,* 120.

10. Sir Walter Besant, *Gaspard de Coligny* (London, United University Club, 1879), 9–17.

11. Frederick J. Baumgartner, *France in the Sixteenth Century* (New York, St. Martin's Press, 1995), 83.

12. *Ibid.,* 34.

13. R. J. Knecht, *Catherine de Medici* (London, Longman Press, 1998), 60.

14. *Ibid.,* 120–124.

15. Beik, *A Social and Cultural History, 315.*

16. Soly, et al, *Charles V 1500–1558 and His Time,* (Antwerp, Mercatorfonds, 1999), 21.

17. William D. and Carla Rahn Phillips, *A Concise History of Spain* (Cambridge, Cambridge University Press, 2010), 169.

18. Soly, et al., *Charles V 1500–1558,* 115.

19. Timothy Walton, *The Spanish Treasure Fleets,* (Sarasota, Pineapple Press, 1994), 27.

20. Soly, et al., *The Political World of Charles V,* 135.

21. *Ibid.,* 163.

22. Francis Gardiner Davenport, *European Treaties Bearing on the History of the United States and Its Dependencies* (Washington, DC, Carnegie Institution, 1917)

23. Paul E. Hoffman, *A New Andalucia and a Way to the Orient* (Baton Rouge, LSU, 1990), 167.

24. Christopher Allen, *Santa Elena and America's Lost Century* (Beaufort, S.C., Santa Elena Foundation, 2015),4.

25. Hoffman, *A New Andalucia,* 3–83.

26. Lowery, *The Spanish Settlements Within,* 299–312.

27. R.J. Knecht, *Francis I* (Cambridge, Cambridge Univ. Press, 1982), 329.

28. Eugene Bersier, *Coligny: The Earlier Life of the Great Huguenot*, trans. Annie Harwood Holmden (London, Hodder and Stoughton, 1884), 21, 22.

29. *Ibid.*, 24.

30. R. J. Knecht, *French Renaissance Monarchy* (London, Longman, 1984), 70.

31. Woodbury Lowery, *The Spanish Settlements*, 6–9.

32. Robert F. Marx, *The Treasure Fleets of the Spanish Main* (New York, The World Publishing Company, 1968), 35.

33. Lyon, *The Enterprise of Florida*, 13.

34. Lowery, *The Spanish Settlements Within*, 125.

35. *Ibid.*, 122, 123.

36. Lyon, *The Enterprise of Florida*, 12, 13.

37. *Ibid.*, 13.

38. Hoffman, *A New Andalucia*, 128.

39. Earl J. Hamilton, *American Treasure and the Price Revolution in Spain* (Cambridge Mass., Harvard University Press, 1934), 14.

40. Pedro Menendez de Aviles, Letter to King Philip II of August 21, 1563, The Lawson Collection (University of Florida Smathers Libraries, Special Area and Studies Collection, August 1563), Box 9, No. 25.

41. Lyon, *The Enterprise of Florida*, 14.

42. *Ibid.*, 15.

43. Kenneth Setton, *The Papacy and the Levant: 1204–1571* (Philadelphia, American Philosophical Society, 1984), 628, 645, 649.

44. Kenneth M. Setton, *The Papacy and the Levant*, 657.

45. *Ibid.*, 655.

46. *Ibid.*, 647.

47. *Ibid.*, 665.

48. Bartolome Barrientos, *Pedro Menendez De Aviles*, trans. Anthony Kerrigan (Gainesville, University of Florida Press, 1965) 12.

49. Setton, *The Papacy and the Levant*, 686.

50. A. W. Whitehead, *Full Text of Gaspard de Coligny, Admiral of France* (London, Methuen & Co., 1896), 56, 57.

51. Soly et al. *The Political World*, 118.

52. Geoffrey Parker, *Philip II*, (Chicago, Open Court, 2002), 179.

53. Philip II, *Letter to Don Luis de Velasco*, Vol. II of *New American World*, ed. David B. Quinn (New York, Arno Press, 1979), 201.

54. Besant, *Gaspard de Coligny*, 90.

55. *Ibid.*, 94.

56. Leona Frieda, *Catherine de Medici*, (New York, Harper, 2003), 112.

57. Besant, *Gaspard de Coligny*, 124.

58. Barrientos, *Pedro Menendez de Aviles*, 12.

59. Bersier, *COLIGNY*, 147.

60. Lowery, *Spanish Settlements Within*, 24.

61. Knecht, *Catherine de Medici*, 57.

62. Leonie Frieda, *Catherine de Medici*, 121.

63. Philip II, *Letter to Tristan de Luna*, Vol. II of *New American World*, ed. David B. Quinn (New York, Arno Press, 1979), 221.

64. Bersier, *COLIGNY*, 160.

65. *Ibid.*, 161.

66. *Ibid.*, 174.

67. *Ibid.*, 212.

68. Whitehead, *Full Text of,* 86.

69. Bersier, *COLIGNY*, 214, 215.

70. *Ibid.*, 218, 219.

71. *Ibid.*, 244.

72. *Ibid.*, 297–300.

73. Knecht, *Catherine de Medici*, 76.

74. *Ibid.*, 83.

75. Hoffman, *A New Andalucia*, 273.

76. John White and Jacques Le Moyne, *The New World: The First Pictures of America*, ed. Stephan Lorant (New York, Duell, Sloan & Pearce, 1946), 9.

77. Bersier, *COLIGNY*, 309, 310.

78. *Ibid.*, 309–311.

79. *Ibid.*, 319.

80. Hernando Manrique de Rojas' Report on Expedition to Santa Elena, A.G.I., Seville Santo Domingo, 99, trans. Lucy Wenhold in *Manrique de Rojas's report on French settlement in Florida* (*Florida Historical Quarterly*, XXVIII, 1959). 45–62.

81. Lyon, *The Enterprise of Florida*, 21.

82. *Ibid.*, 29.

83. Jean Ribault, *The Whole and True Discouerye of Terra Florida* (Gainesville, U. of Florida Press, 1964), 97.

84. *Ibid.*, 8.

85. *Ibid.*,

86. Lyon, *The Enterprise of Florida*, 24.

87. Hernando Manrique de Rojas, "Manrique de Rojas' Report on French Settlements in Florida," *Florida Historical Quarterly, XXXVIII:* (1959), 45–62.

88. Rojas, *Report on French Settlement in Florida, 1564*, 313, 314.

89. Besant, *Gaspard de Coligny*, 168.

90. *Ibid.*, 171.

91. Knecht, *Catherine de Medici*, 92–95.

92. Bennett, *Laudonniere and Fort Caroline*, 17.

93. Richard Dunn, *Sugar and Slaves: The Rise of the Planter Class in the English West Indies, 1624–1713* (New York, Norton, 1973) 92. Rene Laudonniere, *Three Voyages*, trans. Charles E. Bennett (Tuscaloosa, University of Alabama Press, 2001), 53.

94. Bennett, *Three Voyages*, 53.

95. Bennett, *Laudonniere and Fort Caroline*, 97.

96. Lowery, *The Spanish Settlements Within*, 53.

97. White and DeBry, *The New World*, 10.

98. Luis Martinez-Ferdandez, "Far beyond the Line: Corsairs, Privateers, Buccaneers, and Invading Settlers in Cuba and the Caribbean (1529–1670)" (Essay written under the auspices of Project of the Plan Nacional de MINESCO, University of Central Florida, 17.

99. Earl J. Hamilton, *American Treasure*, 40.

100. Ernle Bradford, *The Great Siege of Malta 1565* (New York, Open Road, 1961), 39.

101. *Ibid.*, 41, 45, 46, 47.

102. Meras, *Pedro Menendez de Aviles*, 66.

103. Lyon, *The Enterprise of Florida*, 41, 42.

104. *Ibid*, 43.

105. Barrientos, *Pedro Menendez de Aviles*, xix.

106. Archives of the Indies, Patronato 19, Reprinted in Eugenco Ruidfaz y Caravina, La Florida: su conquista por Pedro Menendez de Aviles, 2 vol. (Madrid, 1893), II, 320–326.

107. Philip II and Pedro Menendez de Aviles, *Agreement of March, 1565*, in *New American World*, Vol. II, 384.

108. Lyon, *The Enterprise of Florida*, 56.

109. Lowery, *The Spanish Settlements Within*, 103.

110. Lyon, *The Enterprise of Florida*, 56.

111. *Ibid.*, 59.

112. See Appendix VIII, page 251, for a description of ships and men promised vs. delivered.

113. Lyon, *The Enterprise of Florida*, 67, 68.

114. Marx, *The Treasure Fleets of*, 35, 36.

115. See Appendix VIII, Ships and Men, for detailed projections, p. 206.

116. *Ibid.*, 208.

117. Pedro Menendez de Aviles, *Letter to King Philip II of September 11, 1565*, in *New American World*, Vol. II, 391.

118. Gabriel de Enveja, *The Report of Dr. Gabriel de Enveja to King Philip II*, (Madrid, Royal Academy of History, 9–30-3, 6271)

119. Pedro Menendez de Aviles, *Letter of Pedro Menendez to King Philip II of August 13, 1565*, The Lawson Collection (University of Florida Smathers Libraries, Special and Area Studies Collection, September 2007), Box 9, No. 32.

120. Lowery, *The Spanish Settlements Within*, 120.

121. Lyon, *The Enterprise of Florida*, 73–76.

122. *Ibid.*, 72.

123. *Ibid.*, 73.

124. Pedro Menendez de Aviles, *Letter of May 18, 1565 to King Philip II*, The Lawson Collection (University of Florida Smathers Libraries, Special and Area Studies Collection, September 2007) Box 9, No. 32.

125. Lowery, *The Settlements Within*, 109.

126. Dr. Gabriel de Enveja, *Report to Philip II of June 3, 1565*, Archives of Royal Academy of; History, Madrid, 9–30-3, 6271.

127. Laudonniere, *Three Voyages*, 161.

128. Pedro Menendez de Aviles, *Letter to King Philip II of Spain* October 15, 1565, in *New American World*, (New York, Arno Press, 1979), 399.

129. Lowery, *The Settlements Within*, 95, 96.

130. Archivo de los Condes de Revillagigedo, Canalejas, 47, No.2, reel 106, microfilm at Center for Historic Research, Flagler College, St. Augustine, Florida, image 197.

131. Nelson and Heckrotte, "Navigation Analysis of Jean Ribault Voyage of 1565 from Isle of Wight to Cape Canaveral" (unpublished manuscript, November 7, 2019).

132. See Appendix VIII, *Ships and Men*, for more detailed projections.

133. Gonzalo Solis de Meras, MEMORIAL, trans. Jeannette Thurber Connor, (Deland, Florida, 1923), 74, 75.

134. Meras, *Pedro Menendez de Aviles*, 72.

135. Pedro Menendez de Aviles, *June 22–23, 1565, Inventory of Ships and Supplies for Expedition*, The Lawson Collection (Gainesville, University of Florida Smathers Libraries, Special and Area Studies Collection), Box 9, No. 34.

136. Lyon, *The Enterprise of Florida*, 74–76.

137. Challeux, *Discours de l'histoire de la Floride,* in *New American World,* 371, 372.

138. Howard Heckrotte and Douglas Nelson, "Navigation Analysis of Jean Ribault 1565: Voyage from Isle of Wight to Cape Canaveral" (unpublished manuscript, July 2017), Excel files.

139. Challeux, *Discours de l'histoire,* 372.

140. Douglas Nelson, "Ribault 1565 Track from Isle of Wight to the Canary Islands" (unpublished Manuscript, December 15, 2016) Excel Files.

141. Nelson and Heckrotte, "Jean Ribault's Deduced Log," 2.

142. Nelson and Heckrotte, *Notes on the August 2017 Navigation Plot of Jean Ribault's North Atlantic Crossing: June 14-August 14, 1565* (unpublished manuscript, August 20, 2017), 1.

143. Carla Rahn Phillips, *Six Galleons for the King of Spain* (Baltimore, The Johns Hopkins University Press, 1986), 121–152.

144. Barrientos, *Pedro Menendez de Aviles,* 26.

145. Menendez, *Inventory of Ships,* Box 9, No. 34.

146. *Ibid.,* Box 9, No. 19.

147. Translation of Archives of the Indies, AGI Contaduria 945, Sixth Section.

148. Lyon, *The Enterprise of Florida,* 94.

149. Perez-Mallaina, *Spain's Men of the Sea,* 66.

150. Meras, MEMORIAL, *New American World,* Vol. II, page 428–429.

151. From *Los bastimentos, armas, A.G.I. Escribania de Camara,* 1.024-A.

152. Douglas Nelson and Howard Heckrotte, "Jean Ribault's Deduced Log" (unpublished manuscript, July 2017), p. 2.

153. See Appendix VIII for a more detailed breakdown.

154. Nelson and Heckrotte, "Jean Ribault's Deduced Log" (unpublished manuscript, July 2017), 2.

155. Phillips, *Six Galleons for the King*, 160.

156. *Ibid.*, 159.

157. *Ibid.*, 121.

158. Perez-Mallaina, *Spain's Men of the Sea*, 69.

159. Phillips, *Six Galleons for the King*, 129.

160. Nelson and Heckrotte, "The Lopaz-Menendez Deduced Log" (Unpublished manuscript, July 2017), p. 1.

161. *Ibid.*,

162. See Appendix VII to review Menendez's Ordinances.

163. See Appendix III, "Menendez's At-Sea Instructions."

164. *Ibid.*,

165. Perez-Mallaina, *Spain's Men of the Sea*, 135.

166. *Ibid.*, 237–239.

167. Nelson and Heckrotte, "John Ribault Deduced Log" (unpublished manuscript, July 2017), p. 2.

168. Douglas Nelson, "Notes on Jean Ribault's North Atlantic crossing of June 14-August 14, 1565 (unpublished manuscript, August 2017 plot), p. 2.

169. Lyon, *The Enterprise of Florida*, 101.

170. *Ibid.*, 74.

171. See Appendix VIII for a more detailed breakdown.

172. *Ibid.*, 208.

173. Nelson and Heckrotte, "Navigation Analysis of Menendez Voyage of 1565 from Cadiz to Cape Canaveral," (unpublished manuscript, July 2017)

174. Francisco Lopez de Mendoza, *July 28 to August 9, 1565 Narrative of the Voyage,* The Lawson Collection (University of Florida, Smathers Libraries, Special and Area Studies Collections, September 2007), Box 9, No. 35.

175. Nelson and Heckrotte, "Lopez-Menendez Deduced Log," (unpublished manuscript, July 2017), 1.

176. Douglas Nelson, "Smell of the Sea" (unpublished manuscript, July 2017), 1.

177. Nelson and Heckrotte, *"Notes on hurricanes," from Notes of plot of Jean Ribault's crossing of June 14-August 14, 1565* (Unpublished manuscript, August 20, 2017)

178. Douglas Nelson, "Severe Thunderstorm Warning," *(Ensign Magazine,* December 1999).

179. Lopez de Mendoza, *July 28 to August 9, 1565, Narrative of the Voyage that the Adelantado, Pedro Menendez de Aviles, made to Florida in 1565,* in Edward W. Lawson Collection, Box 9 (Gainesville, Smathers Libraries, 1957), No. 35, 169

180. *Ibid.,* No. 35, 17

181. Nelson and Heckrotte, *"Ribault Deduced Log" (unpublished manuscript, July 2017),* 2.

182. Heckrotte, *"Cadiz to Cape Canaveral" (unpublished manuscript of July 2017)*

183. Nelson and Heckrotte, "Jean Ribault's Deduced Log" July 2017)

184. *Pedro Menendez de Aviles, Letter of August 13, 1565 to King Philip II,* in *New American World, Vol. II* (N.Y., Arno Press, 1979), 390

185. Mendoza, *July 28 to August 9, 1565, Narrative of the Voyage*, 173.

186. Menendez, *Letter of September 11, 1565*, 391.

187. Lyon, *The Enterprise of Florida*, 102.

188. Francisco Lopez de Mendoza Grajales, "*The Founding of St. Augustine.*" in Old South Leaflets Vol. IV. In Early Americas Digital Archive, https://mith.umd.edu/eada/html/display.php?, 7.

189. Menendez, *Letter to King Philip II of August 13, 1465*, in *New American World*, Vol. II, 390.

190. Menendez, *September 11, 1565, Letter to Philip II*, in *New American World*, 391.

191. *Ibid.*, 394.

192. Mendoza, *Letters of Mendoza*, No. 35, 173.

193. *Ibid.*, 173.

194. Pablo Perez-Mallaina, *Spain's Men of the Sea*, 243.

195. *Meras, MEMORIAL*, in *New American World*, Vol. II, 78.

196. Gonzalo Solis de Meras, *Pedro Menendez de Aviles and the Conquest of Florida: A New Manuscript*, ed., trans. By David Arbesu (Gainesville, University of Florida Press, 2017), 39.

197. Meras, *MEMORIAL*, in *New American World*, Vol. II, 431.

198. Gonzalo Solis de Meras, *Pedro Menendez de Aviles*, in *New Manuscript*, ed. David Arbesu (Gainesville, University of Florida Press, 2017), 40, 41.

199. Barrientos, *Pedro Menendez de Aviles*, 37.

200. Francisco Lopez de Mendoza, *Second Excerpt of the Voyage*, Edward W. Lawson Collection (Gainesville, U. of Florida Press, 1957), Box 9, No. 37, 185.

201. Lopez de Mendoza, *Letters of Menendez*, No. 37, 185.

202. *Ibid.*, 186, 187.

203. *Ibid.*, 187

204. Jean Ribaut, *The Whole & True Discouerye*, 17.

205. Laudonniere, *Three Voyages*, 149.

206. Jean Ribaut, *The Whole & True Discouerye*, 18.

207. Laudonniere, *Three Voyages*, 151.

208. *Ibid.*, 153–157.

209. *Ibid.*, 153.

210. Meras, *MEMORIAL, New American World*, 432.

211. *Ibid.*, 432, 433.

212. Barrientos, *Pedro Menendez de Aviles*, 42.

213. *Ibid.*, 43.

214. *Ibid.*

215. Meras, *MEMORIAL, New American World*, 434.

216. *Ibid.*, 432.

217. *Ibid.*

218. E. Ruidiaz and Caravia, La Florida, 2 vols. (Madrid, 1892), II 70–73.

219. Laudonniere, *Three Voyages*, 160.

220. *Ibid.*, 161.

221. *Ibid.*, 161–167.

222. Pedro Menendez de Aviles, *Letter of September 11, 1565 to Philip II*, (*New American World*, Arno Press, 1979), 393.

223. Meras, *New Manuscript*, 48.

224. Lowery, *The Spanish Settlements Within*, 165.

225. Laudonniere, *Three Voyages*, 162, 163.

226. *Ibid.*, 163.

227. Meras, *New Manuscript*, 48.

228. Meras, *New Manuscript*, 50.

229. *Ibid.*

230. Barrientos, *Narrative of September 29, 1565*, in Letters of Menendez, No. 39, p. 207.

231. Lowery, *The Settlements Within*, 170.

232. Menendez, *Letter of October 15, 1565*, in *New American World*, 396.

233. Meras, *New Transcript*, 52.

234. Mendoza, *Narrative of September 29, 1565*, in Letters of Menendez, No. 39, 207.

235. Barrientos, *Pedro Menendez de Aviles*, 50.

236. Meras, *New Transcript*, 53.

237. Meras, *MEMORIAL*, *New American World*, Vol. II, 438.

238. *Ibid.*, 439.

239. Lowery, *The Spanish Settlements Within*, 172.

240. Meras, *New Transcript*, 59.

241. *Ibid.*

242. Barrientos, *Pedro Menendez de Aviles*, 58, 59.

243. Meras, *New Transcript*, 53. Lowery, *The Settlements Within*, 188.

244. Mendoza, *Narrative of September 29, 1565*, in *New American World*, No. 39, 206.

245. Meras, *MEMORIAL*, in *New American World*, 443.

246. Meras, *New Transcript*, 65, 66.

247. *Ibid.*, 68.

248. *Ibid.*, 69, 70.

249. Meras, *MEMORIAL,* in *New American World*, 399.

250. Lyon, *The Enterprise of Florida*, 122, 123.

251. Lowery, *The Settlements Within*, 140, 141.

252. White and LeMoyne, *The New World*, ed. Stefant Lorant (New York, Duell, Sloan & Pearce, 1946) 27, 28.

253. Navarrete, *Coleccion, XIV* (1971), fols. 300-312.; translated by Henry Ware, "Letters of Pedro Menendez de Aviles," Massachusetts Historical Society Proceedings, second series VIII, 440–453.

254. Meras, *MEMORIAL,* in *New American World*, 454.

255. Gonzalo Solis de Meras, *Pedro Menendez de Aviles and the Conquest of Florida*, in *A New Manuscript*, ed. David Arbesu (Gainesville, University of Florida Press, 2017), 120–121.

256. Eugene Lyon, *Santa Elena: A Brief History of the Colony, 1566–1587* (Gainesville, U. of Florida Press, 1984), 4.

257. *Colleccion de documentos ineditos de Indias*, XXIII 242–258; Eugenio Ruidaz y Caravia, *La Florida*, 2 vols. (Madrid, 1893), 415–427.

258. *Colonial Records of Spanish Florida, 1577–1580*, ed and trans. Jeannette Thurber Connor (Deland, The Florida State Historical Society, 1930), 279.

259. Philip II, *December 18, 1559 Letter to Tristan de Luna, New American World* (New York, Arno Press, 1979), 221.

260. Eugene Lyon, *Santa Elena: A Brief History of the Colony, 1566–1587,* Research Manuscript Series, Book 185 (University of South Carolina Press, 1984) page 4.

261. Paul E. Hoffman, "Video Interview with Hoffman and Lyon" (video meeting, Vero Beach, Florida, March 17, 2017.

262. Philip Wayne Powell, *Tree of Hate* (Vallecito, Ca., Ross House Books, 1985), xiii.

263. Lowery, *The Spanish Settlements Within*, 383.

264. William M. Blackburn, *Admiral Coligny and the Rise of the Huguenots* (London, Forgotten Books, 2018), 334, 335, 336.

265. Walton, *The Spanish Treasure Fleets*, 17-30.

266. Carla Rahn Phillips, *Six Galleons*, 12, 13, 14.

267. Walton, *The Spanish Treasure Fleets*, 47–54.

268. Pedro Menendez de Aviles, *Instructions to Sea Captains of January 1562*, in *Letters of Menendez*, Edward W. Lawson Collection, Smathers Libraries (Gainesville, University of Florida Press, 1957) Box 9, No. 22.

269. Eugene Lyon, "Pedro Menendez' Memorial to King Philip II about the Necessity to settle Florida" (unpublished notes from Lyon's personal files). These notes were attached to the memorial in which King Philip II requested that Menendez offer his assessment of the French risk in La Florida. This memorial is housed in the Archives of the Indies in Seville, Spain, under the file: Patronato 19.

270. Archives of the Indies, Patronato 19, Reprinted in Eugenio Ruidfaz y Caravia, *La Florida: su conquista por Pedro Menendez de Aviles*, 2 vol. (Madrid, 1893) II, 320–326.

271. Philip II and Pedro Menendez de Aviles, *Capitalations and Asiento Regarding the Conquest of La Florida*, Coleccion de documentos ineditos de Indias, XXIII, 242–248, Ruidiadz y Caravia, *La Florida*, 2 vols. (Madrid, 1893), 415–427.

272. Lyon, *The Enterprise of Florida*, 49–53.

273. Eugenio Ruidaz y Caravia, *Coleccion de Documentos Inedits de Indies*, XXIII, 2 vol. (Madrid, 1893), trans. J.T. Connor (Delano, Fl.), 259–270.

274. Archivo General de India, Justica 999, No. 2, ramo 9.

275. Archivo de los Condes de Revillagigedo Canalejas 47, No. 2; reel 106, microfilm at Center for Historic Research, Flagler College, St. Augustine, Florida; image 197.

276. Laudonniere, *Three Voyages*, 149.

277. Ribault, *The Whole & True Discouerye*, 17.

Index

About the Author

It took ten years to uncover this story.

Most historians come from colleges and universities. They only have limited time to do their research. When they want to publish their work, they have to follow very strict and "boring" writing guidelines.

The author did not have those handicaps. When he retired, he had both the time and loving wife that would be needed to attack such a difficult project. But like a die-hard explorer, he would also not be stopped by countless obstacles.

In the late 1960s, he discovered that the U.S. Navy was about to scrap the country's most decorated WW II battleship, the *U.S.S. South Dakota*. It did not take him long to organize a state-wide effort to return much of the battleship to South Dakota and build a national WW II museum for our Navy vets.

In 1973 the White House tried to get the rights to buy and display the famous 23-sided Paris Peace Talks Table. It was on this table that the U.S. negotiated the end of the Vietnam war. The White House failed in its attempt to acquire this famous piece of furniture. The author made a direct call to the French Prime Minister. He got the rights to the table for his country.

The author also had the problem-solving skills to put this gargantuan puzzle together. Before he retired, he was president of Citizens Utilities, a Fortune 500 company that had extensive holdings in communications. He was also co-chairman of Europe's Hungarian Telephone Company.

When he was asked, *"What was it like spending ten years to uncover this story?* he simply said, *"It was like solving 100 complex puzzles that were interconnected to 1,000 smaller puzzles."*

American Conquistador is an action-adventure story that is more Robin Hood than Robin Hood. It is jam-packed with intrigue, piracy, and swashbuckling.

Daryl Ferguson introduces a young peasant who, by Spain's 16th-century standards, will never rise any higher in Spain's society. But he does. He becomes, arguably, the nation's most colorful and important conquistador.

This is an *HISTORICAL THRILLER* that has never been told before. The author makes you one guarantee: You will never forget this story . . . for one reason. The story is **TRUE**. It actually happened.

Made in the USA
Monee, IL
07 August 2022

11172128R00175